ody- and image-space

D1477473

ie last decade has seen renewed interest among philosophers and
eorists in the writings of Walter Benjamin. In *Body- and Image-Space*
grid Weigel, one of Germany's leading feminist theorists and a
nowned commentator on the work of Walter Benjamin, argues that the
ception of his work has so far overlooked a crucial aspect of his
ought – his use of images. Weigel argues that it is precisely his
actice of thinking in images that holds the key to understanding the
ll complexity and topicality of Benjamin's theory.

Bilddenken, or thinking in images, and its relation to the body are
ntral to Benjamin's work. Weigel illuminates points of contact
tween this approach and psychoanalytical modes of observation and
ıggests that there also are affinities between Benjamin's thought and
ıntemporary French theory, notably the work of Foucault and Kristeva.

Focusing on those parallels, the author demonstrates the productiv-
y of Benjamin's theoretical approach for contemporary gender
:udies, cultural theory and philosophy. At the same time, her reading
:eestablishes the buried links between early Critical Theory and post-
tructuralism, between German high modernism and French post-
ıodernist theory.

Body- and Image-Space will be invaluable to anyone interested in
;ender theory, post-structuralism, cultural anthropology and philo-
ophy.

Sigrid Weigel is Professor of German Literature at the University of
Zurich.

Warwick Studies in European Philosophy

Edited by Andrew Benjamin
Senior Lecturer in Philosophy, University of Warwick

This series presents the best and most original work being done within the European philosophical tradition. The books included in the series seek not merely to reflect what is taking place within European philosophy, rather they will contribute to the growth and development of that plural tradition. Work written in the English language as well as translations into English are to be included, engaging the tradition at all levels – whether by introductions that show the contemporary philosophical force of certain works, or in collections that explore an important thinker or topic, as well as in significant contributions that call for their own critical evaluation.

Body- and image-space

Re-reading Walter Benjamin

Sigrid Weigel

Translated by Georgina Paul
with Rachel McNicholl and Jeremy Gaines

London and New York

First published 1996
by Routledge
11 New Fetter Lane, London EC4P 4EE

Simultaneously published in the USA and Canada
by Routledge
29 West 35th Street, New York, NY 10001

© 1996 Routledge for the English translation

Typeset in Times by
Ponting–Green Publishing Services, Chesham, Bucks

Printed and bound in Great Britain by
Redwood Books, Trowbridge, Wiltshire

British Library Cataloguing in Publication Data
A catalogue record for this book is available from the
British Library.

Library of Congress Cataloguing in Publication Data
Weigel, Sigrid.
    Body- and image-space: re-reading Walter Benjamin
        p.   cm. – (Warwick studies in European philosophy)
        1. Benjamin, Walter, 1892–1940 I. Series.
    B3209.B58W45   1996
    193–dc20   95–26618
                                                                CIP

ISBN 0–415–10955–8 (hbk)
ISBN 0–415–10956–6 (pbk)

Contents

Translator's note

The source of all quotations from Walter Benjamin's *Gesammelte Schriften* (ed. Rolf Tiedemann and Hermann Schweppenhäuser, Frankfurt am Main: Suhrkamp, 1980–9) is indicated in the text by the short reference *GS* followed by volume (roman numeral), part (arabic) and page number. Where a published English translation has been quoted, the source is indicated alongside the German reference (see the bibliography for a list of abbreviations used). Occasionally such translations have been modified, in which case this is noted. The translations of all passages with a reference to the German source alone are the translator's own.

Introduction

Distorted similitude – Benjamin as theorist

The subject of this book is Walter Benjamin as theorist – not as philosopher of history or art, not as historian or critic of literature. The central focus of the study is the specific way in which Benjamin thinks and the figurations in which that thinking takes on form. For in his writings, as in those of no other theorist, the manner of thinking and the manner of writing cannot be seen as separate since they – beyond the dualistic opposition of content and form – come together in a third: namely, in the image, which Benjamin himself referred to as a 'third' (*ein Drittes*) (*GS* II.1, 314; *Ill* 207). In an image, however, that in Benjamin's thought does not have the status of a reproduction (*Abbild*), a 'mental picture', or the like, but rather that of a constellation, a heteronomous and heterogeneous similitude, in which figures of thought correlate with those of history or of experience and reality (Chapter 4).

The fact that the reception of Benjamin has taken place within a kind of division of labour between different disciplines has led to the separation of his writings between the discourses of philosophy and literary history, and to the siting of his theorems within these disciplines' respective traditions, categories, and paradigms.[1] The result has been that precisely that field in which Benjamin was first and foremost operative – his thinking-in-images (*Bilddenken*) – has, like a blind spot, been passed over or circumscribed. Yet this thinking-in-images should not be regarded as a supplement to his work, as a particular, additional, or even aesthetic quality to his theorizing which can without consequence be overlooked in the philosophical or sociological reception of his writings – as overlooked it has been. Nor should it be seen as an archive of metaphorology or rhetoric: this is to divert attention away from the epistemological or historico-theoretical status of his thought-images (*Denkbilder*) in favour of a repeated reading of them as metaphorical images, or illustrations, or even as translations of problems that could otherwise be conceptually formulated.

Rather it is this thinking-in-images, the reference to those figurations in which the idea of reality is formed and the images of history are handed down, above all, however, the theoretical and linguistic work on these figurations, the observation of their origins and conditions of possibility, their implications, exclusions, and reverse sides, which constitutes the specificity of Benjaminian theory. As a result, the traditional *oppositions* within established epistemes – above all that between content and form, but also that between theory and practice, politics and art, context and text, individual and collective, and so on – are not treated discursively by him, but, in his thought-images and figurations, cease to obtain altogether, are not integrated or sublated, but quite literally cease to obtain, in that they are represented in that third, the image. Thus his writings are concentrated on the conceptualization and representation of the phenomena that interest him, on the search for and the work on the readability and representability of a dialectic residing within things and within existence. The images of our perceptions and ideas, and the metaphors with which we are surrounded, are seen by Benjamin as 'body- and image-space' (*Leib- und Bildraum*) in which our reality is engendered (*GS* II.1, 309–10; *OWS* 239; Chapter 2), a body- and image-space which, transformed into the writing-space of a profane illumination, he traverses in his thinking and writing.

It is precisely in the encounter with the image-space of our thought and action, in the entry into Benjamin's thinking-in-images and the thought-images of his theory that the contemporaneity and latent meaning of this theory is to be found. Here is the real *Aktualität*[2] of Benjamin, here, where the 'world of universal and integral actuality' is opened up (*GS* II.1, 309; *OWS* 239) – whereas in commemorative lectures on 'Benjamin's *Aktualität*' this genuinely Benjaminian concept of actuality is regularly misrecognized (Chapter 1), a symptom of the more general misrecognition of the central significance of images for his theory.[3] For Benjamin, images are not the object, but rather the matrix and medium of his theoretical work.

If Benjamin is to be considered here as a theorist, it is not in the sense that a theoretical *system* is to be reconstructed. Rather, the concern of this study is a genesis of his thought-figures and -images, the consideration of the origins and traces of his work on particular theorems and their convergence in specific constellations. For it is striking how certain images, rhetorical figures, paradigms, or even individual words – like those collector's pieces or precious objects with which Benjamin compares the individual images of archaeological memory-work (*GS* VI, 486; *OWS* 314) – pervade his writings, how they in places dominate his texts, sometimes to disappear for long periods, only in order suddenly to re-emerge in slightly, but always highly effectively, modified or distorted form, or in completely changed constellations. For the history of his theoretical enterprise can also be described as the history of a fascination: as the fascinated, almost magical absorption in and occupation by specific images and phenomena, and as the intellectual work on the implications in terms of meaning and on the cultural conditions of possibility of this fascination. If Benjamin proceeds from the assumption that there is 'no imagination without innervation' (*GS* IV.1, 116; *OWS* 75), in doing so he is significantly modifying Aristotle's famous dictum that there is no thought without a mental image: for in this way he grounds thought in processes of excitation whose omission from theoretical consideration deprives reflection of its own matrix. As such, his thinking-in-images (*Bilddenken*) is also founded in an image-desire (*Bildbegehren*) in a way pre-eminently suited to pointing a way forward out of the aporias of the discourses of ideology critique.[3]

Reflections, theses, and figurations from other authors, whether of scientific or of poetic literature, are seldom integrated into the discourse or argument of Benjamin's own theoretical writings, just as the discussion of meta-theoretical or theoretical-historical problems are even more seldom to be found there (an exception is in the sections on different theories of memory in the Baudelaire book). Rather, Benjamin's specific manner of theorizing is structured by practices of quotation and of the rediscovery and distorted imitation of particular figures of thought, often in completely changed thematic contexts. A reconstruction of 'influences' or philosophical traditions in which his thought may be considered to stand will therefore always fail to grasp its specificity.

The examination in this book of the genesis of a number of thought-images in Benjamin's writings is not, either, undertaken as a 'perfective' study of those images, but rather in the spirit of interest in his *work* on and with particular concepts. In the course of this book there is mention of caesurae in the conceptualization of certain phenomena (for example with regard to the structure of memory) or of reformulations of certain theorems (such as that of his language theory, the Messianic, or the mimetic); what is meant is not a discursive or explicit derivation so much as a *re-formulation* in a quite literal sense of the word: a *different* formulation, a shift in the linguistic configuration, or the modified representation of an image which has already frequently been used in his own earlier work. Because, in Benjamin's work, the manner of thinking and the manner of writing are not to be separated, the genealogical examination of his figures and images of thought *is* at one and the same time an analysis of the development of his theory. And if theorems which in Benjamin's texts often remain implicit or concealed in the form of quotations are here linked to particular authors (for example to Freud, whose name is, however, used here as a cipher for psychoanalytical thinking as well as an author name) or discussed in terms of particular (theoretical) concepts, it is not with the aim of describing traditions of influence, but rather in order to consider Benjamin's theory in the light of current theoretical discourse.

In this context, Benjamin's concept of 'readability' (*Lesbarkeit*) is applied to his own writings. The 'historical index' which characterizes the given time in which images become readable means that many of his thought-images can, in the Now of current theoretical discourse, attain a new, or at any rate different cognizability (*Erkennbarkeit*) than, for example, in post-1968 discourse.[4] In particular in the light of so-called French theory, Benjamin's writings may attain a new readability which can break with an identificatory siting of his work within certain lines of tradition and thus also with the repeated complaints about the incompatibilities and contradictions (between 'Marxist' and 'theological' elements, for instance) which have always accompanied such an approach. Above all, those theorems which have been developed in the field of the critique of rationality and its reflections on the 'order of things', on the structures of the imaginary and the symbolic, on the paradigm of writing and reading, on the constitution of the subject under the sign of a 'return to Freud', in short, in the field of a structural re-reading of psychoanalysis, but also current cultural-anthropological paradigms, such as gender difference and cultural memory: these form the theoretical horizon within which the re-reading of Benjaminian thought is practised in this book.

Within this theoretical horizon, though, the most important role is undoubtedly played by Freud, or more generally psychoanalysis. This applies to a contemporary reading of Freud as providing the condition of possibility for the re-reading of Benjamin's thought-figures such as is set out here, but also to the affinity between Benjamin's thinking and certain Freudian models of cognition (in particular dream structure, the topographical structure of memory, and the dialectic of consciousness and the unconscious) and the significance of these for the genesis of Benjamin's own thought-figures. This affinity with figures of thought from psychoanalysis does not represent a discrete thematic area within this book, but forms a leitmotif throughout the study. In this respect it is addressed at a number of points, for example in the theses on a psychoanalytic reformulation of Benjamin's theory of language magic in the early 1930s and of his theory of Messianism during the same period (Chapters 2, 9, and 10). But it is set out in concentrated and exemplary form with reference to the generation of his concept of memory which took place around 1930 – that is, between the first phase of the *Passagen* (1927–29)[5] and his resumption of work on the project from 1934 onwards – a period in which clear traces of Benjamin's reading of Freud, and the use of psychoanalytical terminology, become visible in his writings (Chapter 8).

Correspondences between Benjamin and the aforementioned French theory are also demonstrated explicitly and *en détail* here via the example of selected authors from that field, specifically Michel Foucault and Julia Kristeva (Chapters 3 and 5). These analyses are to be understood as being of model character: their target is a blind spot in contemporary theoretical discourse; namely, the buried links between the *early* Critical Theory of the Frankfurt School and post-structuralism.[6] A number of contributory factors might be mentioned to explain why these links have for the most part been disregarded hitherto. In the first place, there is the perhaps overly forcible appropriation of the Benjaminian inheritance by the Frankfurt School, and the marginalization of his work, comparable to a second exile, in the history of Critical Theory following the death of Adorno.[7] This is particularly marked in the phase of the 'socio-philosophical' reformulation of Critical Theory which took place in the Habermas era and which was characterized by a strong tendency towards the reduction of the category of the 'aesthetic'[8] and the rejection of all aspects associated with it. As a consequence, Benjamin's work on thinking-in-images fell by the wayside.

A further contributory factor was the belated reception of Benjamin in France, which only really gathered momentum after the publication of the *Passagen* project in 1982[9] and even today bears the features of a selective reading of his work. This is the case, for example, in Derrida's reading of Benjamin's 'Critique of Violence' in which he talks of a correspondence between Carl Schmitt and Walter Benjamin (Derrida 1990: 979, 1015), although only one letter is known to exist, written when Benjamin sent Schmitt a copy of his book on Baroque drama. Derrida's re-reading of Benjamin's legal-philosophical text under the aspect of *meaning* – whereby the accent falls on the *topoi* of the making, or positing, of the law (*Setzung*) and the suspension of the law (*Entsetzung*) – contains illuminating ideas. But his contribution to the question of the 'limits of representation' in the context of the history of the Shoah is based on too schematic a notion of Benjamin's theory of language.

Nevertheless, this and de Man's reading of Benjamin, which has far more problematical features (Chapter 9), have evidently awakened new interest in Benjamin's work in Anglo-American and international theoretical circles, with the curious effect that in some cases the Franco-German relationship in philosophical discourse has been constituted as a triangular one through the presence of an Anglo-American mediator.[10] And if German reception of contemporary 'French theory', in particular of post-structuralism, has in part taken place via a transatlantic loop, the transformer, so to speak, of deconstruction, for the German-language context something like a return via the detour of a double translation has occurred, since many of the most influential texts by Derrida, Kristeva, Foucault, and others are based on readings of German classics, such as Heidegger, Husserl, and Freud, but also Hölderlin and Kafka *inter alia*. If the authors of early Critical Theory have so far been missing from this list, the omission has recently begun to be rectified, at least in the case of Benjamin, although here, too, the double translation has not remained without its repercussions.

While the triad of French, Anglo-American, and German debate within theoretical discourse that has been briefly sketched here forms the horizon for the re-reading of Benjamin's writings undertaken within this book, the intention is not to present a 'deconstructionist' reading of his texts – at any rate, not if this term is brought into association with the model of that reading by de Man which seeks to integrate Benjamin's translation essay into the history of rhetoric at the cost of the expulsion of his Messianism (Chapter 9). It is true that the way Benjamin operates with images, the way he transforms them into dialectical images, to the extent that in this process they are subject to illumination from within and interrupted, arrested in their functioning, could be termed 'deconstructive' in the sense of Derrida's *Of Grammatology*: that is, in the sense of a practice in which established structures are inhabited from within and are at the same time erased (Derrida 1976: 24). Certain suggestive parallels might also be found between Derrida's description of deconstruction as the 'final writing of an epoch' which both effaces and allows to remain visible (1976: 23) and Benjamin's technique of 'redeeming criticism' (*rettende Kritik*). But Benjamin's writings resist being read as deconstructive in a rhetorical sense to the extent that the target of his deconstructive approach to images is not images as tropes, but rather constellations. This method apprehends not only the representation, but also at the same time what is *not*, nor can be, represented – the reverse side of the thought-figures, the dialectic of things and of history. In this way image-desire and thinking-in-images are in Benjamin always tied to the 'weak Messianic power' of an historical hope.

The re-reading suggested here does, however, find common cause with a deconstructionist reading of Benjamin where the issue is to counter the situating of his thought in relation to established ideologemes or '-isms'. The well-known debate about elements of 'Marxist' and 'theological' thinking in Benjamin's work was – this as an example – for a long time instrumental in concealing that this pair of terms does not describe an antagonism in his texts, but rather that certain conceptual approaches and *topoi* drawn from *both* fields are reformulated by him in the figures of a *third* field, namely, in figurations which have their origin in psychoanalytical concepts (the structure of the unconscious, for example, or the dialectic of consciousness and the unconscious). In Benjamin's writings, these psychoanalytical figures are, in a kind of imitative distortion, subject to partial double-exposure with, or superimposition upon, ideas drawn from quite other fields – the relation between the philosophy of history and Messianism, for example, as will become clear in the re-reading of the 'angel of history' as a dialectical image set out here (Chapter 4).

Instead of the hitherto overly emphasized contradictions in Benjamin's thought, this re-reading aims to illuminate a series of distortions – distortions that are the product of his work on theorems and thought-figures both pre-existing and developed by himself in the course of that work: a distortion of historical materialism, for example (Chapters 1 and 3), or of language magic (Chapters 8 and 9). The central significance of distortion also becomes apparent where Benjamin undertakes a superimposition of 'distortion' (*Entstellung*), a modality of representation within dream structure, and 'redemption' (*Erlösung*), a term taken from Judaic Messianism, as when, in his essay on Kafka, distortion is understood as being simultaneously a form of forgetting, as a kind of symptom, marking a difference from redemption (Chapters 2, 9, and 10). It is indeed possible that it is precisely this psychoanalytical reformulation of the Messianic which, as a more scandalous trace beneath the mask of the explicit and critical reformulation of historical materialism, is concealed – and was intended to remain concealed – in the figures of the Messianic *and* of psychoanalysis in his text 'On the Concept of History'. At any rate it is to be noted that the author confined the sentence to the effect that the dialectical image was to be defined as the involuntary recollection of redeemed mankind (*GS* I.3, 1233) to his preliminary sketches for the text and did not incorporate it into the work on a version suitable for publication.

Yet it is not the case that psychoanalysis represents an immovable reference point for the reformulations, superimpositions, and distortions in Benjamin's theoretical development which are to be described here. Rather, the modes of observation drawn from psychoanalysis appear in his writings in a patently rematerialized form – applied as they are to the first material of human existence, the body (Chapter 2). This is clear both in his emphasis on the language of things and of the body, and also in his concept of 'body- and image-space'. In Benjamin's *modus operandi* with psychoanalytical figures a kind of reversal takes place, however, since the corporeal origins, lost in the course of the development of psychoanalytical theory, are brought back more strongly into focus, albeit without reversing the break with the model of a simple and straightforward decipherability of bodily signs and with the idea of the engrammatic facilitation (*Bahnung*) which had taken place in the course of this same development. In other words, Benjamin takes into account the representational structure of the unconscious: its production of distortions or 'picture-puzzles' (*Vexierbilder*). This reversal undertaken by Benjamin can be seen as a 'reversal of all kinds of ideas and forms' (*Umkehr aller Vorstellungsarten und Formen*) (Hölderlin 1992: II, 375) after the model of Hölderlin's reading and translation of Greek tragedy in which, through looking back and considering the 'wild origination' (*wilde Entstehung*) of a form of rationality, the Oriental elements denied and repressed in Greek art were once more brought to the fore (1992: 375, 925).

 The re-reading of Benjamin proposed here is structured throughout around a number of concepts and figures which have hitherto tended to be disregarded in the reception of his work – concepts and figures which the author himself did not necessarily place at the centre or in the foreground of his texts, but which – this is my thesis – form the armature for that hidden 'complete revolutionary turn' (*vollkommene Umwälzung*) which 'the mass of my thoughts and images, with their roots in the far distant past of my unmediatedly metaphysical, indeed, theological thinking, had to pass through' (Benjamin 1978: 659). They are concepts and figures which give theoretical grounding to the accentual shifts and caesurae between the so-called early and late phases of his work – between the studies on the history of literature and the 'ur-history of modernity', between 'pure language' and 'picture-puzzles', between images and dialectical images – and in which these shifts and caesurae take on form. These concepts and figures, which represent as it were the points of intersection of Benjamin's thinking-in-images, are discussed here from a number of different perspectives, and thus reappear throughout the book in various contexts which in turn lend them different nuances of meaning.

In this respect they also form the points of intersection of this study, and a number of quoted passages will be encountered on more than one occasion.

Apart from the category of 'body- and image-space', one of the most significant of the points of intersection in the various texts of Benjamin's to be discussed here is the concept of distortion (*Entstellung*). Distortion is namely not only one of the central terms of psychoanalysis to be taken up by Benjamin, and is not only used by him in connection with Messianic redemption. In the figure of 'distorted similitude' (*entstellte Ähnlichkeit*), it also forms the pivotal point for his reformulation in the 1930s of his earlier theory of language, and as such is one of the points of origin for the development of the category of 'non-sensuous similitude' (*unsinnliche Ähnlichkeit*) (Chapters 3, 8, and 9).[11] This latter category has its place in the context of the development of Benjamin's concept of memory which is systematically examined here for the first time. And in the context of the 'distortion into allegory' (*Entstellung ins Allegorische*), with which the figure of the whore in the *Passagen* project takes on the role of *the* allegory of modernity, distortion is also centrally significant to the discursive and imaginary shifts in the concept of the 'feminine': the female inhabitants of the has-been (*das Gewesene*) and of silence in Benjamin's early writings here undergo a transformation into the threshold-dwellers who, in the body- and image-space of the *Passagen*, occupy the constellation of awakening – who can, then, in the figurative language of modernity, be seen as the female custodians of a dialectic of consciousness and the unconscious (Chapters 5 and 6), that dialectic in which resemblances become instantaneously, 'in the flashing of an eye', cognizable (Chapter 8).

The 'distortion into allegory' which takes place – in analogy with the language of the unconscious – in Benjamin's project on an 'ur-history of modernity' brings with it, too, a distortion of allegory itself as still featuring dominantly in his work on German tragic drama or *Trauerspiel* (Chapter 7). In this manner the distorted similitude that emerges in the context of his project on modernity can also be seen as the return of a repressed resemblance whose historical disappearance may be situated, against the foil of Foucault's *Order of Things*, at the transition point from a *ternary* to a *binary* sign system. Benjamin, by subjecting things to an allegorical gaze in the *Trauerspiel* book and in so doing effecting their transformation into excitatory writing, rescued, as it were, the repressed resemblance from that transitional point in the history of language at the very moment of its historical disappearance, in order ultimately to lend its return in distorted form central significance for modernity (Chapters 3, 7, and 9): as distorted similitude.

Politics of images and body

'the first material on which the mimetic faculty
is put to the proof . . . the human body'

1 Benjamin's 'world of universal and integral actuality'

COMMEMORATION AND MISRECOGNITION

'The actuality of Walter Benjamin' (*Zur Aktualität Walter Benjamins*)[1] is one of the most popular titles of books and lectures on Benjamin's writings – (first used by Unseld 1972) – and one of the issues most frequently addressed in the history of their reception. The phrase generally signals an appropriation of his theoretical formulations and ideas which expresses itself in a combination of commemoration and historicization. For the discussion, under the heading of Benjamin's *Aktualität*, of the contemporary relevance of his work to a given time implies an assumption of the historical limitation and restricted validity of his thought which is then resolved in the presentation of a variously relativized or modified validity for the present moment. If it is not my concern here to enter once more into a consideration of Benjamin's *Aktualität* in this sense, then this is not because I wish to suggest a universal, suprahistorical validity, but rather because the nature of the question, following as it does the paradigm of the appropriateness of theory to the historical situation, already involves a misrecognition of Benjamin's understanding of that term. That the question can be posed at all implies a disregard of his specific conceptualization of *Aktualität*. Indeed, it is my contention that to enter into a discussion of the *Aktualität qua* contemporary relevance of Benjamin's thought is already to preclude the possibility of engaging with *Aktualität* as he conceived it.

It is possible that, because of this focus on contemporary relevance, current discussion of critical social theory is being deprived of precisely those impulses which, not yet fully considered, could – in actuality! – constitute the specific contemporaneity of his thought. What is at stake here is not the historical appropriateness of particular analytical utterances or individual theoretical formulations, nor the compatibility of the many different philosophical, cultural, and epistemological references contained in his works. The issue is the more fundamental one of the manner of philosophizing, thinking, analysing, of the *attitude* adopted towards ideas and constellations encountered, of the modes of approaching and working with the signs and the material of history and culture – in short, of the 'work of presence of mind incarnate' (*Werk leibhaftiger Geistesgegenwart*) (*GS* IV.1, 142; *OWS* 99, translation modified).

For at the basis of Benjamin's concept of *Aktualität* there lies the theory of thinking and acting in images. The theory takes as its starting point the fact that the primary mode and the primary material of thought and ideas are images. From this Benjamin develops a concept of action in which, as thoughts become em-bodied *in actu* – he speaks of the interpenetration of body- and image-space (*GS* II.1, 310; *OWS* 239) – thinking and acting as it were become one and a world of 'universal and integral' *Aktualität* is opened up, as he writes in his 1929 essay on Surrealism (*GS* II. 1, 310; *OWS* 239). Instead of a 'materialistic theory of society' in its usual sense, then, we are dealing here with a theory which establishes a relation of immediacy to the material of the social or the symbolic. This is not materialism *avant la lettre*, but quite literally a *re-reading* of the material – things, writing, gestures, for example – which, having progressed through the school of political and anthropological materialism, introduces into the political sphere its primary matter – the body – while at the same time emphasizing the manner in which this matter is constituted and structured as image.

Yet whenever the question of Benjamin's *Aktualität* is posed, notably on the occasion of jubilee celebrations, as recently once more at the Benjamin centenary, it is always from the point of view of the usefulness of Benjamin's thought for problems of current interest and concern or of the extent to which his theoretical observations can be appropriated for the purposes of contemporary analysis and reflection. In his opening address to the international Benjamin colloquium in Osnabrück in 1992, for example, Irving Wohlfarth discussed the validity of Benjamin's 'historico-philosophical' reflections following the 'death of socialism' – or rather the collapse of real existing socialism – in order, having undertaken a few corrections here and there, to recuperate Benjamin for today's concerns (Wohlfarth 1993). A questionable recuperation, it seems to me, since the attempt to fit past theories to current conditions and discourse misses the point of Benjamin's concept of *Aktualität* and thus passes up the chance of considering the present differently in the light of – or with the attitude of – Benjaminian *Aktualität*. This is not, then, redeeming critique, but rather a misrecognition of Benjamin's ideas, since a genuine reading of *Aktualität* in his writings would of necessity reveal the inappropriateness of that particular approach.

The popular question concerning Benjamin's *Aktualität* participates in a form of thinking which produces theoretical tradition and development via a series of authors' names and their relation to one another: genealogy is thus presented in terms of the history of the works of great authors, and in terms of heritage and continuity in the development of theoretical positions and analytical perceptions. In this respect it comes as no surprise that Wohlfarth attempted to link his revised, post-socialist Benjamin to Habermas, and in so doing concluded his representations by explicitly naming that hidden influence on his lecture. Habermas himself began his own famous lecture on Benjamin's *Aktualität*, held twenty years previously at the eightieth anniversary celebrations, by setting out a genealogy in which he positioned himself in the line of direct descent from Benjamin, albeit via the mediation of Peter Szondi who, as he said, 'undoubtedly would have stood here today in my place' (Habermas 1972: 31) and Adorno, the 'heir, critical partner and forerunner all in one' (1972: 30) – a position, incidentally, which he proposed to share with Benjamin's editors, Tiedemann and Schweppenhäuser. Counter to the custom of such honourable mentions, however, Benjamin had formulated in his notes on the concept of history that the manner in which something from the past is honoured as heritage is more calamitous than its loss could be (*GS* I.3, 1242).

If in what follows I turn attention once again to Habermas' commemorative lecture of 1972, it is not in order to continue the debate which it engendered in Benjamin studies about the mystical or theological versus the Marxist aspects of his writing, nor to reassess Benjamin's reflections from the point of view of the paradigms of ideology critique and materialist cultural theory such as dominate Habermas' approach to him. It is not my intention either to criticize – or even refute – Habermas' theses, for instance the one that Adorno was 'certainly the better Marxist' (Habermas 1972: 54) – a contention whose rhetoric might be explained in terms of the climate of argument which characterized the historical constellation after 1968.[2] Rather, it is my concern, through the re-reading of the text of that lecture, to reconstruct the exact moment from which the misrecognition of Benjamin's concept of *Aktualität* springs. And it is only in respect of this trace that Habermas' text is once again presented here.

BREAKS AND BLIND SPOTS IN READING

At the beginning of his lecture Habermas briefly mentions the concept of *Aktualität*, quoting in this context the passage from the 'Announcement of the Journal *Angelus Novus*' (*Ankündigung der Zeitschrift Angelus Novus*) in which Benjamin explains the ephemeral nature of true *Aktualität* with the aid of the Talmudic legend of the countless angels who every moment are created, only to pass once again into nothingness once they have sung their hymn before God (*GS* II.1, 246). Apart from this passing reference, however, the concept for some time plays no major role in his argument. Habermas' primary concern is, rather, the discussion of the relation between Benjamin's concept of criticism and the understanding of art in ideology critique. It is only in the sixth section, in which he sets out to show how 'Benjamin assimilates Marxian categories for his own purposes' (Habermas 1972: 51) and in which he argues that Benjamin's attempt to link politics and art failed, that Habermas turns finally to the question of Benjamin's *Aktualität*:

> Benjamin's contemporaneity [*Aktualität*] does not lie in a theology of the revolution. Rather, his contemporaneity unfolds before us if we attempt vice-versa to 'enlist the services' of Benjamin's theory of experience for historical materialism.
>
> (1972: 56)

It is useful to observe more closely the rhetorical construction of this, in terms of his argument, constitutive shift from Benjamin's concept of *Aktualität* to the discussion of Benjamin's *Aktualität qua* contemporaneity. In order to substantiate his dismissal of a theology of the revolution, Habermas refers in the passage which precedes this one to the Surrealism essay of 1929, quoting from it Benjamin's critical objections to notions of 'poetic politics' and pointing to his fundamental rejection of Surrealist experiments in which

> art was transferred into expressive action and the split between poetic and political action was dialectically abolished [*aufgehoben*] ... Politics as representation or even poetic politics – when Benjamin saw these realizations he could no longer close his eyes to the differences of principle between political action and manifestation.
>
> (1972: 55)

And he continues with Benjamin's own words:

this would mean the subordination of the methodical and disciplinary preparation for revolution entirely to a praxis oscillating between training and celebrating its imminent onset.

(1972: 55; *GS* II.1, 307)[3]

If one turns to the passage in question in the Surrealism essay, one finds in the first place that Benjamin is not discussing the differences of principle between political action and manifestation here, but rather distancing himself from Surrealist concepts to the extent, and only to the extent, that they lay *exclusive* emphasis on the intoxicating elements of revolutionary activity, an emphasis which Benjamin goes on to call 'romantic prejudice'. His subsequent critical, even sarcastic commentary on 'poetic politics' is not aimed at the politics *as* representation with which Habermas equates it (1972: 55), but rather at a politics which avails itself of 'poetic' methods, by which he means those methods which have their origin in poetic writing, notably metaphor:

> For what is the programme of the bourgeois parties? A bad poem on springtime, filled to bursting with metaphors. . . . And the stock imagery of these social democratic club-poets?
>
> (*GS* II.1, 308; *OWS* 237, translation modified)

There follows the famous passage on pessimism, on mistrust in all forms of mutual understanding (*Verständigung*), and the call 'to expel moral metaphor from politics and to discover in the sphere of political action a total, hundred per cent image-space [*den hundertprozentigen Bildraum*]' (*GS* II.1, 309; *OWS* 238, translation modified). It is precisely here, where this image-space is opened up, that Benjamin discloses his concept of *Aktualität*, namely a 'world of universal and integral actuality'. The whole direction and argumentation of Benjamin's text on Surrealism, his discussion of the possibilities available to his time for the politicization of art, provide a pathway to an idea of *Aktualität* defined in terms of body- and image-space.[4]

Habermas, however, chooses not to pursue this trace in the section of his lecture which itself culminates in a concept of *Aktualität*. Instead, he breaks off his reading of Benjamin's Surrealism essay with the quotation about the 'methodical and disciplinary preparation for revolution', from which he concludes that Benjamin had,

> [p]rompted by the contact with Brecht, . . . therefore dissociated himself from his earlier anarchistic inclinations, seeing instead the relationship between art and political praxis primarily from the point of view of the organizational and propagandistic *utilizability* [*Verwertbarkeit*] of art for the class struggle.
>
> (1972: 55, translation modified; my emphasis)

Such an interpretation cannot readily be supported from the evidence of Benjamin's texts after 1929. Above all, the criterion of utilizability is alien to Benjamin's thought, perennially concerned as he was, be it in the contemplation of language, history, art, or of the object-world of modernity, with moments of immediacy. Moreover, the opposition of anarchism and organization has its origin rather in the archive of opposing terms which structure Habermas' text throughout: poetry and politics, art and class struggle, theology and Marxism, mysticism and enlightenment. And the figure of *integration* (*Vereinigung*), in his talk of what Benjamin attempted to integrate (1972: 51), has its basis, like the question of the *relationship* of, for example, theory and practice or politics and art, in an attitude and in a form of thinking which initially have to constitute that which is to be related as separate fields or areas. Benjamin, by contrast, in his concentration on images, proceeds from another modality in which all that is material and all that is intelligible, in which world and knowledge mediate.

No less significant in this context than the incompatibility of the basic approaches is the observation that the point at which Habermas breaks off his reading of Benjamin and his failure to take account of Benjamin's concept of *Aktualität* are located at precisely that stage in his lecture where he introduces his own concept of *Aktualität*. The blind spot in his reading, the closing-off of an *Aktualität* in a 'hundred per cent image-space' thus at the same time marks the emergence of the question about Benjamin's *Aktualität*, in pursuit of which Habermas once again picks up the trace of genealogical argumentation. The mention of the name of Brecht in Benjamin's averred liberation from 'anarchistic inclinations' had served a corresponding purpose, of course, but in the seventh and final section of his lecture, in which the services of Benjamin's theory of experience are to be enlisted for historical materialism, Habermas' aim is to set out a theory of linguistic communication (a project on which he was engaged in the early 1970s) 'which *brings* Benjamin's insights *back* into a materialist theory of social evolution [*die Benjamins Einsichten in eine materialistische Theorie der sozialen Evolution* zurückbringt]' (1972: 59, translation modified; my emphasis).

If the gesture of bringing back into the fold something which had gone astray here leads directly into his own theoretical project, Habermas' blind spot in his reading of Benjamin is also symptomatic – and this is the only reason why it is of interest here – in that it acts as a shield, preventing the encounter with Benjamin's thinking-in-images (*Bilddenken*) which is not readily translatable into the categories of philosophical discourse. It is a barrier hindering access to the 'hundred per cent image-space' in which the division between subject and object, including that between the philosophizer and the object of his discourse, does not obtain – quite apart from the fact that there could be no greater incompatibility than between Benjamin's theory of language, based on immediacy and mimesis, and Habermas' communicative model.

The blocking out of *images* and of Benjamin's work on thinking-in-images can also be observed at those points in Habermas' lecture where, in his presentation of Benjamin's theoretical utterances, 'images' and 'looking' are replaced, even suppressed, by 'thoughts' and 'thinking'. Habermas speaks, for example, of the 'sudden flash of contemporary immediacy [*Aktualität*] in which a thought takes power and holds sway for an historical instant' (1972: 32), while Benjamin famously speaks of *images* that appear in a flash: '*It is only as an image*, which flashes up in the moment of its cognizability, never to appear again, that the past can be apprehended' (*GS* I.2, 695; *Ill* 257, translation modified; my emphasis). Similarly there are passages in the lecture where Habermas misrecognizes thought-images (*Denkbilder*) central to Benjamin's theory, as when he speaks of the 'messianic promise of happiness' (Habermas 1972: 45), a conflation of Messianism and the striving after happiness, where Benjamin by contrast assigns the search for happiness to the order of the profane, representing its relation to the Messianic in the thought-image of two counter-directional forces which, although in opposition to each other, can mutually propel each other on a single path (*GS* II.1, 204; *OWS* 155), an image of a 'counter-striving disposition' (*gegenstrebige Fügung*).[5]

THINKING-IN-IMAGES, THE BODY, AND *AKTUALITÄT* IN BENJAMIN'S WRITING

This representation in terms of a thought-image of a constellation that is difficult to apprehend conceptually should not be confused with poetic writing, nor is it a supplementary quality of Benjamin's philosophical discourse. Rather, it indicates a mode of philosophizing which invalidates philosophical discourse as meta-discourse. Benjamin's image-space is not about metaphor – so-called figurative or even 'non-literal' (*uneigentlich*) speech – in which an image takes the place of a concept or thought that could also be expressed otherwise. For the precondition of the model of *Aktualität* put forward in the Surrealism essay is precisely the differentiation from metaphor, the 'distinction between metaphor and image' (*GS* II.1, 308; *OWS* 238). What is under discussion here is not, then, the 'encoding' (Habermas 1972: 40) of meanings in images, but the insight that memory and action find articulation in images, that ideas are structured as images, and that what is at stake is therefore a praxis that can operate with images – a *politics of images*, not a figurative or metaphorical politics.

In Benjamin's political image-space, ideas and actions, the imaginings of and their representation by the actors/agents are contingent upon one other. Moreover, for Benjamin, where the subjects themselves embody their ideas *in actu*, image-space conjoins with body-space. This scene of history, the creation of the 'political and factual reality' of the *physis* in that image-space 'with which profane illumination makes us familiar' (*GS* II.1, 310; *OWS* 239, translation modified), represents the instant of a materialized, embodied now-time (*Jetztzeit*). The scene becomes for him a 'world of universal and integral actuality' to the extent that the Now of cognizability (*Jetzt der Erkennbarkeit*) here coincides with the Now of a corporeal representation or action. 'Politics as representation' would therefore be the exact opposite of 'poetic politics'; it would be *Aktualität* in its true sense: presence of mind incarnate (*leibhaftige Geistesgegenwart*). In this, Benjamin anticipated a number of ideas in the current debate on 'performance'. And yet his theory never runs into danger of forgetting the body.

This scene, the (revolutionary) moment in which image- and body-space coincide, signifies as it were Benjamin's *idea* of *Aktualität*. For Benjamin, the representation of an idea can, as he sets out in *The Origin of German Tragic Drama*,

> under no circumstances be considered successful unless the whole range of possible extremes it contains has been virtually passed in review. . . . The idea is a monad – that means briefly: every idea contains the image of the world. The purpose of the representation of the idea is nothing less than an abbreviated outline of this image of the world.
>
> (*GS* I.1, 227–8; *OGT* 47–8, translation modified)

The closing sequence of the Surrealism essay, which projects an interpenetration of body- and image-space, representing this in the corporeal innervations of the collective, can thus be read as a monad of a 'world of universal and integral actuality'. In this sequence two theoretical operations of Benjamin's intersect which could respectively be described – on the one hand in relation to psychoanalysis, on the other to historical materialism – as materialized re-readings and radicalizations of previously existing theoretical concepts.

Sigmund Freud began developing his theory of the unconscious in the first instance, namely in the context of his theory of hysteria, on the basis of the physical symptom as a mnemic symbol (*Erinnerungssymbol*). In *The Interpretation of Dreams* he went on to describe the language of the unconscious, exemplified in dream images, as a system of meaning with a specific syntax and different modalities of dreamwork. In the course of his expositions of the functioning of the psychic apparatus, however, one of the modalities, namely the 'consideration of representability' (*Rücksicht auf Darstellbarkeit*), was pushed ever further into the background; and this touches on the question of the material of representation. Benjamin follows Freud's lead in the way he focuses on bodies, things, commodities, monuments, topography, and so on, reading these as wish-symbols and as materializations of collective memory; and in so doing, he restores matter to its central significance for psychoanalysis and for the means of expression of a language of the unconscious.[6] And conversely: he brings to the reading of Marxism a manner of observation derived from psychoanalysis – which accounts for his emphasis on the expressive relationship (between economics and culture) rather than the causal connection that Marx attempted to delineate, and gives rise to his specific, psychoanalytically based reading of the images of history.

With this, Benjamin took quite literally the phrase that 'the world has long possessed the dream of a thing, and must only possess the consciousness of it in order to possess it in reality' and laid at the basis of this quotation from Marx, which he noted down in the *Passagen* project (*GS* V, 583; see *N* 55), Freud's concept of the dream. His idea is that, through the deciphering of materialized wish-symbols (which, however, like all signs in the unconscious, can only be represented as distortions), the images of history become recognizable and readable. This means that in Benjamin's work, through a superimposition or double-exposure of the Freudian paradigm 'consciousness–unconscious' over the Marxian paradigm 'being–consciousness',[7] the concept of consciousness undergoes a metamorphosis which transforms it into the concept of 'presence of mind' (*Geistesgegenwart*). And presence of mind is as it were the attitude of the subject which permits *Aktualität*.

It is this which enables Benjamin to maintain that actualization, not progress, should be the basic principle of historical materialism (*GS* V, 574; *N* 47). Moreover, it is in this principle of actualization that his theses and thought-images on the concept of history are grounded. It has become customary to refer to these as the 'Theses on the Philosophy of History' (*geschichtsphilosophische Thesen*), a label which once again tends to suppress the work on thinking-in-images that is of such central significance for Benjamin's writings.

IMAGES OF POLITICS – THE POLITICS OF IMAGES: READING MARX

The manner in which Benjamin reformulates historical materialism in the *Passagen* project and in his text 'On the Concept of History' (*Über den Begriff der Geschichte*) could well be described as a quite literal distortion (*Entstellung*) – distortion here in the Freudian sense of that term, which refers to the image-writing (*Bilder-Schrift*) of memory in which excitations or the processing of experience within the psyche have left their mark. The abandonment of the epic element of history (*GS* V, 592; *N* 65) and the breaking down of history into images rather than into stories (*GS* V, 596; *N* 67) are the ways in which the blasting of an object of history out of the historical continuum occurs, and are therefore elements essential to the dialectical representation of history – brought about by the impulse of *Aktualität* (*GS* V, 587; *N* 60). If *Aktualität* is as it were the charge which effects the blasting of the continuum or the standstill of a 'constellation saturated with tensions' (*GS* V, 595; *N* 67), then it is through *Aktualität* that the monadological structure or constitution of history as image is produced. In relation to Benjamin's concept of history and to his re-reading of history as memory-scene (*Gedächtnisszene*),[8] *Aktualität* thus becomes the pre-condition for the dialectical representation of historical states of affairs (*Tatbestände*) (*GS* V, 587; *N* 60), as for the readability of the images of history (*GS* V, 577; *N* 50). This thinking-in-images is the core of Benjamin's *theory* of history which, if it is translated into a *philosophy* of history and robbed of the concepts of *Aktualität* and image, is reduced once more to the recognizable and familiar.

Benjamin's distortion of historical materialism can paradigmatically be demonstrated in the manner in which he throws a different light on the images of the collective imaginary from that provided by the Marxian interpretation. He effects, for example, a shift of the 'necromancy' which for Marx was an indicator of false consciousness into a practice of quotation, a form of action in political image-space. Where Marx, in his famous opening passage to the 'Eighteenth Brumaire of Louis Bonaparte', describes the references made by actors on the political scene to figures and images from past historical events (the French Revolution's to ancient Rome, for example) as 'self-deceptions' (Marx 1979: 104) and 'superstition' (1979: 106), as false consciousness therefore, Benjamin gives to the same constellation, in the context of his images of history, a quite different inflection, but without setting his text in direct opposition to Marx's or evaluating Marx's analysis as a false one. Already in his mode of writing, then, Benjamin effects a caesura in the face of a discourse characterized by the binary opposition of 'true' and 'false', presenting instead, in a thought-image containing an implicit intertextual reference to Marx's 'Eighteenth Brumaire', a *different* reading of the historical constellation, as here in section XIV of 'On the Concept of History':

> History is the object of a construction whose site is not homogeneous, empty time, but time filled by the presence of the now [*Jetztzeit*]. Thus, to Robespierre ancient Rome was a past charged with now-time which he blasted out of the continuum of history. The French Revolution viewed itself as Rome reincarnate. It quoted ancient Rome the way fashion quotes costumes of the past. Fashion has a good nose for the actual [*das Aktuelle*], no matter where it stirs in the thicket of the erstwhile; it is the tiger's leap into the past. This leap, however, takes place in an arena where the ruling class has the command. The same leap under the open skies of history is the dialectical one that Marx conceived of as revolution.
>
> (*GS* I.2, 701; *Ill* 263, translation modified)

The tiger's leap into the past, as a movement which overleaps the continuum, creates immediacy in relation to the past, actualizes or quotes an image from the archive of historical memory – 'quotes' here in the sense of invoking or summoning up rather than that of making a scholarly reference to some authority. This *topos* demonstrates how closely linked *Aktualität* and quotation are for Benjamin: both are ways of working politically with images outside of the historical continuum. This praxis can also be seen in the way Benjamin himself uses quotations, deconstructing the concept of tradition or heritage. He quotes Marx's idea of revolution as a dialectical leap, and yet at the same time no greater difference could be created than that between Marx's interpretation of the political image-space of the French Revolution and Benjamin's thought-image.

It is not only that Marx, in using the vocabulary of theatre and costume – tragedy, farce, disguise, mask – and of borrowing and translating, connects with it a negative evaluation of false or non-genuine expression; nor only that, in his talk of nightmare, of the resurrection of the dead, and of the ghosts of the revolution, he situates the images of the past on the darker side of reason. He also explicitly formulates a concept of history entirely orientated towards the future, in which all recollection of the past is evaluated negatively and every reference to provenance or descent[9] must be obliterated from memory – just as the dead are. Here recollection is equated with dullness or stupefaction:

The social revolution of the nineteenth century cannot draw its poetry from the past, but only from the future. It cannot begin with itself before it has stripped off all superstition about the past. Earlier revolutions required recollections of past world history in order to dull themselves to their own content. In order to arrive at its own content, the revolution of the nineteenth century must let the dead bury their dead. There the words [*Phrase*] went beyond the content; here the content goes beyond the words [*Phrase*].

(Marx 1979: 106)

This negative assessment of the past and of recollection is, moreover, linked to a logocentric terminology, based on the opposition of spirit (*Geist*) and spirits (*Geister*). The 'spirits of the past' (1979: 104) stand in the way of the new spirit; and language is an instrument of the 'new spirit', free and pure only where it is without recollection:

In like manner a beginner who has learnt a new tongue always translates it back into his mother tongue, but he has assimilated the spirit of the new language and can freely express himself in it only when he finds his way in it without recalling the old and forgets his native tongue in the use of the new.

(1979: 104)

If, in Marx's strict separation of history and recollection, political image-space becomes of necessity 'poetry' or a metaphorical field – whereby a conventional understanding of metaphor as 'non-literal' or 'figurative' speech obtains – it is presumably not by chance that this is combined with a use of imagery by Marx himself which is to be read, not as quotation, but as a re-inscription and reproduction of traditional metaphors, for example when notions of purity in the concept of the historically new are expressed in terms of the commonplace comparison of nation and violated woman: 'A nation and a woman are not forgiven the unguarded hour in which the first adventurer that came along could violate them' (1979: 108).

When Benjamin places a quotation, by contrast, as an invocation of *das Aktuelle* 'in the thicket of the erstwhile', it is in the context of a concept of history which understands the construction of history as work in and with the images of recollection[10] and which founds the cognizability of the past in a model of memory, thus ultimately equating memory and historiography: 'To articulate the past historically . . . means to seize hold of a memory as it flashes up at a moment of danger' (*GS* I.2, 695; *Ill* 257). It is in this 'concept of history', founded in images of the past that are to be read as recollections, rather than in Benjamin's critique of an historically specific and temporally limited ideology of progress, that the 'genuine actuality' (*echte Aktualität*) of his writings should be seen.

2 'Body- and image-space'
Traces through Benjamin's writings

THE PASSAGE THROUGH 'BODY- AND IMAGE-SPACE' IN 'SURREALISM'

It is not the person standing at the source who can tap the full power of 'intellectual currents'; rather, it is the one standing in the valley who generates energy from the gradient or distance from the source – this image of the power station which dominates the opening of Benjamin's 'last snapshot of the European intelligentsia', as the sub-title of his 1929 essay on Surrealism has it, is replaced at the end of the essay by another image, similarly drawn from the field of mechanics: that of the 'face of an alarm clock that in each minute rings [anschlägt] for sixty seconds' (GS II.1, 310; OWS 239) which is exchanged by the Surrealists for the play of human features. Whereas in the first image the subject draws on an energy generated by a movement external to himself, in the closing image the mechanical movement has as it were become part of him: his face has itself become mechanical, is in a state of perpetual vibration or ceaseless ringing, so that time is completely filled by a combination of sound and movement – and thus ceases to obtain as a category.

This image occurs at the end of a text which in terms of its style mimetically performs the transformation of the Surrealist revolt into revolution that it invokes, a text which develops as at an increasingly accelerated pace until it explodes in an uninterrupted striking of the alarm (Wecker-Anschlag). Yet at the same moment that the image of the ringing alarm clock freezes sound and motion into permanence, the movement of the text comes to an abrupt standstill. And while the 'alarm clock that in each minute rings for sixty seconds' has on the one hand the precisely opposite implication to the shots fired at the tower clocks during the July revolution 'pour arrêter le jour', of which Benjamin writes in the fifteenth section of his text 'On the Concept of History' (GS I.2, 702; Ill 264), it is also the case that both – the functioning of the alarm clock, intensified into immeasurability, as also the violent arresting of the tower clocks in order to make 'remembrance' possible – have the same ultimate effect. 'Irrités contre l'heure', both are strikes (*Anschläge*) against clocks, strikes of the now-time (*Jetztzeit*) against the measured, continuous, linear progression of time – or 'homogeneous, empty time', as Benjamin will call it in the historico-theoretical theses. Yet between these two images a difference may be remarked upon, readable as an allegory of the difference in conceptual armatures that give the texts of 1929 and 1940 their respective characters: *body- and image-space* in 'Surrealism', and the *dialectical image* in the theses on the concept of history.

If the later text is concerned with the way that history is conceived and constructed, with recollected or quoted moments of the past, with images of what is past or correspondences between now-time and what has been (*das Gewesene*), which are represented and become cognizable in dialectical images, in the earlier text it is a quite literally incorporated image that rings in the elimination of time: the image here takes possession of the body of the subject. In the exchange of the play of features for the face of the clock, image-space has become body-space. The strike against time is thus simultaneously a strike against the notion of the opposition between the organic and the mechanical, between the human being and the mechanical device. The boundary between the two is here eliminated – in a manner which produces a profound impact, for the face is the very epitome of the 'humanity' of the human being – just as the 'best room' is eliminated in a 'world of universal and integral actuality' which opens itself up in the course of this exchange (*GS* II.1, 309; *OWS* 239). It is not by chance, then, that the image of the alarm clock follows a passage in which Benjamin develops and condenses his ideas concerning body- and image-space.

The exchange of the play of features for the clock face occurs at the conclusion of a passage in the text which as it were bears the name 'body- and image-space'. The passage begins with the 'distinction between metaphor and image', with the lead-up to this point passing through a number of conceptual stages: through 'profane illumination', understood as a 'materialistic, anthropological inspiration' which is the result of the 'overcoming of religious illumination' (*GS* II.1, 297; *OWS* 227) and which is embodied in the types of the reader, the thinker, the loiterer, and the *flâneur* (*GS* II.1, 308; *OWS* 237), and from here through the 'substitution of the political for the historical view of what has been' (*GS* II.1, 300; *OWS* 230, translation modified), the 'contrast to the helpless compromises of "sentiment" [*Gesinnung*]' (*GS* II.1, 304; *OWS* 234), and a 'dialectical optic that perceives the everyday as impenetrable, the impenetrable as everyday' (*GS* II.1, 307; *OWS* 237).

If these stages are for the most part presented in a terminology related to perception, vision, or *optics* – as opposed to opinion or sentiment – with the 'distinction between metaphor and image', that is, with the inception of the passage on 'body- and image-space', the text introduces a *spatial* dimension. Here an *image-space* (*Bildraum*) is opened up into which the subject (Benjamin speaks of the artist or the revolutionary intelligentsia), in the discovery of 'hundred per cent image-space', himself enters and in which he as it were assumes functionality. In this image-space which 'can no longer be measured out by contemplation', the distance and boundary between subject and image no longer obtain, to the extent that the subject has entered into this image-space by becoming part of it, literally with his body:

> wherever an action puts forth its image and is that image, absorbing and consuming it, wherever closeness looks at itself through its own eyes, this sought-after image-space is opened up, the world of universal and integral actuality, where the 'best room' is eliminated.
>
> (*GS* II.1, 309; *OWS* 239, translation modified)

In this space the individual, following his dialectical partition through 'political materialism' and 'physical nature', can remain with 'no limb unrent', thus rendering this image-space at the same time a body-space (*Leibraum*).

The coincidence of image- and body-space is described by Benjamin as a process of putting forth or of absorption, a process which, with the total absence of distance and the construction of a self-related closeness ('where closeness looks at itself through its own eyes'), blasts apart the dialectical constellation of closeness and distance which is elsewhere so significant for Benjamin's thought,[1] thus dissolving the boundary between subject and object. The reader can no longer be distinguished from the agent, nor the one who deciphers an image from the one who represents or in actuality *is* an image. In the continuation of the passage, this is similarly applied to the collective, for in the transition from a metaphysical to an anthropological materialism (a transition which does not occur without leaving its trace) there remains, as Benjamin notes, 'a residue. The collective is a body too' (*GS* II.1, 310; *OWS* 239). In this way image-space becomes indistinguishable from the body collective to the extent that the reality of the latter is produced in an image-space which in turn refers to the corporeal materiality of the collective as its matrix. In order to represent this idea, the text has recourse to the neurologico-psychoanalytical conception of energy as a bodily load or charge:

And the *physis* organized for it in technology can, in accordance with all its political and factual reality, only be produced in that image-space with which profane illumination makes us familiar. Only when here, in profane illumination, body and image-space so interpenetrate that all revolutionary tension becomes bodily collective innervation, and all the bodily innervations of the collective become revolutionary detonation, will reality have surpassed itself to the extent demanded by the *Communist Manifesto*.

(*GS* II.1, 310; *OWS* 239, translation modified)

Following this portrayal of an explosive charge-become-flesh in the body of the revolutionary collective comes the closing image of the alarm clock which thus describes a further break with what goes before it, namely the abrupt transition from the *body* to the *mechanical device*.[2] In the course of Benjamin's text on Surrealism the gradient of the power station has generated an energy which, in the passage through 'body- and image-space', has gathered force to such a degree that the image invades the body, whereupon body and image become one, resulting, in effect, in the leap into a mechanical state.

'BODY- AND IMAGE-SPACE' AND 'DIALECTICAL IMAGE'

This reading demonstrates a very close connection between Benjamin's talk of body- and image-space and the revolutionary gesture of the essay on Surrealism. The composition of the text stands in chronological proximity to the first phase of Benjamin's work on the *Passagen* project (1927–29), in the context of which he also set out his conception of the *dialectical image*, something he would develop further in the second phase of the project (1934–40). The proximity between the two concepts is, however, more than merely chronological. For just as the talk of body- and image-space proceeds from the distinction between metaphor and image, so the dialectical image is derived from a differentiation from the archaic image.[3] In both concepts representation (*Darstellung*) and idea (*Vorstellung*) coincide, and both have in common that they break the dimension of time out of the linear order in which it is traditionally structured. In the combination of image, body, and space, the category of time as the fourth dimension of culture is entirely absent, eliminated; while in the dialectical image, time as a linear progression is suspended when, in the 'Now of cognizability' (*Jetzt der Erkennbarkeit*), past and present come together unmediated, that is, with no distance between them. In both cases it is the achievement of presence (*Vergegenwärtigung*), as opposed to empathy (*Einfühlung*), that is at stake: a technique of *closeness*, a metabolic exchange between matter and image. The description of putting forth and absorbing in the Surrealism essay has its counterpart in the *Passagen* project in 'the true method of making things present to ourselves', of 'thinking of them in our space (not ourselves in theirs)' (*GS* V.2, 1014).

Here, the body- and image-space resembles a dream image that has become reality or a materialized primal fantasy (*Urphantasie*),[4] two types of images that are structured by the fact that the subject himself participates in the scene that he imagines. But further: in body- and image-space, both matrix and material of expression and representation are one. By contrast, the dialectical image is a *read* image, an image in language, even if the material of representation can here be very various: from physiognomy via dream images, the world of objects, to architecture, encompassing both the organic and the inorganic. Benjamin sees all gathered together in the 'landscape of an arcade. The organic and the inorganic world, base necessity and audacious luxury enter into the most contradictory of alliances, the merchandise hangs and shoves in as unrestrained a confusion as images in the wildest dreams' (*GS* V.2, 993). In view of the correspondences between outer world and dream world, the arcade in the city of modernity becomes for Benjamin the topographical paradigm of his investigation. Here he reads the world of objects as one would a dream, whereby the opposition of inner and outer is sublated in a dialectical constellation as he observes the *outward* topography in terms of the *inward* body of the collective. The dreamer on the journey through the body,

> Just as the sleeper though – in this respect like the madman – sets out on the macrocosmic journey through his body, while the sounds and sensations of his own inside, which to the healthy, waking man unite in the surge of health – blood pressure, the movement of the entrails, heartbeat, and muscular sensation – bring forth in his extraordinarily sharpened senses, *translating* and explaining them, delusion and dream image, so also is it with the dreaming collective which in the arcades and passageways [*Passagen*] becomes engrossed in its own inwardness. We must follow in its footsteps in order to construe the nineteenth century, in its fashions and advertising, its buildings and its politics, as the result of its dream history.
>
> (*GS* V.1, 491–2; my emphasis)

> [Variant in the earlier sketches:] the dreaming collective which becomes engrossed in the arcades and passageways as in *the inside of its own body*.
>
> (*GS* V.2, 1010; my emphasis)

In seeing the production of dream images as the result of physiological processes, or rather, in seeing dream images as a *translation* of corporeal processes, the *Passagen* project in its second phase follows the Freudian model of the unconscious, transferring this model to the collective and its body, the city; in the variant from the first phase of the project, by contrast, the dream still appears as a sphere within the subject or collective.[5]

Here, in Benjamin's notes for his ur-history of modernity, the body- and image-space of the collective is transposed into the arcades and passageways of the city which the author enters as a reader in order to decipher them, whereas the textual passage through body- and image-space in 'Surrealism' generates the collective as a detonating mechanism: a truly 'dialectical fairyland'.[6]

In the history of the composition of Benjamin's texts, the origins of the categories 'body- and image-space' and 'dialectical image' are linked together as by communicating tubes. The way having been prepared for them by a number of thought-images (*Denkbilder*) in 'One-Way Street' (1928),[7] both categories emerge from his writing at the end of the 1920s, with 'body- and image-space' tied more to the idea of a 'profane illumination', and the 'dialectical image'[8] to the constellation of awakening. Both are theoretical constructions originating in Benjamin's efforts to bring together the perceptions of both psychoanalysis and materialism for the purposes of analysing modernity.

In both cases Benjamin undertakes a *material* grounding or materialist inflection of *psychoanalytical* methods of observation. In the body- and image-space of 'Surrealism' this results in a materialization of the image in corporeal innervations, that is, in an enfleshment of expressive matter, whereby the human body becomes the material of imagery – a quite literal, no longer allegorical, form of embodiment. In the dialectical images of the *Passagen* project, on the other hand, we find a materialization of the language of the unconscious, the spatialization of dream structure, that is, a materialization of the imaginary in the organic and inorganic external world, or body social (*Gesellschaftskörper*).

The increasing concentration on the dialectical image and the constellation of awakening in the *Passagen* project is justified by Benjamin as a 'Copernican turning-point in remembrance' or as a 'Copernican turning-point in the perception of history' (*kopernikanische Wendung in der historischen Anschauung*) which he considers a matter of urgent necessity since the 'natural and bodily aids to remembrance' have been lost (*GS* V.1, 490). Where the body's aids to memory – one speaks today of *Körpergedächtnis*, corporeal memory –

have disappeared, the author shifts his work of recalling and deciphering onto the world of things as the material of the collective unconscious
– what is nowadays called the social imaginary. But even here Benjamin
still attempts to perceive the relation of body-space to image-space: 'In
the nineteenth century, construction has ... the role of the bodily
process, over which the "artistic" designs of architecture are laid like
dreams over the framework of physiological processes' (*GS* V.1, 494).

In the Surrealism essay he attempted to eliminate this difference
between framework and covering, and between construction and art –
perhaps because the basic structure and that which covers it cannot be
clearly distinguished in body-space, but perhaps also to introduce,
within the revolutionary gesture of the text, the notion that the artistic
process is itself a construction, thereby implicating it in the processes
of history. In his text 'On the Concept of History', Benjamin would
write that 'History is the object of a construction'. Composed in 1940
in exile and in the face of the totality of Nazi fascism, the theses are
cast as a reflection on ways of looking at history and its revolutionary
constellations, and see history as the subject of a *theoretical* construction. The gesture of the 1929 text, however, referring to the
Surrealists and programmatically exceeding their practice, is still
emphatically in favour of a revolutionary *praxis* of art.

THE GENESIS OF 'BODY- AND IMAGE-SPACE' IN BENJAMIN'S WRITINGS

The formulation 'body- and image-space', to my knowledge only to be
found in this specific form and combination in the Surrealism essay,
appears in the context of the development of Benjamin's theorems as a
point of convergence where formerly separate lines of thought meet.
The concept of *image-space* is to be found, for example, in the
unpublished notes 'On Painting' (*Zur Malerei*) (*GS* VI, 113–14) in
which Benjamin distinguishes between different kinds of painting,
referring not only to the method of representation, but also to the
relation between the 'visual space of a contemplated scene' and a
'correlatively opposed' and concealed image-space. This is in keeping
with his attentiveness to the materiality and spatiality of images and
writing as also to the non-representable which they point towards, an
attentiveness borne out by other notes and sketches,[9] but which takes
on theoretical shape at the latest in his book on German tragic drama,
inter alia in his remarks on Johann Wilhelm Ritter. Nevertheless,
while the painting is described in the notes 'On Painting', probably

written in 1921, as a correlation of fantasy and reproduction (*Abbil*,
the reproductive function plays no part in Benjamin's later conceptiʋɴ
of images. In Benjamin's writings the term 'image' (*Bild*) appears in
a whole range of different combinations and contexts, and ultimately
his talk of graphic image (*Schriftbild*) and dream image (*Traumbild*),
of the images of history (*Bilder der Geschichte*) and the mnemic image
(*Erinnerungsbild*), of thought-images (*Denkbilder*) and dialectical
images (*dialektische Bilder*) has as its basis a concept of images which
– aside from the controversy concerning the relation between 'material
and mental image' – goes back to the original and literal sense of the
word: image as likeness, similitude, or resemblance (*Ähnlichkeit*).[10]
The specific combination of *image* and *space* probably plays its most
significant role in the context of his writings on memory, among which
the textual form of 'Berlin Childhood Around 1900' is the most
obvious example of his calling to mind, 'making present', image-
spaces and the topography of mnemic images.[11]

The traces in Benjamin's writings of *body* – appearing both specifically as the corporeal (*Leib*) and under the more general term for body,
or mass (*Körper*) – and of *body-space* are rather less obvious and more
intricate. Since the publication of the 'Miscellaneous Fragments'
(*Fragmente vermischten Inhalts*) in volume VI of the *Gesammelte
Schriften* (1985) it has at any rate become clear what a significant role
reflections on the corporeal played already in Benjamin's early notes
on psychology and anthropology written shortly after the essay (similarly not intended for publication) 'On Language as Such and on the
Language of Man' (1916). Marlen Stoessel's observations on the
'forgotten human dimension' (*das vergessene Menschliche*) which, in
her view, characterizes his reading of the creation myth as 'language
magic' (*Sprachmagie*), since here the origin of human language appears
as a disembodied process, must now be revised at least in so far as
Benjamin was himself evidently aware of this forgotten dimension and
devoted attention to it elsewhere in his writings. In the first instance, as
an anthropological schema of 1918 demonstrates, he assigned the
corporeal and language to two different spheres of individual existence
which he nevertheless conceived as being simultaneous. In this schema,
body and language form the opposing cardinal points of a semicircle
from which the circles of human existence then variously extend.
However, in sketches from the same period, written under the influence
of his studies of Freud, the central concern is precisely the relations
between language, perception, the corporeal, and the body. Here *direct*
links to his theory of language magic are to be found, for example:

The relation of the human form to language, that is, the way in which God works within the human being, giving him form and shape, is the object of psychological study. Corporeality, in which God works in him linguistically in an immediate – and perhaps unintelligible – way, properly forms part of this study.

(*GS* VI, 66)

Benjamin is interested in this context in the connection between corporeality and language both with regard to bodily signs – for example in his notes 'On Shame' (*Über die Scham*) of 1919–20 (*GS* VI, 70) – and to perception, the history of which he links, in the note 'Perception and the Corporeal' (*Wahrnehmung und Leib*) (*GS* VI, 67), to 'corporeal changes' (*Veränderung des Leibes*). In this same note he also discusses the phenomenon of the inaccessibility to the perception of the subject of his own body. His reflections on shame are carried further in those 'On Blushing in Anger and Shame' (*Über Erröten in Zorn und Scham*) of 1920–21 (*GS* VI, 120), which in turn make reference to his sketches 'On Painting or Sign and Mark' (*Über die Malerei oder Zeichen und Mal*) composed in 1918 (*GS* II.2, 603–4). The result is a network of comparative reflections on different signs – in the image, on the body, or in the face – which in terms of their materiality and matrices are quite distinct from one another. In this sense it is already at this early stage, as opposed to only later in the 'body- and image-space' of 1929 or in the two essays of 1933 in which he develops the ideas contained in his essay on language of seventeen years earlier, that Benjamin modifies his reflections on a theory of language to take account of the 'forgotten relation of man to his origin in matter' that Stoessel remarks upon in the text of 1916 (Stoessel 1983: 69).

It is, however, not only this recently published material which corrects the overall picture drawn by Stoessel. On the one hand it is true that in the essays of 1933, the 'Doctrine of the Similar' and 'On the Mimetic Faculty', Benjamin now explicitly takes theoretical account of the body, integrating it into his modified version of the theory of language magic. Moreover, it is clear from these essays that the concept of 'non-sensuous similitudes' (*unsinnliche Ähnlichkeiten*) developed by Benjamin in this context emerged from a distinction from lost 'corporeal resemblance' (*Leibähnlichkeit*) (*GS* VI, 193). Nevertheless, this can hardly be linked to the 'substantialization of what Benjamin calls *aura*', as Stoessel maintains (1983: 16), and, indeed, the 'forgotten human dimension' generally becomes ever less clearly defined in the course of her study, successively related as it is to man's origin in matter, to the way man is made, to human physicality, to the feminine, and to work.[12]

It seems rather to be the case that in his early language theory Benjamin does not as yet differentiate between the motifs of aura – the raising of the eyes, for example – and those of magic and immediacy, whereas the immediacy in the conception of body- and image-space has lost its auratic character, since here the distinction between the perceiver and the perceived, the naming and the named, and between man and nature has been eliminated in so far as body-space and image-space are themselves indistinguishable. That this has nothing to do with the 'reinstitution of the paradisiac unity of conception [*Empfängnis*] and spontaneity' (Stoessel 1983: 175) is already indicated by the fact that the materialization of image-space in the body of the collective is apparently only conceivable for Benjamin in terms of a mechanical image, as the previously discussed image of the alarm clock suggests. As the 'first material on which the mimetic faculty is put to the proof . . . the human body' (*GS* VI, 127), lost as the material of mimesis in the course of human development, makes its reappearance in a constellation of revolutionary action and here displays its mimetic force, it is not *nature* that the human body comes to resemble, but *things*. In short, the coincidence of body- and image-space in modernity appears in terms of an instantaneous 'corporeal resemblance' to an image from the sphere of mechanics.

It is also problematical to describe, as Stoessel does, Benjamin's early language theory in terms of the notion of a pre-Oedipal 'magical communion between man and nature in the divine *logos*' which might be represented as an Oedipal triangle (Stoessel 1983: 139). Even if one were to understand the relation between God, nature, and man in the description of Adamite language as triadic (like that between father, mother, and son), the essential element that determines the Oedipal structure is here absent, namely the prohibition of immediacy between the bodies of mother and son. Benjamin's theory of language magic is at this early stage in his work to be seen rather as a pre-analytical conception, as the proposal of a theologico-linguistic, not a psycho-analytico-corporeal immediacy.[13] In the development of his thought, however, reflections on the body do indeed become important shortly afterwards, and then in the context of his studies of Freud. And when Benjamin thereafter refers to the body, it is always to the *body in/of language* (*Körper [in] der Sprache*), whether in the motif of the symbolized and dismembered body, of bodily signs, postures and gestures, the lost mimetic faculty, the bodily aids to (involuntary) recollection, or in the motif of distortion (*Entstellung*). In one of the

more extended texts on the theme of corporeality and the body, the
'Schemata on the Psychophysical Problem' (*Schemata zum psycho-
physischen Problem*), possibly written around 1922–23 (*GS* VI, 78),
Benjamin discusses the function of an as it were corporeal *différance*
coming from psychic excitation, and describes the body as an instrument of differentiation and discrimination:

> For all living reactivity is bound to the faculty of discrimination
> [*Differenzierung*], the foremost instrument of which is the body. This
> attribute of the body should be seen as fundamental. The body as a
> discriminatory instrument [*Differenzierungsinstrument*] of vital re-
> action, and only the body, can simultaneously be understood in terms
> of its psychic animation. All psychic activity can be differentiatedly
> localized in the body, as the anthroposophy of the ancients attempted
> to set out, for example in the analogy of body and macrocosm. One
> of the most important determinants of the body's differentiatedness
> [*Differenziertheit*] is perception.
>
> (*GS* VI, 81–2)

The discussion, together with the differences of pleasure and pain, of
the spatial relations of the body, of closeness and distance, and of dream
reality and perception in this text already brings together many of the
motifs which will later be investigated in detail and explained in more
concrete terms in relation to media history in the production complex
of Benjamin's work on modernity. In a note on his essay 'The Work of
Art in the Age of Mechanical Reproduction', Benjamin writes explicitly: 'The observation that the first material on which the mimetic
faculty is put to the proof is the human body could with greater
emphasis than hitherto be rendered fruitful for the ur-history of the arts'
(*GS* VI, 127). Here Benjamin suggests a perspective for research which
was only to be followed up in the 1980s with the many studies of the
language and history of the body written in that decade.

To return, however, to the origin of body- and image-space in
Benjamin's early anthropological writings. An apparent anticipation of
the later notion – comparable to that of the shock effect or impact
(*Chock*) – of a body that has lost its distinctive boundaries, such as
encountered in the body-and image-space of the Surrealism essay, can
be found in the early sketch 'On Horror I' (*Über das Grauen I*). In this
sketch Benjamin describes the state of distraction and absent-
mindedness (*Geistesabwesenheit*) or mental absorption in things external to the self in terms of a loss of power within the body, or a
disembodiment. In such a state the body is

left without the dividing, distinguishing distance between the corporeal < and > the mental, which expresses itself in the fact that the human body in a state of distraction has no distinct boundary. What is being perceived, above all when it is registered in the face,breaks into the body under these circumstances. .... A human being can, in a state of extreme terror, go so far as to imitate that which terrifies him.

(*GS* VI, 76)

The same constellation, a kind of apotropaic mimesis, which Benjamin ascribes to the effect of warding off horror, will reappear later, once he has moved on from the metaphysical construct of the body–mind relation[14] to a more consistent use of psychoanalytical terminology, in the simultaneity of shock or impact (*Chock*) and the defence against shock or parrying of impacts (*Chockabwehr*) as described in the Baudelaire book – for example, with reference to Baudelaire's 'eccentric grimaces' (*GS* I.2, 616; *Ill* 165). And, comparable with the shock effect of film or the new experience made possible by the camera whereby the 'optic-unconscious' becomes perceivable and the postures and attitudes of the individual in any given split-second are made visible, it is already in the body- and image-space of 'Surrealism' that 'an unconsciously penetrated space is substituted for a space consciously explored by man' in the way that Benjamin will analyse in his 'Work of Art' essay (*GS* I.2, 500; *Ill* 238–9). The difference is that in the 'Surrealism' essay the process does not take place on the screen, is not represented in terms of body-space in the film image, but happens rather to the collective and in the space of political action – and, not least, in the space of an as yet pre-fascist constellation. To this extent the passage through body- and image-space could also be read as an experiment in giving a revolutionary inflection to terror in modernity, in the course of which the state of the distracted or absent-minded body has become the concept of *Aktualität* as presence of mind incarnate (*leibhaftige Geistesgegenwart*).

FORGETTING AND REDEMPTION: THE PSYCHOANALYTIC REFORMULATION OF THE MESSIANIC

In the essay on Kafka of 1934, by contrast, the focus is more on the aspects of alienation and forgetting associated with the body: 'the most forgotten alien land is one's own body' (*GS* II.2, 431; *Ill* 132). Here Benjamin examines the significance of gestures in Kafka, reading his literary work as a 'codex of gestures' which cannot be comprehended symbolically. This is formulated most memorably in the Talmudic legend in which the village whose language cannot be understood is interpreted as being one's own body, an alien territory which 'has gained control over [modern man]' (*GS* II.2, 424; *Ill* 126). What is being addressed here is a language of the body in which the forgotten, while visible, is not readily decipherable – the body, then, as material and matrix of the language of the unconscious.

It is in this context that we find an image which reads as the reverse side of the revolutionary notion of body- and image-space, an image in which the coincidence of representation and perception manifests itself in the same material, in the body – but now as fear.

> In the *Penal Colony* those in power use an archaic apparatus which engraves ornate letters on the backs of guilty men, multiplying the cuts and increasing the ornamentation to the point where the back of the guilty man becomes clairvoyant, able itself to decipher the writing from whose letters it must learn the name of its unknown guilt. It is, then, the back upon which this is incumbent.
>
> (*GS* II.2, 432; *Ill* 133, translation modified)

The *profane illumination* which led to the body- and image-space of 'Surrealism' can thus also be read as a counter-proposal to the violent practices of *clairvoyancy* depicted in this text, and on this basis in turn as a concept based in *Chockabwehr*, the defence of oneself against shock.

If the Kafka essay is thematically structured by the relation between the body and forgetting, it is also linked by its interest in the significance of the body in the context of a language of the unconscious to other works of the 1930s, notably the *Passagen* project and the Baudelaire book, in the latter of which the theme reappears in the discussion of permanent traces, of *mémoire involontaire*, and in the reference to the memory images (*Gedächtnisbilder*) deposited in parts of the body such as described by Proust (*GS* I.2, 613; *Ill* 160). In the Kafka essay, it is the term 'distortion' (*Entstellung*), derived from the Freudian theory of the unconscious, which is used to describe the connection between the body, things, animals, and the forgotten:

> Odradek is the form things assume when they are forgotten. They are distorted. The 'cares of the family man', which no one can identify, are distorted; the bug, of which we know all too well that it represents Gregor Samsa, is distorted; and distorted, too, the great animal, half lamb, half kitten, for which the 'butcher's knife' might be 'a release'

[*Erlösung*]. These figures of Kafka's are, however, linked via a long series of figures with the prototype of distortion, the hunchback.

(*GS* II.2, 431; *Ill* 133, translation modified)

This reference to the body and to things, to both the organic and the inorganic, as the material of distortion (a modality in the structure of the unconscious) represents one of the variants with which Benjamin accomplishes his materialist inflection of psychoanalytical modes of observation. In the Kafka essay, which in many respects, not only with the motifs of the storm and of reversal (*Umkehr*), anticipates the text on the concept of history composed six years later, distortion is also conceived of in terms of its difference from redemption: 'the forgotten always touches on the best, for it touches on the possibility of redemption [*Erlösung*]' (*GS* II.2, 434; *Ill* 136, translation modified). In this way, Benjamin is able to inscribe his reading of Judaic Messianism into his fusion of materialism and psychoanalysis: 'No one says that the distortions, to set aright which the Messiah will one day appear, are those of our space alone. They are also certainly those of our time' (*GS* II.2, 433; *Ill* 135, translation modified). And those of the body, one might add, a body which, understood here as memory, makes manifest its/a difference from its origin – and from Benjamin's early version of language magic.[15]

This little man [the little hunchback] is the inmate of distorted life; he will disappear with the coming of the Messiah, of whom a great rabbi once said that he would not wish to change the world by force, but would put it to rights in slight ways.

(*GS* II.2, 432; *Ill* 134, translation modified)

If distortion here marks the difference from redemption, it is also the case that the psychoanalytical reformulation of the Messianic idea simultaneously eliminates the possibility of a clear opposition between 'true and false life'. The implication is that in an unredeemed state no 'true' or complete image of history can be attained, or as Benjamin will later write: 'only a redeemed mankind is granted its past *in full abundance*' (*GS* I.2, 694; *Ill* 256, translation modified; my emphasis); and: 'The Messianic world is the world of universal and integral actuality, and only in this world is there a universal history' (*GS* I.3, 1235); or again: 'The genuine conception of universal history is a Messianic one' (*GS* V, 608). Yet the idea that historiography, in deciphering its sources, should pay particular attention to the form of their distortions is one which even today most historians – at any rate those working in German – would doubtless regard as a pretty tall order.

3 Communicating tubes
Michel Foucault and Walter Benjamin

THE ARTS OF EXISTENCE: ANTIQUITY
AND MODERNITY

In one of his last works, the second volume of *The History of Sexuality*, published in 1984, Michel Foucault makes a footnote reference to the author of the Baudelaire study (Foucault 1987: 11). This is, to my knowledge, Foucault's only explicit mention of Benjamin, although his earlier works, too, show evidence of a considerable closeness to Benjamin's thinking, be it in the concept of 'similitude' in his archaeology of the human sciences, in his reading of Nietzsche, or generally in his approach to history, for which the break with the continuum, the reference to corporeality, and the critique of historicism are of fundamental significance. This footnote can also be read as a footnote to the Franco-German constellation in philosophical discourse in the post-1945 period, and particularly to the belated reception of Benjamin in France.

> It is not quite correct to imply that since Burckhardt the study of these arts and this aesthetics of existence has been completely neglected. One thinks of Benjamin's study on Baudelaire. There is also an interesting analysis in Stephen Greenblatt's recent book, *Renaissance Self-Fashioning* (1980).
>
> (1987: 11)

This footnote is, in terms of the history of philosophy, symptomatic in that it configurates that typical triad[1] by which *contemporary* theory in France and the United States is placed in relation to *historical* theoretical works from Germany. At the same time, the allusion to Benjamin is of considerable importance, since Foucault sees the Baudelaire study, together with Burckhardt's Renaissance book, as a building block for the history of the 'arts of existence' and of those technologies of the self

by which men not only set themselves rules of conduct, but also seek
to transform themselves, to change themselves in their singular being,
and to make their life into an *oeuvre* that carries certain aesthetic
values and meets certain stylistic criteria.

(1987: 10–11)

Thus for the construction of the history of the subject as a history of
problematizations and techniques of the self – in particular with regard
to sexual conduct – through which 'the individual constitutes and
recognizes himself *qua* subject' (1987: 6), Foucault names authors
whose works might be seen as forerunners to his own study of the
'problematization' (1987: 10) of sexual conduct in Greek and Greco-
Roman antiquity. The techniques of the self are described as 'etho-
poetic' (1987: 13) practices which shape the body and its relationship
to others. Drawing a contrast between his own approach and that typical
of ideology critique, Foucault characterizes his project as archaeological and genealogical: archaeological with reference to the forms
of the problematizations themselves, and genealogical in terms of the
'formation [of the problematizations] out of the practices and the
modifications undergone by the latter' (1987: 12).

Simultaneously with the proposal of a *genealogy* and archaeology of
techniques of the self and modes of constituting the subject, then,
Foucault situates his own work as it were in a *genealogy* of the history
of these arts of existence. With this he places his last major project, the
analysis of the genealogy of 'desiring man' (1987: 13) deriving from
antiquity, *inter alia* in proximity to the work on an 'ur-history of
modernity' with which Benjamin was occupied for more than the last
ten years of his life and nearly half a century before Foucault. This
constellation effects a double inversion in/of the genealogy. From the
position of historiographical and theoretical *posteriority* to Benjamin,
Foucault's study of antiquity forms from an historical perspective as it
were the *pre-history* of those arts of existence which for Benjamin
found expression in the attitudes of Baudelaire as a hero of modernity.

Indeed, numerous correspondences can be observed between the two
projects. Benjamin, for example, compares the modern author who
exposes himself to the impacts and sensations of the city, parrying these
and giving them form in his literary work, with the hero of antiquity,
while Foucault, drawing an analogy between the self-constitution of the
subject and political structure, between the ethics of pleasure and the
organization of the city, makes reference to Plato's formulation that 'the
"paradigm" of the city is laid up in heaven for him who wants to
contemplate it' and that 'looking upon it the philosopher will be able

to "set up the government of his soul"' (1987: 71).[2] Then again, Foucault gives emphasis to the frequent occurrence of battle metaphors (the battle with one's own desires; the notion of the conqueror and the conquered in a dramaturgy of the practices of pleasure) in the ancient world's problematization of the arts of existence, while Benjamin characterizes the modern author as a fencer (*GS* I.2, 570; *CB* 68), the creative process as a duel, and the defence of the self against impacts that it entails as combat (*GS* I.2, 616; *Ill* 165). But over and above this, there are correspondences in the dramaturgy of the sexes as presented by each. Foucault examines discourses in which the male subject sees the use of pleasure primarily in terms of the *mise en scène* of the relationship with the male sexual partner and in which the relationship with woman remains marginalized, since this is considered only in terms of economy (that is, relations between the sexes are considered only in terms of the reproductive function). Benjamin, on the other hand, presents as it were a reverse mirror image: the modern author on 'the sacrificial path [*Opfergang*] of male sexuality' (*GS* I.2, 670), that is, Baudelaire, who, in his renunciation of that which is defined as natural, namely the bourgeois model of femininity which reduces woman to her role in the family and her function as mother, stylizes the lesbian with her sexuality liberated from the reproductive function as a heroine of *modernité* (*GS* I.2, 594, 667; *CB* 90). In the *topos* of the 'recurrence of the same', that in the relationship of modernity to antiquity which is *new* – and which, according to Benjamin, is won by Baudelaire from the 'always-the-same' (*Immerwiedergleichen*) (*GS* I.2, 673) – can be seen as bearing the mark of gender difference. For there is between the constellation investigated by Foucault and the one investigated by Benjamin a clear displacement from male to female homosexuality – albeit without a corresponding change of perspective from the male to the female subject, for: 'In his image of modernity he [Baudelaire] had a place for it [lesbian love]; in reality he did not recognize it' (*GS* I.2, 596; see *CB* 93). This remark of Benjamin's draws our attention to another difference, the difference in writing. For where Foucault examines prescriptive texts, discourses in which the male subject constitutes himself as author and composes his text as an exposition of his own arts of existence or as a reflection on these, Benjamin refers to an author whose texts are not drafts for living. Rather this author is, by giving form to the crisis of perception and experience in modernity, operating in the image archive of a collective memory.

Despite the concurrence and continuity of the male perspective, there nevertheless seems to lie in the aforementioned displacement a motif for the chiasmus in the trajectories of the two authors' historical interests – or perhaps rather of their vision and their 'historical sense' (Nietzsche) – and of the genealogies of their intellectual projects. If Foucault's studies originated in modern thought for which the relation between sign and subject has become problematical and in an archaeology of knowledge (*Les mots et les choses*, trans.: *The Order of Things* 1966), the goal of his progression into so-called ancient history in his last major project is a constellation in which the male constitutes himself as subject both of sexual and of discursive practices. Benjamin, by contrast, took as his starting point readings of historical literature (primarily the literature of the Romantic and Baroque eras, but also of Goethe and Hölderlin) and went on to concentrate on texts from the nineteenth and twentieth centuries (those of the Surrealists among others, but particularly those of Proust, Kafka, and Baudelaire). His readings of the latter became for him, in the context of the *Passagen* project which grew out of them, fragments of an 'ur-history of modernity' for which literature and written texts – in accordance with the theorem of readability – took their place alongside other scenes and figures. Apart from the author as hero, whom Benjamin understands as the 'true subject of *modernité*' (*GS* I.2, 577; see *CB* 74), there are other heroes, multifarious types and figures of the modern city whose positions are distributed among both sexes.

PORTRAIT OF THE AUTHORS IN THEIR ARCHIVES

It is with these differing constellations that each of these two authors, Foucault and Benjamin, seems to have arrived at his own singular position, at the distinguishing mark of his own experience and attitudes. At first sight no greater contrast seems to be imaginable than that between the *images* and the *discursive methods* of the two thinkers: between the penetrative gaze and resolute bearing of the one and the contemplative, somewhat dreamy gaze and stylized gestures of the melancholic of the other; between Foucault's lucid and systematic analysis of discourses on the one hand and Benjamin's subtle literary thought-images on the other – although both these portraits would no doubt have appealed to Benjamin as illustrations of the physiognomy of the brooder (*Grübler*) beneath whose gaze the continuum disintegrates. Similarly no greater contrast could be imagined than that between the professor of the History of Thought Systems at the renowned Collège de France, whose lectures were often transmitted by loudspeaker to the foyer because of the overflow from the lecture theatre, and the freelance writer who failed in his attempt at the *Habilitation* at the University of Frankfurt, who – not only after 1933

Figure 1 Photograph of Michel Foucault by Michèle Bancilhon

as a Jewish exile – was obliged to expend considerable diplomatic effort every time he sought to publish, and for whom his material conditions became such a concern that by the time of the Paris exile the loss of his fountain pen drove him to the brink of despair.

I hope that I might be permitted this brief sideways glance at the portraits of the two authors since both attributed central significance to the *location* and the *stance* of the historian for the construction and reading of the images of history – stance here in a sense that goes beyond opinion or conviction.[3] Foucault discusses this under the heading of 'historical sense' as the necessary affirmation of 'knowledge as perspective'; for historians this includes the 'elements in their work which reveal their grounding in a particular time and place, their preferences in a controversy, and the inevitability of their passions'

Figure 2 Photograph of Walter Benjamin by Germaine Krull, reproduced by permission of Museum Folkswang in Essen, Germany

(Foucault 1977: 156–7, translation modified). Referring to the place of perception, Benjamin speaks in a similar way of the 'Now of cogniz-ability' (*Jetzt der Erkennbarkeit*). In this way he makes the image of what has been dependent on the (psychological) preoccupations of the present observer or reader, the 'subject of historical cognition'; de-pendent, then, on the present lighting and the developer which deter-mine the readability of the images. 'The read image, by which is meant the image in the Now of cognizability, bears to the highest degree the stamp of the critical, dangerous moment which is at the basis of all reading' (*GS* V.1, 578; see *N* 50–1). Benjamin's historian, too, finds himself confronted with the passionate, although in Benjamin this is already part of the pastness of things themselves: 'To be past, to be no longer works passionately on things. The historian entrusts his work to this effect. He is directed by this power and recognizes things as they are to a moment of being-no-longer' (*GS* V.2, 1001).

For both Benjamin and Foucault the most important place of work and at the same time the most essential object of their study was the *archive*, though not understood in its traditional sense as 'the sum of all the texts that a culture has preserved as documents attesting to its own past, or as evidence of a continuing identity' (Foucault 1972: 128–9, translation modified). If Foucault, in his approach to the history of discourses, sees the archive as taking on concrete form in those systems 'that established statements as *events* (with their own conditions and domain of appearance) and *things* (with their own possibility and field of use)' (1972: 128; my emphasis), then it could be said that Benjamin quite literally proceeds from the things and the events themselves and is, as it were with a reverse perspective, in search of their statements. This is at any rate the case in his ur-history of modernity in which he, rather than (re)constructing historical discourses, adopts the stance of the collector of quotations and of the reader. On the other hand, his *Trauerspiel* book could be taken as the description of an archive of German tragic drama in a Foucauldian sense,[4] since Benjamin's concern in it was the *idea* of tragedy, whereby 'idea' is understood as inner structure and configuration, as image of all virtual tragedies, as 'the whole range of possible extremes it contains' (*GS* I.1, 227; *OGT* 47). And for Foucault the archive is 'first the law of what can be said, the system that governs the appearance of statements as unique events' (Foucault 1972: 129).

Their work on the archive regularly took both of them to the institutionalized archive, the place in which tradition was preserved, which meant, in concrete topographical terms, above all to the Bibliothèque Nationale where both of them would periodically disappear behind veritable mountains of books – so that they might well never have encountered each other even if their visits to the archive had not been decades apart. Foucault, however, seems to have been a lot more successful in systematizing or ordering his archive, and in doing justice in his writing to Benjamin's dictum that history was the object of a *construction* which was preceded by *destruction* (*GS* V.1, 587; *N* 60). At any rate his books reduced considerably in volume over his lifetime – compare, for example, *The Order of Things* or the works on prison, madness, or the institution of the clinic with the second and third volumes of *The History of Sexuality* – while the wealth of quotations from documents researched for the archive made way increasingly for his historical construction, for his own writing. For Benjamin, by contrast, the possibility of presenting his construction evidently threatened to evade him in the mass of material gathered for his *Passagen* project, although he was constantly producing different schemes for ordering it. In the end, it seems that he expended ever greater effort in dislodging individual quotations and fragments from his sources only to become entangled in the net of their multiple cross-references.

THE END OF DISCOURSE AND THE RETURN OF LITERATURE

This is no doubt related to the fact that Benjamin's attempt to write an ur-history of modernity was located historically precisely at that point of transition[5] which Foucault describes in *The Order of Things* as the place of literature's appearance and as the moment in which language ceased to function as representation, so that the radical reflection on language became increasingly the central focus of philosophy (Foucault 1970: 303ff.). Foucault here differentiates between a 'language that says nothing, is never silent, and is called "literature"' (1970: 306) and discourse – *discourse*, that is, in the sense of a unity of general grammar in accordance with the model of simple representation such as pertained in the Classical age. He understands literary language as a kind of counter-discourse (p. 44), and thus literature as the reappearance of language 'in a multiplicity of modes of being, whose unity was probably irrecoverable', of language 'in an enigmatic multiplicity' (1970: 304, 305).

If Foucault devoted his attention in his last works to an historical constellation in which he found *discourses* in their least ambiguous form, namely in prescriptive texts,[6] Benjamin by contrast tested his theory of deciphering and readability not only on the ambiguous *literary* texts of modernity, but extended it to other cultural 'texts': to the topography of the city, to architecture, interiors, objects, fashions, and so on. In comprehending these as the dream-writing (*Traumschrift*) of the collective, he was concerned to decipher at origin the dream of a past epoch from the wish-symbols of the previous century which had been laid in ruins 'even before the monuments which represented them had crumbled' (*GS* V.1, 59; *CB* 176). With his reading project Benjamin oversteps precisely that boundary of knowledge that Foucault associates with the end of discourse and the simultaneous reappearance of a language of multiple meaning. For as a result of the fragmentation and dispersion of language, every effort to come to terms with the break with the methods of the Classical order tends simply to complete it, since in the systematic or analytical attempt to define this language in its totality the break is repeated. In this respect the question is raised of a completely new form of thinking which is different from the closure of systematic knowledge: 'To discover the vast play of language contained once more within a single space might be just as decisive a leap towards a wholly new form of thought as to draw to a close a mode of knowing constituted during the previous century' (Foucault 1970: 307).

If Foucault draws attention with the heterogeneity of discourse and language to a question which has proved of structural significance to all contemporary theory based on linguistics or semiotics, and which in the process has produced an array of formal variants aimed at reducing the gap and the antagonism between academic discourse and literariness,[7] Benjamin's writing is already situated in immediate relation to this heterogeneity. His *Passagen* project, the attempt at representing an ur-history of modernity through a collection of quotations and thought-images, might well be seen in terms of the first of the methodological variants suggested by Foucault, namely as a 'leap towards a wholly new form of thought'. Benjamin was indeed working on this with, for example, his representation of the whole through the fragment, which was methodologically concretized in the theorems of allegorical perception and the monadological structure of phenomena.[8]

In this form of thought the quotation attains a linguistic materiality and independence which make it readable in a variety of ways, but also resistant to the purpose of constructing history. The quotation embodies as it were language as literature, broken out of one discourse in order, as a fragment, to become part of another, different form of writing. For the quotation

> summons the word by its name, breaks it destructively from its context, but precisely thereby calls it back to its origin. . . . In the quotation the two realms – of origin and destruction – present themselves before language. And conversely, only where the two realms interpenetrate – in the quotation – is language consummated. In the quotation is mirrored the language of the angels in which all words, startled from the idyllic context of meaning, become mottoes in the book of Creation.
>
> (*GS* II.1, 363; *OWS* 286, translation modified)

But by indicating its own origination in the *topoi* of context and break, the quotation also resists participating in the construction of a new totality.

LOST SIMILITUDE

This approach to the quotation suggests links with Benjamin's theory of *language magic (Sprachmagie)* which came out of his reading of the Book of Genesis – of Holy Scripture understood not as meaning handed down nor as 'revealed truth' (*GS* II.1, 147; *OWS* 114), but as a mythical primal scene describing the emergence of language and sense. According to this theory the immediacy (*Unmittelbarkeit*) or magic of Adamite language, described as a translation of the silent language of nature or of things into the language of man, is lost in language's fall from paradise whereby language takes on an instrumental and communicative character. As a result of the Fall its magic side thereafter only becomes visible through its symbolic side in momentary flashes. Thus man's mimetic faculty passes into writing and language, and from then on can only find expression in the form of what Benjamin calls 'nonsensuous similitudes' (*unsinnliche Ähnlichkeiten*).[9]

It is with respect to this idea that Foucault – surprisingly, and even in the formulations chosen – comes particularly close to Benjamin, namely in his account of *lost* similitude in the second chapter of *The Order of Things*. This chapter could be read as a subsequent historicization of Benjamin's mythically derived theory of language. The severance from language magic which appears in Benjamin's work in a *mythical* primal scene, in the expulsion from paradise, is made concrete by Foucault as an *historical* movement, and situated by him at the transition from the Renaissance to the Classical age, the epoch of representation. It is identified, then, as the first of the two historical ruptures examined in his *Order of Things*. For the epistemes of the sixteenth century which were displaced in the process of transition are described by him in terms of the paradigm of similitudes:

> The world is covered with signs that must be deciphered, and those signs, which reveal resemblances and affinities, are themselves no more than forms of similitude. To know must therefore be to interpret: to find a way from the visible mark to that which is being said by it and which, without that mark, would lie like *unspoken speech, dormant within things.*
>
> (Foucault 1970: 32; my emphasis)

Moreover, where once there was a 'space inhabited by immediate resemblances', a vast open book bristling with written characters and magic signs (1970: 27), in the seventeenth century the kinship of language and world was dissolved and the primacy of the written word broken, that 'uniform layer, in which the *seen* and the *read*, the visible

and the expressible, were endlessly interwoven' (p. 43), with the result
that words and things became separated, and order came to dominate
over interpretation.

> on the one side, we shall find the signs that have become the tool of
> analysis, marks of identity and difference, principles whereby things
> can be reduced to order, keys for a taxonomy; and, on the other, the
> empirical and murmuring resemblance of things, that unreacting
> similitude that lies beneath thought and furnishes the infinite raw
> material for divisions and distributions.
>
> (1970: 58)

However, the lost similitude had as little to do with representation
(*Abbildung*) as did the lost immediacy of Benjamin's paradisiac
language. On the contrary, it was the 'invisible form of that which from
the depth of the world made things visible', so that the visible was a
sign of invisible analogies, the cipher of a silent language which
required deciphering. In terms of the history of language, Foucault
describes this loss of similitude as a transition from a *ternary* to a *binary*
system of signs, as a transition, then, from a sign system 'containing
the significant, the signified, and the "conjuncture" (the *tygkanon*)'[10]
to an arrangement of signs defined 'as the connection of a significant
and a signified' (1970: 42). It is this sign system that dominates
representation and what Foucault calls the Classical age. Moreover,
'nothing, except perhaps literature – and even then in a fashion more
allusive and diagonal than direct' can recall 'even the memory of that
[earlier] being', or, more precisely, nothing except literature in its
manifestation as 'the reappearance of the living being of language'
(1970: 43) on the threshold to modernity.

Yet in the manner in which Benjamin takes up precisely this
possibility of the reappearance of a lost similitude and ambiguity of
language, there also enters into his work another recollective trail
tracing back to Holy Scripture as memory and to the tradition of Jewish
writing, from which is taken a model of non-representational similitude. This trail is also followed by Foucault in his section on 'The
writing of things' in which he refers explicitly to the Hebraic tradition
and to the Cabala, and in which his account draws even closer to
Benjamin's reading of Genesis and its cultural presuppositions. Both
writers refer to the divine origin of language, and both see in the
proliferation of languages, the confusion of tongues at Babel, a caesura.
But where Benjamin posits the 'Fall of language-mind' (*der Sündenfall
des Sprachgeistes*), Foucault speaks of the first *raison d'être* of
language:

In its original form, when it was given to men by God himself, language was an absolutely certain and transparent sign for things because it resembled them. . . . All the languages known to us are now spoken only against the background of this lost similitude, and in the space that it left vacant. There is only one language that retains a memory of that similitude, because it derives in direct descent from that first vocabulary which is now forgotten; because God did not wish men to forget the punishment inflicted at Babel; because this language had to be used in order to recount God's ancient Alliance with his people; and lastly, because it was in this language that God addressed himself to those who listened to him. Hebrew therefore contains, as if in the form of fragments, the marks of that original name-giving.

(1970: 36)

In Foucault's own writings, in which in the course of his studies language as literature disappeared increasingly into the background while language as discourse took on ever greater importance, this passage remains an episode. The title under which this passage appears, 'The writing of things', is nevertheless extraordinarily apposite as a title for a mode of thought that moves in the space between both of the quite different forms of recollection of lost similitude mentioned by him: between the Cabala and (modern) literature. It was in this space that Benjamin worked and in which the trail of his own writing partially lost itself. For it was here, in a space which perhaps rather resembled an abyss – a space opened out by correspondences between two different forms of recollection, the trace of a forgotten tradition of writing on the one hand and the appearance of another kind of similitude, a distorted or 'non-sensuous similitude' on the other – that he was operating with his project on readability.[11] So that Foucault in his historiography of discourses retrospectively staked out and described the boundaries between which Benjamin's 'wholly new form of thought' found its origin.

ORIGIN AND THE BODY IN HISTORY

Since in the previous section the theme of 'origin' was touched on a number of times, this section will focus on the meaning of origin and its theoretical location in the concept of 'real history' (*echte Historie*) in both authors. The most explicit concurrences in the theoretical projects of Foucault and Benjamin are namely to be found in their approach to the writing of history and in their anti-historicist reflections on *discontinuity* and the concept of *origin*. This emerges most clearly from a comparison of Benjamin's theses 'On the Concept of History' and *Konvolut* N of the *Passagen-Werk* with Foucault's essay on 'Nietzsche, Genealogy and History' which he wrote in 1971 for a volume in homage to Jean Hyppolite.

The work of historiography involves for both Benjamin and Foucault above all the renunciation of unity, totality, and the absolute, and it implies the necessity of systematically blasting apart historical continuity. In differentiating between 'effective' or 'real' history (Nietzsche's *wirkliche Historie*) and that of the historians, Foucault states:

> The traditional devices for constructing a comprehensive view of history and for retracing the past as a patient and continuous development must be systematically dismantled. . . . History becomes 'effective' to the degree that it introduces discontinuity into our very being – as it divides our emotions, dramatizes our instincts, multiplies our body and sets it against itself.
>
> (Foucault 1977: 153–4)

If the reference here to the body suggests a link to the 'body- and image-space' of Benjamin's essay on Surrealism where 'no limb [of the inner man's] remains unrent' (*GS* II.1, 309; *OWS* 239), the idea of blasting apart the continuum finds numerous parallels in Benjamin's writing, for example in his formulation 'That the object of history should be blasted out of the continuum of historical progression is demanded by its monadological structure' (*GS* V.1, 594; see *N* 66).

The 'glance that distinguishes, separates, and disperses' postulated by Foucault (1977: 153) as necessary to the fulfilment of this intention recalls Benjamin's demand in the Surrealism essay for the 'substitution of the political for the historical view of what has been' (*GS* II.1, 300; *OWS* 230, translation modified). And Benjamin's dictum that the writer should as far as is possible distance himself from the process of transmitting tradition, or his claim that it is the task of the historical materialist 'to brush history against the grain' (*GS* I.2, 696–7; *Ill* 259) make common cause with Foucault's programme of turning history against its own provenance, of liberating it from the metaphysical or anthropological model of memory, of constructing 'a counter-memory – a transformation of history into a totally different form of time' (Foucault 1977: 160).

Nietzsche, to whose text *On the Use and Disadvantage of History for Life* Foucault here refers and from which Benjamin also took the motto for the twelfth of his theses 'On the Concept of History', is without any doubt a common point of reference for the two authors,[12] even if his works do not take on the same central significance as informants on modernity for Benjamin as they do for Foucault. A number of Benjamin's and Foucault's projects could be viewed in relation to Nietzsche's famous dictum:

> Until now everything that has given existence colour has as yet had no history: or where is there to be found a history of love, of greed, of envy, of conscience, of piety, of cruelty? Even a comparative history of justice, or even merely of punishment has been until now totally lacking.
>
> (Nietzsche 1980: III, 41)

In this the work of both stands in opposition to the 'complete denial of the body' in philosophy (Foucault 1977: 156). For both Benjamin and Foucault the body is not outside history, nor is it understood as nature in opposition to culture. The body, too, has a history, it is simultaneously a matrix of history and a site in which history takes place.

Foucault followed up this insight in a whole series of projects: the studies on madness, on the practices of discipline and punishment, on the regulation of sexuality, and finally on the constitution of subjectivity in the ancient world and in early Christian culture. But it was Benjamin already who anticipated the relevance of history to materiality and corporeality which has become so important in contemporary theory – even if this aspect of Benjamin's work has hitherto, with the exception of the allegory of the corpse in the *Trauerspiel* book, been largely ignored in Benjamin reception.

In his essay on 'Nietzsche, Genealogy and History', Foucault focuses above all on Nietzsche's approach to the concept of origin (*Ursprung*) in order to demonstrate his distance from the idea of historical beginning or a first identity, and to differentiate between the two aspects of *descent* (*Herkunft*) and *emergence* (*Entstehung*). The concept, so important to his work, of genealogy is explained here in the context of a discussion of *Herkunft* and *Entstehung*, whereby the body is dealt with primarily under the aspect of *Herkunft*.

> The body – and everything that touches it: diet, climate, and soil – is the domain of the *Herkunft*. The body manifests the stigmata of past experience and also gives rise to desires, failings, and errors. These elements may join in a body where they achieve a sudden expression, but as often, their encounter is an engagement in which they efface each other, where the body becomes the pretext of their insurmountable conflict.
>
> The body is the inscribed surface of events (traced by language and

dissolved by ideas), the locus of a dissociated Self (adopting the illusion of a substantial unity), and a volume in perpetual disintegration. Genealogy, as an analysis of descent, is thus situated within the articulation of the body and history. Its task is to expose a body totally imprinted by history and the process of history's destruction of the body.

(Foucault 1984: 83)

Such a close association of descent (*Herkunft*) and body is absent in Benjamin's writings. In Benjamin the interpenetration of body and history always occurs in an image-space, so that the body as matrix of history is always already structured as an image; the *physis* in 'all its political and factual reality' can only be produced in image-space (*GS* II.1, 310; *OWS* 239), and body- and image-space cannot be separated.[13] Yet Foucault's concept of the heterogeneity of descent – symptomized by the dissociation of the self, by dispersion, and so on (Foucault 1977: 145–6) – is supported indirectly by Benjamin through his *negation* of a construction of *Herkunft* which promotes unity or identity, or which serves a political or ideological purpose, for example where he emphasizes the artificial nature of recollection produced for the proletariat.[14] The dimension which Foucault in the Nietzsche essay terms descent, 'the ancient affiliation to a group' (1977: 145), is produced in Benjamin's interpretation primarily through expectation or recollection, through 'that secret agreement between past generations and the present one', that '*weak* Messianic power . . . , to which the past has a claim' (*GS* I.2, 694; *Ill* 256).

The reflections of both authors on the concepts of *Ursprung* and *Entstehung* come still closer. While in Foucault's reading *Herkunft* refers to descent (*provenance*) and is related to the network of subindividual marks which intersect in each individual in the same way as the inscriptions of events in the body, he sees *Entstehung* as emergence: '*Entstehung* designates *emergence*, the moment of arising [*surgissement*]. It stands as the principle and the singular law of an apparition' (Foucault 1977: 148). In the German translation of this passage, 'apparition' is rendered by the word *Aufblitzen* (appearance in a flash), a leitmotif word in Benjamin's writings, thereby creating an association which in view of his work on the concept of origin appears fully supportable. In Benjamin's 'Epistemo-Critical Prologue' to *The Origin of German Tragic Drama*, in which he finds himself on a curious threshold – still employing a metaphysical terminology, but already engaged in a thought process which breaks with metaphysics – the term *Ursprung*, likewise distinguished from 'beginning', is also discussed in terms of emergence:

Origin [*Ursprung*], although an entirely historical category, has, nevertheless, nothing to do with genesis [*Entstehung*]. The term origin is not intended to describe the process by which the existent came into being, but rather to describe that which emerges from the process of becoming and disappearance [*dem Werden und Vergehen Entspringendes*]. Origin is an eddy in the stream of becoming, and in its current it swallows the material involved in the process of genesis.

(*GS* I.1, 226; *OGT* 45)

Foucault's understanding of the one variant in Nietzsche's concept of origin, *Entstehung* in the sense of emergence, thus resembles Benjamin's concept of origin in the sense of the emergent (*das Entspringende*), which Benjamin distinguishes from the concept of *Entstehung* as beginning or genesis. This discussion of origin in the *Trauerspiel* book is still related to ideas and content. In his work on modernity, however, Benjamin is concerned with the historical originary phenomena – for example, the Paris arcades – in whose topography material, concrete, and symbolic meanings intersect.

SCENE AND IMAGES OF HISTORY

Origin in both authors should strictly speaking be envisaged in terms of an event which is perceived *scenically*, as an emergence onto the historical scene, as an appearance, or as a primal scene. 'Emergence is thus the entry of forces; it is their eruption, the leap from the wings to center stage' (Foucault 1977: 149–50). Foucault also speaks here of the 'place of confrontation' – although, in order to avoid being drawn by the word 'stage' into an association with the *metaphorical* image of history as theatre, he simultaneously characterizes this place as a non-place: 'In a sense, only a single drama is ever staged in this "non-place"' (1977: 150). (The German translation of Foucault is here more explicitly theatrical, speaking of an *auf diesem ortlosen Theater gespielten Stück*, a drama staged in an unlocated theatre.) The reference to drama and staging serves to indicate, rather, the *topoi* of performance, ritual, regulated procedures, and combat, the complex mechanisms within which history takes place and in which masquerade[15] represents a specific practice for dealing with the rules of the unlocated theatre, for 'The isolation of different points of emergence does not conform to the successive configurations of identical meaning; rather, they result from substitutions, displacements, disguised conquests, and systematic reversals' (1977: 151).

Since all these *topoi* could be subsumed under the (psychoanalytical) heading of distortion (*Entstellung*), Foucault's description of historical emergence and his characterization of the effects of the rituals of history as marks and recollective traces which are engraved on things and within bodies (1977: 150) indicate that his concept of history, his counter-memory, is also grounded in a model of memory in which this appears both in the form of permanent traces and as the scene of writing.

Such an approach owes much to the scenic nature of psychoanalytical thinking, or, more precisely, to the topographical description of the relation between perception-consciousness and the unconscious by Freud and to the conception of memory as a 'scene of writing' (Derrida). Using the example of the Baroque *Trauerspiel*, which he saw as an expression of a vision of history *as* tragic drama, of an attitude towards history which makes of history a tragedy, Benjamin described a *mise en scène* in which history 'merges into the setting' (*in den Schauplatz hineinwandert*) (*GS* I.1, 271; *OGT* 92), in which, therefore, history appears not in the temporal dimension, but as a scene. The historical scene and the scene of writing are thus identical for him, since the scenic images of history become readable images – like writing. Already here, then, he established his interest in scene and topography and in the significance of constellations as the decipherable image-spaces of history which he would later develop in the *Passagen* project and the text 'On the Concept of History'.[16]

The images of history only become such read and readable images – or what Benjamin termed 'dialectical images' – through an attitude of reading which is constituted by discontinuity as a fundamental practice of historiography. Such a practice requires, apart from the 'glance that distinguishes, separates, and disperses', an inversion of the 'relationship that traditional history ... establishes between proximity and distance' (Foucault 1977: 155), or a 'dialectical optic that perceives the everyday as impenetrable, the impenetrable as everyday' (*GS* II.1, 307; *OWS* 237).

It is in this inversion of the optic that Nietzsche's postulate of the use of history for life might find its fulfilment, since the difference between the historiography of the historians and that of the actors/agents falls away when reading and action, interpretation and agency coincide. Just as for Benjamin, commenting on the manner in which the French Revolution saw itself in relation to the Roman Republic,[17] the practice of quotation becomes the tiger's leap (of revolution), so for Foucault a specific interpretative practice becomes the precondition of a change in historical direction:

But if interpretation is the violent or surreptitious appropriation of a system of rules, which in itself has no essential meaning, in order to impose a direction, to bend it to a new will, to force its participation in a different game, and to subject it to secondary rules, then the development of humanity is a series of interpretations.

(1977: 151–2)

In the analogy of interpretation on the one hand and reading/quotation on the other, a clear distinction is nevertheless visible which is characteristic for the difference between the work of Foucault and Benjamin. Where Foucault stresses *rules*, Benjamin works almost exclusively with *images*.

With reference to the significance of images, a further inversion in the genesis of the theoretical reflections of both authors can be observed which corresponds to the one described earlier concerning the relationship of language as discourse to language as literature. On the one hand, the thought processes of Benjamin and Foucault meet in their interest in the dream as a specific medium of experience and cognition, and in the image beyond its mere representative function or the history of pictures, whereby the concept of similitude marks the point at which the contrary directions of their theoretical trajectories intersect. Yet within the framework of a scenic model of history – above all in the context of a reformulation of the historical scene (for example, in *The Origin of German Tragic Drama*, where history merges into the setting) as the scene of memory (for instance, in the *Passagen-Werk*) – images and their readability become for Benjamin the most important medium of history, whereas in Foucault's work on the history of discourse, images become ever less central, even if they had played an important role in his earliest theoretical reflections where the influence of psychoanalysis was still in evidence.

In an unusual combination of ontological, phenomenological, and psychoanalytical terminology, Foucault had, in his 1954 introduction to Ludwig Binswanger's *Traum und Existenz* (*Dream and Existence*), described the dream as the origin and precondition of imagination (*Imagination*), and on this basis discussed the relationship between image and imagination. In explicit contrast to Freud's *Interpretation of Dreams*,[18] Foucault here sets out a dialectic in which the image as crystallization functions as an indication of the moment of the collapse – or as it were paralysis – of imagination (whereby the 'phantasm' is the most extreme form in which the imagination becomes locked in the image), while imagination is described in terms of an 'iconoclastic' movement, as a kind of ontal activity which in relation to the wishes and the existential course of the subject breaks, destroys, and consumes the images (Foucault 1992: 78ff.). His interest is thus focused here on that transition point from the ungraspable excitations which he calls imaginings (Freud speaks of innervations or facilitations) to crystallized images – that is, the transition for which the moment of awakening, the threshold between dreaming and wakefulness which is the prominent location of Benjamin's *Passagen* project, takes on a paradigmatic significance. If Foucault here states 'that the image is a view on the imagination of dreaming' and that it is in this way that the waking consciousness grasps its dream moments (1992: 89), then the remembered dream image could be characterized, with Benjamin (and Freud), as the representative of dreaming in the waking consciousness,[19] whereby Foucault also emphasizes the *distance* of the image from imagination (1992: 90). And it was this distance – seen as distortion – that increasingly came to determine the direction of Benjamin's reading of images, at least from the end of the 1920s.

While Foucault examines the process of imagination from the point of view of production, as an activity which precedes the image and is arrested in it, Benjamin approached from the other direction, attempting to retrieve the dialectic from the immobilized images by reading them in such a way that that which had preceded them, gone into their formation, and disappeared in them became once again visible. For in Benjamin's reading the image is 'dialectic at a standstill' (*GS* V.1, 577; *N* 50). Moreover, the visible appearance of that which is arrested within the image can only take place in a flash. 'The dialectical image is one that appears in a flash [*ist ein aufblitzendes*]. It is thus, in the image that flashes up in the Now of cognizability, that the has-been can be grasped' (*GS* V.1, 591–2; see *N* 64).

In some respects Benjamin here achieved that step which Foucault – again retrospectively, although theoretically as a precondition – identifies as the blind spot of phenomenology, since Benjamin developed a theory of articulation which according to Foucault was only possible by 'going beyond phenomenology' (Foucault 1992: 28): 'Phenomenology has succeeded in allowing images to speak; but it has not given anyone the means of understanding their language' (1992: 29).

4 Thought-images
A re-reading of the 'angel of history'

BENJAMIN'S CONCEPT OF IMAGES

From his theory of readability and his definition of dialectical images as read, it is clear that Benjamin regarded images in terms of their property as writing (*Schrift*) rather than as representations. As such, Benjamin's concept of images has nothing to do with the history of material images, nor with a 'mental image' that is distinguished from the material image in its characterization as derivative or secondary, not proper (*uneigentlich*). Rather, his thinking goes back to a tradition of the image which precedes that of the function of pictorial representation and which 'sees the *literal* sense of the word *image* as a resolutely non- or even anti-pictorial notion' (Mitchell 1984: 521). Benjamin himself describes the image as a constellation of resemblances (*Ähnlich-keitskonstellation*) which is figured in a third (*ein Drittes*), beyond a form–content relation. It is at any rate in order to establish this distinction that he recounts his story of the stocking, a story taken up again in 'Berlin Childhood Around 1900':

> Each pair had the appearance of a small bag. Nothing gave me such pleasure as to plunge my hand as deep as possible into its inside. I did not do this on account of the warmth. What drew me into its depths was 'what had been brought me' [*das Mitgebrachte*] which I always held in my hand in the rolled up inside. When I had clasped it in my fist and assured myself as best I could of the possession of the soft, woollen mass, the second part of the game began which brought the unveiling. For then I applied myself to unwrapping 'what had been brought me' out of its woollen bag. I drew it ever closer to myself until the perplexing thing happened: I had taken 'what had been brought me' out, but 'the bag' in which it had lain was no longer there. I could not put this process to the test often enough. It taught me that form and content, the wrapping and what is wrapped in it are

the same thing. From this lesson I learned to draw the truth out of poetic writing [*Dichtung*] as carefully as the child's hand took the stocking out of 'the bag'.

(Benjamin 1987: 58)

He had related this same story already in his essay on Proust, where he then goes on to describe the image as a third or third thing (*ein Drittes*). This passage, which is concerned with Proust's 'impassioned cult of similarity', begins with the concept of similarity or resemblance (*Ähnlichkeit*), and leads finally – via a number of detours – to that of the image. Taking the concept of similarity as his starting point, Benjamin here makes reference to the dream world 'in which everything that happens appears not in identical but in similar guise, opaquely similar to itself' (*GS* II.1, 314; *Ill* 206, translation modified), in order then to illustrate this 'structure of the dream world' in the story of the stocking. With this he introduces the concept of the 'third' which in turn leads into the analogy with Proust's image-desire (*Bildbegehren*). For just as children

cannot get enough of changing at a *single* stroke these two things: the bag and what is in it, into a third thing: the stocking, so Proust could not get his fill of emptying at a single stroke the display dummy [*die Attrappe*], the ego [*das Ich*], in order to keep on bringing in that third: the image, with which his curiosity, no, his homesickness was assuaged.

(*GS* II.1, 314; *Ill* 207, translation modified)

It is this image, according to Benjamin, that bears Proust's 'fragile, precious reality' – and not only this. The image, as third, as the non-material appearance of a resemblance comparable in structure to the dream image, is for Benjamin the shape in which experiences, history, and reality become cognizable, in which they are made visible, as in a mnemic image.

If Benjamin understands the image as a constellation, as that 'in which the has-been [*das Gewesene*] comes together in a flash [*blitzhaft*] with the Now to form a constellation' (*GS* V.1, 578; see *N* 50), then the image here describes a heterogeneous, or heteromorphous, relation of resemblances.[1]

The image is the general term, from which various particular resemblances and correspondences subtend (*convenientia, aemulatio, analogia, sympathia*), which conjoins the world with 'figures of knowledge'.

(Mitchell 1990: 21)

According to Mitchell, it was only with the invention of artificial perspective in the Renaissance period and with the accompanying illusion of a pictorial representation that was true to life that the material image and the function of representation came to dominate the conceptualization of the image. This meant that other types of image now came to be defined as mental or spiritual, and thus as secondary or metaphorical. By contrast, Benjamin's concept of the image actualizes a biblical or Judaic tradition that had been submerged in the course of this historical development. It is a tradition in which the image figures as a synonym for likeness, resemblance, or similitude (*Ähnlichkeit*), and expressly for a non-material and non-sensuous similitude.[2] Moreover, within this tradition images are also understood as being readable, as being a form of writing.

This concept of the image may also go some way to explaining why in Benjamin's ur-history of modernity, in which the mode of observation is so dominated by images and which is grounded in a theory of images, painting plays such a minor role. And where Benjamin does devote attention to particular works from art history, such as Dürer's *Melancolia* or Klee's *Angelus Novus*, these images become for him meditative images, as he termed them following a visit to an exhibition of Klee's work (Benjamin 1978: 283), or thought-images, which accompany and preoccupy him over a long period of time.[3] They are for him thought-images (*Denkbilder*) in a double sense: as images in relation to which his thoughts and theoretical reflections unfold, and also as images whose representations are translated into figures of thought (*Denkfiguren*) – 'translated' here in the primary sense that Benjamin had attributed to it in the context of Adamite language, namely, as the translation of the language of things into that of words.

THOUGHT-IMAGES

The thought-image (*Denkbild*) – a word used by Benjamin as a kind of generic term for his own shorter text-pieces – can be seen as lying at the heart of his work on thinking-in-images (*Bilddenken*). His thought-images are as it were dialectical images in written form, literally constellations-become-writing (*Schrift-gewordene Konstellationen*) in which the dialectic of image and thought is unfolded and becomes visible. They are in the first instance linguistic representations of those resemblances which conjoin 'the world with "figures of knowledge"' (see above), that is, texts proceeding from those images and figurations in which the act of thinking is performed and in which history, reality, and experience find their structure and expression: *representations of ideas (Darstellungen von Vorstellungen)*, executed in such a way that in the linguistic imitation of the idea the petrified movement in it is restored, made fluid again. Here, with the aid of the mimetic faculty, the image, understood as dialectic at a standstill, is transformed into writing, that is, set in motion, in such a way as to reveal the origin of the idea and what has gone into its production: what has preceded it, entered into it, disappeared in it, and, simultaneously with the expression of an idea through the image, become, as its reverse side, invisible and invalidated. Thus this writing mimetically re-enacts the constitution of meaning in the image.

The dialectic at work here does not follow a triadic formula; its line of (written) descent goes back not so much to Hegel as to Hölderlin, in whose work a like attempt is to be found at the precise linguistic description of a dialectical process and its illumination in all its aspects – aspects which in the very course of this process change their status and position. Indeed, Hölderlin's text 'Das Werden im Vergehen' could be taken as a model of this, his linguistic representation of a constellation of origination and emergence (*Entspringen*) which mimetically re-enacts the dialectical movement inherent in this process, doing so by describing the movement as a reciprocal transformation from the status of the possible to that of the real or the ideal:

> But the Possible which enters into Reality when Reality disintegrates [*sich auflöst*], this has effect, and it has as its effect both the sensation of disintegration and the recollection of what has disintegrated. . . . The new life is now real, that which was destined to disintegrate, and has disintegrated, possible, ideally old, the disintegration necessary and bearing its particular character between Being and Non-Being. But in this state between Being and Non-Being the Possible becomes now everywhere Real, and the Real Ideal, and this is in the free imitation of art a fearful, and yet a divine dream.
>
> (Hölderlin 1992: II, 73)

If in what follows Hölderlin lends particular emphasis to the recollection of the disintegrated in the new, as also to the gap and contrast between new and old, it is – from the perspective of what has entered into reality – only the backward glance to what has disappeared in the process described that makes possible the 'recollection of what has disintegrated'. And it is precisely this kind of recollection that is central for Benjamin's thought-images. The constitution of meaning of which he is in pursuit is quite different from a 'grammatology' orientated around the modern conceptualization of the sign. It is not a *différance*

(Derrida 1976) operating with a range of linguistic material that he is concerned with, but the origin of ideas and their crystallization in linguistic figurations: linguistic images (*Sprachbilder*) which precede and provide the basis for the archives of metaphor, rhetoric, and iconography. In this way Benjamin identifies language, too, as the location of those images defined by him as dialectic at a standstill, and will only allow these dialectical images the status of *genuine* images (*echte Bilder*) (*GS* V.1, 577; *N* 50). They have a bearing on that image-writing (*Bilder-Schrift*) in which the images of the world become the view of the world. And with his 'thought-images', Benjamin himself produced and wrote such images, in order by so doing to deconstruct ways of thinking and ideas or imaginative concepts (*Vorstellungen*) handed down through the centuries.[4]

Yet thought-images are also read images, readings of images in written form, in which the character of images as writing – whether these be paintings, mnemic images, dream-images, wish-images materialized in architecture or in objects – becomes literally transformed into writing. It is in his thought-images that it becomes most patently apparent that Benjamin's manner of writing and manner of thinking cannot be seen as separate, that his thinking-in-images constitutes his specific and characteristic way of theorizing, of philosophizing, and of writing, and that his writings cannot be seen in terms of a dualistic opposition of form and content. Rather, the many constellations that run like leitmotifs through his writings demonstrate how, from the tensions between poetic language and conceptual meta-discourse, he won his own singular style of writing, so to speak a third thing beyond the dualistic opposition of literature and philosophy. The emergence and construction of this third place can be observed in the development of individual figures over what is frequently a long period of time, as also in the construction and procedural method of individual texts.

A fine example in this respect is the text 'On the Concept of History'. The series of eighteen, or rather twenty, short text-pieces, not really theses as such, do not so much set out an historico-philosophical programme as present reflections on *conceptualizations* of history, or thought-images on the way history is conceived – that is, on the notion of history itself. This is made extremely clear by Benjamin through such formulations as: 'the puppet *called* "historical materialism"' (*GS* I.2, 693; *Ill* 255), the '*conception* of progress' (*GS* I.2, 701; *Ill* 262), or 'the *notion* of a present' (*GS* I.2, 702; *Ill* 264; my emphases).

The text opens with the much-discussed image of the automaton, the knowledge of which is introduced as an *on dit* – 'The story is told of . . .'[5] – and which is described in detail, following which a 'philosophical counterpart' is imagined: note a *counterpart*, not a comparison. 'One can imagine a philosophical counterpart to this device' (*GS* 1.2, 693; *Ill* 255). As the many attempts at interpreting this passage demonstrate all too clearly – attempts that turn Benjamin's sentences over and over in order to try to wrest from them some unequivocal meaning[6] – this notion of a philosophical counterpart to the image of the automaton cannot be subsumed in a simple equation or unambiguous transferral – *metaphora* – between the object described and the philosophical concept. On the contrary, via the correspondence between concrete thing and philosophical counterpart, Benjamin circumscribes precisely that field in which the image is constituted as a resemblance between the figures of the external world and those of abstract knowledge. This is the field of his writing in which he develops his thought-images, images located in a space beyond the opposition of poetic language and philosophical discourse, in a different sort of language, the language of thought-images that operate with the received figurations of thought. Yet these thought-images do not stand at the beginning of his writing, but are rather the result of many and varied detours – for method is detour (*GS* I.1, 208; see *OGT* 28) – and arise 'from the centre of his image-world'.[7]

GEGENSTREBIGE FÜGUNG: THE ANGEL OF HISTORY

An example of this is the figure of the 'counter-striving disposition' (*gegenstrebige Fügung*)[8] in which the thought-image of the angel of history culminates – itself figuring a non-synchronicity between *his* position and perception and *ours*, which simultaneously gives expression to the non-synchronicity or incompatibility of philosophy of history and Messianism – and which has a whole series of precursors in the shape of similar constellations, linguistic figures, and images with which Benjamin evidently worked on this *topos* of a counter-striving disposition.

In 'The Diary' (*Das Tagebuch*) (1913), a *poetic* text full of metaphor, the writing 'I' is situated within a counter-movement of things and time and in the midst of unfolding events which surround it like a landscape – in the midst, then, of a *mythically* perceived environment.[9] The same constellation as appears here in the medium of a subjective, literary text and in a metaphorical language will reappear in a number of very different texts and linguistic figures – for example, as a conceptual image in the context of a philosophical discourse on the relation between philosophy of history and the Messianic in the 'Theologico-Political Fragment' (*c.* 1920–21). Here, following a passage emphasizing the difference between the Messianic and the historical dynamic, Benjamin writes:

> The order of the profane has to be erected on the idea of happiness. The relation of this order to the Messianic is one of the essential lessons of the philosophy of history. For it is this that forms the basis of a mystical conception of history, raising a problem that can be represented figuratively [*in einem Bilde sich darlegen läßt*]. If one arrow points to the goal towards which the profane dynamic acts, and another marks the direction of Messianic intensity, then certainly the quest of free humanity for happiness runs counter to the Messianic direction; but just as a force can, by its movement, propel another forward that is moving in the opposite direction, so too the profane order of the profane [*die profane Ordnung des Profanen*] assists the coming of the Messianic kingdom.
>
> (*GS* II.1, 203–4; *OWS* 155, translation modified)

What is here still termed a 'lesson of the philosophy of history' and represented (*dargelegt*) figuratively – that is, as an *illustration* of a conceptually formulated insight in terms of a figurative description – can be seen as a kind of experiment on the path towards the elaboration of thought-images within Benjamin's writings. The attempt at portraying, or illustrating, a philosophical problem with the aid of arrows pointing in different directions or counter-directional forces propelling each other forward has something of the character of the representation of a conceptually formulated figure in terms of a geometrical or topological image. Benjamin's endeavour to capture dialectic in the image can already be seen here, an endeavour in which he will, however, only really achieve success with his read or written images.

In this respect, the thought-image of the angel of history can be read in direct succession to the 'Theologico-Political Fragment'. This probably most frequently quoted section from Benjamin's text 'On the Concept of History', in which he sets out his critique of conventional historicism as well as of the progressive trajectory of historical materialism, has been repeatedly read as a metaphorical image,[10] but not as a dialectical one. This is symptomatic of the more general misrecognition of Benjamin's thinking-in-images and is not without its repercussions, for it is in this section that the many different lines of thought developed in his work converge and that his quite singular and specific reflections on history, progress, the hope of redemption, and on the image itself are figured in a *single* constellation. This thought-image can thus be understood as an allegory of Benjamin's specific theoretical work. If it is read as a *metaphorical* image – for example, when Klee's

Angelus Novus is taken as a figurative representation of the 'angel of history' – Benjamin's thought-image is not seen as dialectic at a standstill; instead, such an interpretation immobilizes, freezes the dialectic contained in the image.

For a start, the motto, the quotation from a poem by Gershom Scholem, is often overlooked or disregarded in readings of this kind. These lines of poetry are, however, an important component of the movement of the text, since they mark a reference point for the constellation in which that movement culminates. For in fact this ninth section 'On the Concept of History' (*GS* I.2, 697–8; *Ill* 259–60) presents us with not one, but three angels who are very different indeed. The first is the one in Scholem's verse:

> *Mein Flügel ist zum Schwung bereit,*
> ich kehrte gern zurück,
> *denn blieb ich auch lebendige Zeit,*
> *ich hätte wenig Glück.*
>   – Gerhard Scholem, *Gruss vom Angelus*

> [My wing is ready for flight,
> *I would like to turn back.*
> If I stayed timeless time,
> I would have little luck.]

The lyrical 'I' of the poem quoted is identical with the voice of the angel here. In this turn back to the origin in search of salvation, it is the tone of disappointment in the quest for happiness (in the order of the profane) and the pathos of a positively evaluated about-turn that determine the lyrical rhythm.[11] In contrast to this very eloquent angel of Scholem's, the second angel referred to, the one in Klee's painting, is mute. Benjamin says of him that he is called – that is, that the artist called him – *Angelus Novus*. .

A Klee painting named 'Angelus Novus' shows an angel looking as though he is about to move away from something he is fixedly contemplating. His eyes are staring, his mouth is open, his wings are spread.

In Benjamin's description, this angel has Medusa-like features: an open mouth, staring eyes, a frozen gaze. But to this account of Klee's painting, the description of the angel depicted in it, and the name given to it by the painter, Benjamin adds an association of movement: he looks 'as if he were about to . . .'. With this formulation the text makes reference to the perceptual logic of the 'as if' in the supposed simple reproduction characteristic of material images. In the frontal view of the picture, however, which has the angel's face turned towards the viewer, this movement is only imagined; that is, it is added to the representation through the act of looking. The real movement enters the text, though, with the third angel, the angel of history. The *Angelus Novus* depicted by Klee is not equated with the angel of history, let it be noted, nor is it interpreted as a pictorial representation of it. What is presented is now a purely *imagined* image:

> The angel of history must look like this. His face is turned toward the past. Where *we* perceive a chain of events, *he* sees one single catastrophe which keeps piling wreckage upon wreckage and hurling it in front of his feet. The angel would like to stay a while, awaken the dead, and make whole what has been smashed. But a storm is blowing from Paradise that has got caught in his wings, and its strength is such that the angel can no longer close them. This storm drives him irresistibly into the future, to which his back is turned, while the pile of debris before him mounts up to the heavens. What we call progress: that is *this* storm.
>
> (Translation modified)

The movement in the text is brought about above all by several changes of perspective: a shifting between the way the viewer sees the angel and the perspective and wishes of the angel himself – 'the angel would like to stay a while' – and between 'us' and 'him' in relation to the wreckage at his feet and to the future to which his back is turned, but towards which he is driven by the storm. In the course of the text, the non-synchronicity between 'us' and the angel is made present in a representation that functions polyperspectivally and on multiple levels: as a topographical and spatial constellation ('*where* we perceive . . ., he sees') and as a bodily one (through the references to the face, feet, and back), a temporal one ('irresistibly' – here in the sense of 'incessantly', '*while* the pile . . .'), a material one (the dead, wreckage), a mythical one (the storm blowing from Paradise), and a conceptual or historico-philosophical one ('What we call progress').

IMAGE-DESIRE AND THE TURN BACK

Through this constellation, whose multidimensional relations clearly differentiate it from the description of a picture or a pictorial representation, the contrast between the two preceding angels as quoted from Scholem and Klee – the lyrically articulated desire to turn back of the one and the mythically conceived, Medusa-like frozen posture of the other – is carried over into a dialectical textual movement. It is true that this textual movement is tripartite in structure, and yet it does not culminate in a synthesis, but in a constellation of non-synchronicity. Here the incompatibility of the desire for healing – to 'make whole what has been smashed' – and the paralysis of terror is reflected, while the non-synchronicity and ultimate irreconcilability of a positivistic understanding of history, which sees history as a chain of events and as a continuum, with the perception of wreckage and catastrophe is figuratively represented in the thought-image. The storm blowing from Paradise that is called 'progress' – the originary moment of an *historical* movement through which history is finally and irreversibly separated from Paradise and thus from a mythical place – marks a situation in which Messianism and the philosophy of history cannot be made to tally with each other.

It is clear that in this text, in contrast to the 'Theologico-Political Fragment' of twenty years previously, the image no longer serves as an illustration of an historico-philosophical 'lesson'; namely, the relation of the order of the profane to the Messianic (*GS* II.2, 203; *OWS* 155). Rather, taking as his starting point on the one hand a poetic image and on the other a painted one, both of which can be seen also as wish-images (*Wunschbilder*), Benjamin evolves a thought-image whose figuration can no longer be translated into conceptual terminology or meta-discourse. And in this, the reflection of the images of (his own) imagination at the same time embraces the 'processing' or working-through (*Bearbeitung*, a Freudian term) of the wishes bound up in these images, and thus also the work on, and with, fascination and image-desire (*Bildbegehren*).

For with his text on the angel of history it seems probable that Benjamin was working out and reflecting the history of a fascination of his own that had bound him to Klee's painting for nearly twenty years, doing so in a dialectical image that at the same time represents an awakening from a magical fixation on the painting as expressed in a form of continuous 'beviewing' (*Beaugenscheinigung*).[12] It is doubt-less not by chance that the time-span during which Benjamin was in possession of Klee's painting corresponded to that of the hidden history of the origin of this text (written in 1940, shortly before his involuntary suicide), as indicated in a letter to Gretel Adorno. Referring in this letter to the text, he writes that it is his concern 'to write down a few thoughts of which I can say that I have kept them with me, indeed, kept them from myself, for nigh on twenty years' (*GS* I.3, 1223). There is, too, an idea of Klee's in a note in his 'Paedagogical Sketchbook' (*Pädagog-isches Skizzenbuch*) (1925) which could be taken as a comment on his

Angelus Novus – 'The human being is half winged creature, half prisoner' (Klee 1990: 100) – a note that follows the pattern of dichotomous concepts of imagination and identity, which in Benjamin's thought-image of the 'angel of history' is wrenched from its paralysis as a metaphor of existence and set in motion of a kind that, in the representation of non-synchronicity, does not seek resolution in reconciliation.

The radicality of Benjamin's thinking lies precisely in his work on such constellations – in the transformation of conventional images, traditional metaphors, and his own linguistic figures into thought-images, a transformation which does not simply adjudge and denounce the former as false consciousness. He himself describes this work as a reflection in moments of awakening, and it is a reflection that does not neutralize or rationally resolve the desire condensed in these pre-existing images. Rather, the desire is incorporated into the thought-image, so that it becomes both allegorical practice and redeeming critique (*rettende Kritik*) in one.

Moreover, the figuration in which Benjamin's text finds its culmination and in which the non-synchronicity of our perception and the gaze of the angel of history is represented corresponds precisely to the theoretical figure of non-synchronicity in Freud's model of memory as set out in the allegory of the 'mystic writing-pad' (*Wunderblock*).[13] The non-synchronicity between consciousness and the writing that flashes up out of the permanent traces of the unconscious thus forms the basis for the representation of the non-synchronicity with which Benjamin is preoccupied. Even the formulation 'chain of events' might be traced back to Freud. In his essay 'On Screen Memories' (*Über Deckerinnerungen*) of 1899, it says: 'The reproduction of life as a connected chain of events is not achieved before the age of six or seven, in many not until the age of ten' (Freud 1964: 531–2; see Freud 1953: III, 303). The non-synchronicity only becomes visible via the *topos* of the turn back or reversal (*Umkehr*), a figure which is again to be found in Hölderlin. The turn back organizes a form of perception which – positioned in the flow of time, but adopting a stance opposed to it – directs the gaze towards what has disappeared in that flow, towards what has been destroyed in history, the elements that have been used – and consumed – in the process of artistic production, in short, towards 'what passes away in the becoming' (*das im Werden Vergehende*). Precisely this is what Hölderlin put to the test in his reading and translation of Greek tragedy. Here he focused attention on the 'wild origination' (*wilde Entstehung*) of a form of rationality in order to accentuate the 'oriental element' (*das Orientalische*) which, he maintained, had been denied .

within Greek art[14] – but not in such a way as to repudiate the Greek tradition or its importance for him. What was at stake, as Hölderlin himself formulated it, was a 'reversal of all kinds of ideas and forms' (*Umkehr aller Vorstellungsarten und Formen*), but not a complete reversal, for 'A complete reversal in these is, as is complete reversal generally, where nothing is left to hold onto [*ohne allen Halt*], not permitted to the human being as a creature of intellect [*erkennendem Wesen*]' (Hölderlin 1992: II, 375).

In this respect it is, in Benjamin's historico-theoretical thought-image, precisely the angel, as a non-human being, who endures in the position of the one who turns back, in doing so keeping at least momentarily this perspective open for us too.

Translated by Georgina Paul and Rachel McNicholl

Other – gender – readings

'But women are silent. In whatever direction they listen, the words are unspoken. They draw their bodies closer and caress one another.'

5   Towards a female dialectic of enlightenment

Julia Kristeva and Walter Benjamin

The contemporaneity (*Gegenwärtigkeit*) of Benjamin's theoretical work and of his thinking-in-images (*Bilddenken*) might also, and quite particularly, be found to lie in its relevance to the discourse of gender difference. Since the relations between the sexes could be taken as an emblem of Western culture, and since the feminine has been the privileged figurative material for the representation of so many of its imaginative concepts, ideas, and values, it may well prove that Benjamin's specific way of thinking and philosophizing, his dialectical approach to images and to the desire bound up in them, could point a theoretical way forward out of the aporias in which gender discourse (including feminist gender discourse) has repeatedly found itself ensnared: between the iconoclastic work of enlightenment on the long tradition of images of the feminine on the one hand, and the perpetual reproduction of precisely these same images on the other, between the critique of civilization and the struggle for emancipation, between the rejection of the 'male order' and the continued orientation towards its established meanings and values, between the critique of, and yet desire for, subject position, and so on.

Whenever the question of gender is addressed, gender relations as defined in and by language are always already at work: this is the reason why studies on 'the feminine' or 'the female'[1] and women, or on the history of the sexes, always run up so soon against conceptual limitations in their representations. Since the different positions and *imagines* of men and women within cultural history have become so strongly inscribed in the patterns of thought and modes of expression handed down to us, as well as in the dominant symbolic and imaginary structures, it is a matter of course that theoretical contributions to research in this area in large part reflect the linguistic preconditions of the investigative work in hand. Studies of gender issues are thus always – whether consciously or not, whether explicitly or implicitly – work both about and on the gender-specific meanings which are transported in language and writing, in conceptualizations and value-judgements, in perceptions and perspectives, in the definition of the object of study and what is excluded from it. 'Who is speaking' and 'what position they are speaking from' here have the character of unavoidable questions. Theories of 'the feminine', which must be understood as experiments in examining this correlation explicitly, thus constantly return to the link between language and gender, or to the position of women and the role of 'the feminine' in practices of the constitution of meaning as these have been handed down – though without being able to situate themselves outside the problematic upon which they are at pains to reflect. And so the search for a position from which it might be possible to speak seems constantly to be deferred.

What follows is thus not intended as a contribution to the cultural history of gender relations, but as a reflection on the *way* in which the latter are (or can be) represented at all within various theoretical conceptual frameworks – and in particular in those of Julia Kristeva and Walter Benjamin. This attempt is linked, with regard to current theoretical debate, to a twofold concern: first, to refute the supposed antagonism between 'Critical Theory' and 'French theory' as this is currently embodied in the obvious mutual hostility of the respective theoretical camps on the west German cultural and academic scenes. With this in mind, Kristeva and Benjamin are to be taken as exemplary, and their approaches discussed comparatively in order to mark similarities and differences. The second concern is to make Benjamin's thought fruitful for the theory and history of 'the feminine/the female', or at any rate to introduce it into feminist theoretical debate.

THE PROBLEM OF IMAGINING AND REPRESENTING A FEMALE SUBJECT-POSITION

> I had, of course, been placed *under* him from the word go, and I must have known early on that he would be *my downfall*, that Malina's place had already been occupied by Malina before he installed himself in my life.
>
> (Bachmann 1978: 3, 17; second emphasis mine)

With these reflections the first-person narrator of Ingeborg Bachmann's novel *Malina* (1971), who is to be understood as the voice of a female, nameless 'I', tries to put her *relationship* to Malina into words, her relationship to that superior position of reason which is embodied in the eponymous (male) character. In a subsequent passage, in which she reflects upon the *difference* between herself and Malina, she says:

Then it seems to me that his calm comes from my being too unimportant and familiar an 'I' for him, as if he had excreted me, waste matter, a superfluous piece of humanity, as if I were only made out of his rib and had always been dispensable, but also *an unavoidable dark story which accompanies, wants to complete his story, but which he separates and dissociates from his clear story.* And that is why I alone have something to clarify with him – above all, I must and can only clarify myself in front of him. He has nothing to clarify, no, not he.

(1978: 3, 22–3; my emphasis)

At a later point, in a dialogue with Malina, this passage is supplemented by the assertion of the speaking 'I': 'You came *after me*, you can't have been there before me, you are only thinkable at all after me' (p. 247; my emphasis).

There can be few such acute representations of the dialectic of enlightenment from a female perspective as we find here in Bachmann's novel. The Malina-'I' constellation represents both the asymmetry and the hierarchy of dichotomous gender relationships and their connection to the relationship between the rational and that 'Other' which initially produced it, but which is subjected to and cut off by it. It is no coincidence that it is a *literary* text which manages to give expression to the complicated position of women and the complex function of the feminine in the dialectic of enlightenment, achieving this through the use of many of the expressive possibilities inherent in poetic language. Where feminist critiques of scientific discourse have attempted to express the fate of the feminine in the progression of European science and knowledge in theoretical terms – for example, as the 'simultaneous appropriation and rejection of the feminine' (Fox Keller 1986: 50) – Bachmann's text represents the relationship in question in the image of two dialectically connected, but also separate stories and positions, whose constellation comes into focus through a variety of changing scenarios and illuminations. In this way, the relationship between 'I' and Malina is not only presented as that of two characters, voices, stories, and positions, but also as an historical-temporal and hier-archical-spatial one, as a relationship between preconditions and pos-teriority, between assertion and disappearance, between superiority and decline. The figurations in which the two move are so manifold and multiple that they cannot easily be captured in the singularity of meaning, in the linearity and logical structure of conceptual language and scientific argumentation. This is one reason why interpretations of and commentaries on *Malina* seem to this day to be as it were on the trail of the text, without ever managing to reach it totally, as a whole.[2] Furthermore, the novel does not limit itself to the problems raised between Malina and the narrative 'I'. In the relationship between 'I' and her lover Ivan, it creates a further constellation of the gender relationship. Thus Bachmann deals with the theme of the difference and the relationship between the sexes not only on the level of 'the rational', but also on the level of 'love' – whereby both 'levels' are woven together in the literary fabric, the texture of the novel.

The example of *Malina* is introduced here solely for the purpose of providing a foil for the deliberations that follow: on the tendency within feminist discourse to turn to literary and figurative modes of expression, on the frequently employed references to mythical scenes and artistic figures, on the way myths are used, and on the possibilities and perspectives of thinking in images. For the 'literary' elements in feminist studies do not always have as their basis a creative use of the possibilities of poetic language, such as polyperspective, polyphony, and multiple meaning, or such as difference, figurative expression, and the simultaneity of heterogeneity. Often motives are in play which range from the necessary criticism of the predominant rigidity of scientific discourse to the exposition of global anti-academic and anti-theoretical attitudes, whereby literariness and figurative expression are seen as characteristics of a so-called *feminine* mode of speech and language and as linked *per se* to the promise of greater subjectivity, more concreteness and vitality. It is obvious that this tendency in feminism results in the creation of a new mythology in which 'the feminine' is inscribed as the opposite of the rationality claimed by science. Nevertheless, it is true that borrowing from art and mythology can provide responses to the mythical and artificial structuring of the patterns and history of 'femaleness' (the latter being the object of feminist analysis), and that this offers a way of reacting to the realization that it is by no means a simple matter to conduct enlightened, or enlightening, discourse on the myths of femininity and the female.

This particular dilemma manifests itself, as is so often the case, in its opposite poles. At one extreme, there are the iconoclastic positions which regard all patterns of the feminine and images of women as nothing but seductive illusion, sorcery, or evil deception, positions which take as their implicit reference point a hidden truth or essence of woman as 'self' and which can thus be seen as a variant of the myth of enlightenment. And at the other extreme, there is remythicization, the recourse to the myths of a better female world – myths concerning the matriarchy, for example, or 'secondary myths'[3] such as found in the sociological discipline of women's studies with its tendency towards a positivistic description of (feminine) characteristics which, through the claim to moral superiority and totality, often transpire to be mere reverse mirror-images of masculine concepts. Such polarizations can be explained by the difficulty, indeed impossibility, of women gaining a perspective of their own, let alone an unequivocal perspective, with regard to, and in the debate on, woman: a difficulty that becomes particularly evident whenever rationality, and what it has subdued and repressed, or whenever women's position in and with regard to enlightenment are under discussion. The formation of opposing camps in the current discourse about the 'future of enlightenment' and 'postmodernism', which has produced a clash of opinions on the simple model of *pro* and *contra*,[4] already demonstrates how difficult it is to continue to advance that cultural-historical movement which Horkheimer and Adorno grasped as the dialectic of enlightment in a manner that is productive for the present. And yet the difficulties are considerably aggravated when a female subject enters the story, or when the question of woman's will to knowledge and to selfhood, or simply her participation in public and political life are addressed.

Horkheimer's and Adorno's siting of the feminine on the reverse side of enlightenment and of the preservation of selfhood (*Selbsterhaltung*), alongside Nature as that which has been conquered by and claimed for the self, has in the meantime been concretized and refined by numerous works of feminist analysis, and also confirmed, at any rate as far as the description and analysis of the history of woman's domestication and mythicization of the feminine are concerned.[5] However, when it comes to the history omitted from their text, when it comes to woman's desire for a subject position, and to a speaking position located as it were on the reverse side of enlightenment, it soon becomes tangible how the dialectic is then set into motion in such a way that it is not easy to gain a secure foothold. For woman cannot simply catch up on the process of individuation, nor can the reverse side of history simply be turned into, or declared to be, the obverse. Any attempt to make up lost ground in terms of the self-realization hitherto denied her or to reduce the male subject's head start in the process of enlightenment would have far more serious consequences for woman than the detrimental effects of progress as attested by and for man. Whereas for man the process and practices of laying claim to and subjugating Nature were largely carried out on the material and the images of the 'Other', and above all of the 'other' sex, for woman this work on the process of civilization would affect what is her own: *mater-materia*, the mastering and rationalization of which is the prime goal of the preservation of selfhood; the woman's body as the *skandalon* of a rationally orientated history. The sacrificial structure of the history of enlightenment[6] not only repeats itself more corporeally and closer to the bone, as it were, in the female subject, but woman at the same time also has a share in both the reverse and the obverse sides. As a result, the *female* variant of a dialectic of enlightenment, in addition to reason and its Other, which may from time to time take on a female countenance, introduces what might be described as a *third position* into the dialectic. This is a highly unstable position, of course, which maintains relations with *both* sides, both reason and the Other – which may serve to explain why triadic, and in particular psychoanalytical models, have played so important a role in theories of the feminine.

The position of the *female subject* is not only far more complicated than that of the male one, it also introduces a *doubly reversed* perspective into the dialectic: namely, the perception and speech of the second sex which wishes to occupy the position of the first, but which cannot simply shake off its provenance from the dark reverse side – and which is anyway not altogether certain how desirable that position, so long denied it, really is. The complexity of this constellation seems constantly to elude conceptual articulation. While this explains the search in some areas of feminism for a third position beyond myth and enlightenment, as also the efforts to come up with an alternative concept of (female) subjectivity, neither approach seems particularly promising; for both, at least as far as women in European and North American cultures are concerned, seem more suited to evading than to resolving the problems in question. Instead, out of the acknowledgement of the inadequacies of prevailing academic discourse for the complex constellation of a female dialectic of enlightenment there follows the need for a specific mode of thought and representation: the introduction of a *polyperspectival* and *topographical* dimension to dialectical thinking. Since the position of woman in and in relation to enlightenment cannot be clarified completely and wholly, with final and universal validity, in a *single* analysis, what remains is a – probably infinite – series of observations, in which the many and varied situations and moments of transition may be illuminated in detail.

'DIALECTICAL IMAGE' AND GENDER DISCOURSE

For the purposes of such a project, nothing could be more promising than the recourse to Walter Benjamin's mode of operation with myths and images, and especially his conception of the 'dialectical image': that image that he sees as dialectic at a standstill, a snapshot wrested from the continuum of time which, as the 'Now of cognizability' (*Jetzt der Erkennbarkeit*), bears its previous and subsequent history within itself. Benjamin's dialectical image is without doubt a cognitive one, but it refers in manifold ways to seen images, imaginary images, and the images of the unconscious.

It is not that the past casts its light on the present or the present casts its light on the past: rather, an image is that in which the has-been comes together in a flash with the Now to form a constellation. In other words: image is dialectic at a standstill. For while the relation of the present to the past is a purely temporal one, that of the has-been to the Now is dialectical: not of temporal, but of figurative nature. Only dialectical images are genuinely historical, that is, not archaic images. The read image, by which is meant the image in the Now of cognizability, bears to the highest degree the stamp of the critical, dangerous moment which is at the basis of all reading.

[Variant in N2a, 3, following 'not archaic images':] and the place one encounters them is language. *Awakening*

(*GS* V.1, 578; see *N* 50–1)

Important to the understanding of this note of Benjamin's in the *Passagen* project is the realization that 'reading' for Benjamin refers to far more than just the reading of written text and that 'language' does not only mean written and spoken words. It is not that he 'reduces' social phenomena to a text, but rather that the ability to read, the skill of deciphering is applied to more, and other, than just written material. Benjamin's dialectical image is not one of a *frozen* dialectic either, but rather the snapshot, or instantaneous crystallization, of a movement in which, as a specific constellation is made visible, cognition comes in a flash. In testing his method on a range of subjects and situations from cultural history, most extensively on the Baroque *Trauerspiel*, on nineteenth-century Paris, and on the Berlin of his childhood, he always proved to have a watchful eye for and to pay considerable attention to the positions and functions of the feminine in the world of images and signs which he examined. He did not, however, propose a theory of femaleness, as Christine Buci-Glucksmann would have us believe in her study *Walter Benjamin and the Utopia of the Female*, to which purpose she reinterprets many of Benjamin's dialectical images, or those critical of progress, as Utopian.[7] Of more importance, from today's perspective, than his images of the feminine is his textual practice, the way in which he works with these images, transforms them into dialectical or thought-images.

None the less, it is no coincidence that, long before the theories of 'female aesthetics' or 'the aesthetics of the feminine', Benjamin managed, in one of his thought-images, very successfully to represent the use and destruction of the female in the male myth of creation, thus anticipating in a dialectical image one of the central theses of feminist literary criticism. Under the heading 'After Completion' (*Nach der Vollendung*), he picks up the metaphor of birth in the conceptualization of the creation of 'great works' and describes how the concept of intellectual creation displaces that of natural creation, a process in which the female element necessary to it is consumed and exhausted, while the creator is newly born at the very same moment as the work is completed: as the 'male first-born of the work that he once conceived'. By substituting the work for the mother, the 'master' no longer owes his birth to his origins, but to the completion of his work, so that he appears both independent from and superior to nature.

> He blissfully surpasses nature: for he will now owe this existence, which he first received from the dark depths of his mother's womb, to a brighter realm. His home [*Heimat*] is not where he was born; rather he comes into the world where his home is. He is the male first-born of the work that he once conceived.
>
> (*GS* IV.1, 438)[8]

Here Benjamin describes that construction, bound up in the notion of the *work*, of male creation arising autonomously from *mater-materia*; and he does so by remaining within the image (that of birth), but making it recognizable as a dialectical one. The question as to what consequences this model of creation would have for a female artist is another story, which Benjamin naturally did not write.[9]

The fact that Benjamin's work and his way of thinking have received so little attention in the feminist theory that developed out of 'Critical Theory' or through the break with it (the German journal *Frauen und Film* is an exception) is no doubt due to the belated reception of Benjamin generally as also to the forcible appropriation of the Benjaminian inheritance by the Frankfurt School, which led to the neglect of those aspects of his work which could not be integrated into its orientation towards Western culture and its focus on concepts of rationality and communication.[10] The selective reception of the materialist traces in his work after 1968 did not help. But this absent or blocked reception is also partly responsible for the fact that critical social theory and post-structuralism so often seem irreconcilably opposed to each other, whereas there are, in fact, many points of contact between Benjamin's writings and those of, for example, Michel Foucault and Julia Kristeva.

ANALOGIES IN BENJAMIN'S AND KRISTEVA'S THEORY . . .

Parallels between Kristeva's and Benjamin's theoretical reflections are to be found, above all, in the dialectical conception of the signifying process in Kristeva (1984) and of language in Benjamin,[11] between the way in which Kristeva, in her description of the dimension of the history of the subject, relates the 'semiotic' and the 'symbolic', and Benjamin, in his representation of the dimension of cultural history, relates the magic side of language (the mimetic) and its communicative side: as being distinct from each other and yet linked to each other in their functioning. The prior modality in each case – the modes of articulation of the semiotic *chora* (Kristeva) and the magic of the 'paradisiac language of man' (Benjamin) – passes into and disappears with the emergence of the subsequent modality – that of the symbolic (Kristeva) and that of the mediating language of signs (Benjamin). From then on, the appearance of the preceding modality in the text or in writing is bound to the succeeding, now dominant modality and can be apprehended 'only' as a transgression or breach, or in a momentary flash.

According to Kristeva, the articulations of the semiotic belong to the pre-Oedipal phase, which is characterized by an archaic relationship to the mother. To this extent they are understood as pre-symbolic and pre-linguistic functions, precursors of the discourse which is in turn based on them, but which dissociates itself from them. Since, according to the psychoanalytical model used here, the constitution of the subject is linked to the entry into language/the symbolic, Kristeva writes:

> This is to say that the semiotic *chora* is no more than the place where the subject is both generated and negated, the place where his unity succumbs before the process of changes and stases that produce him.
> (1984: 28)

Only theory, however, can isolate the semiotic as 'prior' in order to specify its functioning, for it does not reach us until after the symbolic 'thesis', that is, after the break which gathers up the semiotic facilitations and stases of drives within the positing of signifiers. As a result of this break, the semiotic is produced recursively, and appears as a breach, a 'second return' of the functioning of drives within the symbolic and as a transgression of its order (1984: 68–71).[12] In this way, the semiotic is expressed as a breach, a transgression, or an explosion within the symbolic. Yet these two modalities of the signifying process cannot empirically be isolated from each other, as it is only through their dialectical relationship that the signifying process becomes possible.

The 'thetic', as a breach or boundary, occupies the same place structurally in Kristeva's theory as the 'Fall of language' in Benjamin's theory of language. Benjamin distinguishes between the 'paradisiac language of man' and the mediacy of language as sign. Referring to the second version of the myth of creation in the Bible and in derivation from the creative language of God, he conceives human language before the Fall as both cognitive and denominative. Its magical character lies in its being able to recognize the silent language of Nature and of things by naming them. This corresponds to the description in the biblical myth of a prior state of language as one of immediacy, as a state in which the communication and the communicated were not yet separated: language magic (*Sprachmagie*), mimesis. The loss of this immanent magic is linked to the origin, in the Fall, of abstraction as a faculty of language-mind (*Sprachgeist*), as to the knowledge of good and evil and the origin of a language which, in communicating *something* outside itself, becomes mere sign. Thus immediacy crosses over into abstraction, giving rise to a new, no longer immanent magic, the magic of judgement, which has its roots in the judging word (*GS* II.1, 152ff.; *OWS* 114ff.).

Nevertheless, the lost mimetic gift of human beings – this was Benjamin's hypothesis – 'gradually found its way into language and writing in the course of a development over thousands of years, thus creating for itself in language and writing the most perfect archive of non-sensuous similitudes [*unsinnliche Ähnlichkeiten*]' (*GS* II.1, 209; *DS* 68, translation modified). After the original magic of language has disappeared and the language of signs has taken over, the magic aspect manifests itself in certain *constellations* or *moments* within the communicative (*mitteilend*) side of language, through which, in a flash, similitude becomes apparent. Thus Benjamin's concept of 'non-sensuous similitudes' is made concrete in the relationship of the lost magical character of language to the predominating language of signs, within which the mimetic only appears transitorily or instantaneously, as it were in the flashing of an eye (*Augen-Blick*). It is in this instant that the picture-puzzles (*Vexierbilder*) of the unconscious and of the not-yet-known are made apparent. The magic side therefore requires the communicative side of language in order to become visible. But as a prior, submerged element of language which reappears in modified form, it cannot empirically be isolated as such. Like the semiotic in Kristeva's theory, mimesis in Benjamin is inextricably bound up in a dialectical conception.

Benjamin's concept of 'non-sensuous similitude' can be compared in its theoretical function with Kristeva's understanding of the semiotic as a 'second return of the functioning of drives within the symbolic'. However, despite the analogies between their respective theoretical understandings of language and signification, and despite the fact that both focus their attention on the break with the creation myth and the consequences of this break, and on lost or prior aspects of writing which, having undergone transformation, now express themselves *differently*, there are nevertheless significant differences between them which must also be considered. Whereas Kristeva's interest in the semiotic is related to her interest in a 'subject in motion' and in a specific textual praxis which attaches importance to discontinuities, rhythm, gesture, and the body of language, Benjamin's interest in the magic of language and in non-sensuous similitude is focused on images and constellations, on history as this can be deciphered in images – in short, on dialectic at a standstill.

... AND DIFFERENCES: KRISTEVA AND THE TRIAD OF PSYCHOANALYSIS

The work of Kristeva has hitherto attained far greater significance within the development of feminist theory than has that of Benjamin. At the same time, the reception of Kristeva has partly compensated for the lack of attention to Benjamin in imparting to feminist theory an obviously psychoanalytical orientation. The reason why Kristeva's theory has become such a central and productive reference in analyses of the highly complex position of woman as she enters history – whether this be the history of the subject or of culture – is undoubtedly that her structural extension of psychoanalysis enables the different positions of the sexes to be represented in a triad. The question of the problematic constellation of a female dialectic of enlightenment corresponds to the question of woman's complicated entry into the symbolic in Kristeva's reflections, posited at first on an ontogenetical level. Here, as in Lacan's theory of the subject, the conflict-ridden stage of development which Freud called the Oedipus complex (and which he saw as part of a teleological model) is expressed in terms of a topographical configuration and seen as the transition from the mother–child dyad to a *triadic* relationship, whereby the prohibition of incest (for both sexes) is understood as the prohibition of the mother or separation from the mother's body. The reference to the Oedipus myth is here no longer intended as an actualizing identification with the figure of Oedipus or as a re-telling of the old story; rather, the myth is read as the primal scene of a constellation that has become a structure.

In contrast to Lacan, Kristeva is particularly interested in the consequences of this constellation for women, both for the girl child[13] and for the fate and the significance of the repressed, prohibited body. Kristeva succeeds in distinguishing a number of different functions and positions of the female – the 'function of the mother', for example, which is associated with the dominant nature of the maternal body in the pre-Oedipal phase, and also the function of woman in the symbolic. This latter she calls the 'woman effect', 'an effect which has neither power nor a language system, but is their mute support' (Kristeva 1976: 167), a silent support of the system, then, which itself makes no appearance – an image which is to be taken quite literally and concretely.

That Kristeva is able to describe the history of the constitution of the female subject, with all the conflicts and contradictions necessarily inscribed into it, is explained by her projection of the conflicts she examines onto the topological model of the subject offered by psychoanalysis, the *triad*. Thus conflicts which occur in the dimension of the history of the subject and of culture are represented in a triadic configuration. Seen from the perspective of the female infant, the female subject is constituted between the poles of identification with the father, or rather with the *law* in the *name* of the father, and identification with the mother, or rather the *body* of the mother. By associating the position occupied by the father at the top of the triangle with the law and the name, and the position occupied by the mother at the bottom, opposite the infant, with the body, by taking into account, then, not only the relations between the sexes, but also at the same time the relationship between the body and the name/law, this model permits the topographical representation of the complex problematic of a female position in the symbolic and thus its conceptualization. With this theoretical approach, which takes as its starting point the triad and its personae, a thinking-in-images is developed in which all kinds of situations and 'solutions' can be figuratively apprehended and represented through the superimposition, or double-exposure, of psychoanalytical primal scenes and their repetitions in or transformations into the symbolic.[14] Especially where she extends her studies to cultural-historical themes, at those points in her work where she leaves the ontogenetical level (as in the afterword to *About Chinese Women* or in the *Tales of Love*), Kristeva makes repeated reference to mythical female figures[15] whose names then denote paradigmatic constellations and 'solutions' in the conflict-ridden process of woman's becoming a subject.

In contrast to popular feminist reception of myths, however, which seeks to lend meaning to the present through the aura of classical mythology, Kristeva does not identify or equate mythical figures or situations with present-day ones. If myths are understood as a social imaginary – on the one hand as the memory of what has not been understood, what has been repressed by reason, and what cannot be named in rational discourse, and yet at the same time as a canon of images which has been handed down over centuries, as a repertoire of, for the most part, tragic stories that have become fixed and set, frozen into 'metaphors of existence' (Heinrich 1985: 338) – then what is of paramount importance when dealing with myths is the manner in which this ambivalence is approached. A metaphorical application which actualizes and reinterprets mythical figures tends to remain within the structure of the imaginary in which, through operations on the level of identification, differences are not discerned or are erased. It is a different matter if we reflect upon the structuring of our perception and experience through the patterns of the imaginary, and read mythical constellations as primal scenes of our history that are preserved in memory.[16]

BENJAMIN: MYTH AND MODERNITY

Just such a thinking-in-images that goes beyond metaphor was developed by Walter Benjamin; it has as its basis his theory of language in which magic, myth, and progressive instrumentalization are significantly arranged in relation to one another. Whereas Horkheimer and Adorno essentially describe magic, myth, and enlightenment as the consecutive stages of an historical development, Benjamin places more emphasis on their non-synchronicities (*Ungleichzeitigkeiten*). His theory of language is marked by mourning for the loss of the magical quality of language, the loss of its immediacy and of that 'paradisiac language' of man, which was cognitive and denominative in equal measure. However, his theory is also shaped by the knowledge of the historical logic of this loss. Grounded in his theory of language is a practice of *reading*, which reveals its full force in his treatment of the myths of modernity; for example when he discovers 'correspondences between the world of modern technology and the archaic symbol-world of mythology' (*GS* V.1, 576; *N* 49), or when he deciphers a dream structure in the topography and architecture of the city and, in so doing, reflects upon elements of the mythical and the unconscious in the history of progress, of technologization, and of the world of commodities and objects.

Benjamin's methodological concern is with the significance of the insights of psychoanalysis for a materialist representation of history which, taking the term 'materialism' literally, would be inclusive of the *matter* providing the precondition of the relations of production – for example, the human body. In seeing, through the category of body- and image-space (*Leib- und Bildraum*),[17] the physical materiality of the human being, the corporeality of the collective as providing the basis for a materialist viewpoint, he distinguishes between the technical organization of the *physis* and its political and factual reality, so that the generation of the *physis* is seen as taking place in an image-space. In other words, he reflects on the significance of the *imaginary* for the reality of the physical. In this respect, Benjamin's reflections reveal parallels with the perspectives of a structural psychoanalysis which focuses on phenomena of social and cultural history.

Precisely because of his interest in the myths of modernity, but also, more fundamentally, because of the historical perspective of his studies, Benjamin's theory can productively complement that of Kristeva for the purposes of examining a female dialectic of enlightenment. His dialectical images create an *historical topography* independent of a graphic model such as that of the triad; they can be read as differently projected superimpositions, as double-exposures of now-time (*Jetztzeit*) and the has-been (*das Gewesene*), in which historical constellations, including those of a history of the female subject, become readable in all their contradictoriness.[18]

With regard to the relationship between myth and enlightenment, Benjamin's work concentrates on moments of transition. One of the central constellations he refers to in this context is that of *awakening*, which he calls the textbook example of dialectical thinking – the threshold between night and day, the transition between the dream and waking consciousness. It is a constellation organized in a highly complex manner – in topographical terms as a transition, in psychoanalytical terms as a threshold, in temporal terms as the 'Now of cognizability', and in historical terms as the superimposition of the has-been and the present moment – and one that seems pre-eminently suited to presenting a dialectical movement at a moment of standstill for contemplation and cognition, as a dialectical image. In such a way as neither to repress them nor to deny their magic, the elements of the mythical and of the unconscious are thus made accessible for reflective viewing. And in this manner Benjamin dissociates himself critically both from a philology which, in the 'beviewing' (*Beaugenscheinigung*) of a text, remains magically fixated on it, and also from mythology,[19] proposing instead his method of 'real reading':

Philology is that beviewing of a text which proceeds detail by detail and which fixates the reader magically on the text . . . . The semblance of complete facticity which clings to the philological study and which puts the researcher under its spell dwindles according to the degree in which the object of the study is constructed in historical perspective. The vanishing lines of this construction converge in our own historical experience. In this way the object is constituted as a monad. In the monad everything comes to life which, regarded as the data of the text, lay frozen in mythical rigidity . . . and so you will find that criticism of the attitude of the philologist is an old concern of mine – and inherently identical with my criticism of the myth.

(Benjamin in a letter to Adorno dated 9 December 1938; Benjamin 1978: 794–5; see Benjamin 1995: 587–8)

With regard to history, this is linked to a renunciation of the idea of continuity and progress. As an alternative to the logic of development characteristic of linear historiography, a reading in the Benjaminian sense opens up *correspondences* between present and past moments which, as he formulated it in his note on the 'dialectical image', are both dialectical and of the nature of an image. Those living in the present day relate to the has-been by 'quoting' moments from the past, blasting them out of the continuum of history and thus 'loading', as with a charge, the Now in which they live, whereby the manner in which these moments are illuminated or charged up arises out of the situation in which they find themselves, out of their passions and desires and hopes (of redemption). 'History is the object [*Gegenstand*] of a construction whose site is not homogeneous, empty time, but time filled by the presence of the now [*Jetztzeit*]' (*GS* I.2, 701; *Ill* 263, translation modified).

For a history of women – as for all historiography which does not share the perspective of the rulers, of 'the heirs of those who conquered before them' (*GS* I.2, 696; *Ill* 258) – Benjamin's historico-theoretical reflections offer a productive stimulus, not least because women have few moments or images from their past which they can quote, since in what has been handed down they have been largely 'forgotten' or repressed as subjects. Whereas the sort of historiography orientated around the concept of development maintains for the most part a persistent silence concerning female subjects, authors, artists, and so on, myths, paintings, and other sources of the imaginary offer to the attentive reader a wealth of correspondences with the experiences and situations of present-day women – as is demonstrated by the quotations from historical and mythical women in those works of contemporary literature whose concern is not to show 'the way it really was' (*GS* I.2, 695; *Ill* 257), but rather to present literary thought-images, constellations of a female dialectic of enlightenment, recollected images of a past of which women, in their moment of awakening (and this moment, too, is one of danger) seize hold.[20]

A READING OF 'THE ANGEL OF HISTORY' FROM THE PERSPECTIVE OF WOMEN

In order to give a more concrete impression of Benjamin's praxis of the 'dialectical image', and specifically in order to relate it to the problems of a female dialectic of enlightenment, the re-reading of the famous image of the 'angel of history' offered in the previous chapter, in which emphasis was given to the *three* different angels and to the dialectic between their positions as this unfolds in the text,[21] can be supplemented with a further reading – one which adopts the perspective of women in the history of female emancipation. The starting point is the reading of the 'angel of history' as a dialectical image and as a constellation of non-synchronicity. When women read this image today, it becomes immediately evident how difficult it is to find a position within its dialectic. The first angel, the lyrical voice in Scholem's poem, offers the possibility of adopting a timeless perspective in which a morally superior 'I' turns its back on the world of today – which can be read as the 'male' or 'patriarchal' world. This would be a version of stepping out of history, as is also figured, for example, in a retrogression to a supposedly happier (matriarchal) prehistory. The second angel, embodied in the frozen horror of Klee's image, lends itself to fascinated viewing, to identification with its mythical rigidity, to the viewer becoming caught under the spell of the myth, entranced into fascinated identification with the position of victim.

The third angel, the angel of history, is, by contrast, explicitly distinguished from 'us'. The presentation of the irreconcilability between the angel's position and 'ours' breaks open the imaginary structure based on the moment of identification which fails to recognize what is heterogeneous. The 'us' can refer to the 'we' who think in terms of progress or, simply but necessarily, to the 'we' of the survivors. Read in political, or indeed feminist, terms, it can, however, also point towards the participation of women in the concept of progress *qua* emancipation. For in the same measure as women have taken (and continue to take) active part in the ruling institutions, such a 'we' cannot simply be identified with 'men' or the 'male system', but must include women in its perspective.[22] Nevertheless, women have much in common with the perspective of the angel as a result of their sex, or, more precisely, as a result of the gender-specific division of labour in Western cultural history. It is they who are chiefly concerned with bodies: both as those who conceive and bear children and as those who care for the sick and the dying and mourn for the dead. But they are not to be compared with the angel of history; for in that they are survivors, participants in this history and this culture, they are forced to turn their eyes away from those of the angel.[23]

It makes a difference, then, whether it is a man or a woman who engages in the reading of this image, and this is precisely what brings into play that *difference* between the dialectic of enlightenment and its female variant which is so difficult to define conceptually – provided, of course, that Benjamin's image of the angel of history is read as a dialectical one. Although it does not serve as a building block for a theory of femininity, Benjamin's philosophy of history does nevertheless provide the premises for a representation and contemplation of the history of the female subject beyond the illusions created by emancipatory discourse or the refusal of history. As such, his reflections offer an important complement to the possibilities of Kristeva's theory wherever the problems posed have to be carried over from the field of psychoanalysis into that of history.

Translated by Rachel McNicholl and Georgina Paul

6　From images to dialectical images

The significance of gender difference in Benjamin's writings

While the previous chapter was concerned with the possibilities opened up for a theoretical reflection on constellations of gender difference by the dialectical movements of Benjaminian theory and by his specific thought-figures, the focus in this chapter is on Benjamin's own work on gender images. Here it becomes evident that images of femininity, creation myths, and metaphors of sexuality form one of the most important archives from which the genesis of dialectical images in his work can be reconstructed, and in which his work on the transformation of images into dialectical images is most clearly profiled. One might even say that, within the framework of his theoretical work, Benjamin's gender-images represent as it were the allegory of his allegorical method. For it is not only that certain types of the feminine are explicitly put forward in the *Passagen* project and in the Baudelaire book as 'allegories of modernity'; it is also the case that the method of (detour to) the modern allegory or allegory of modernity is designated by images of the feminine. The Benjaminian attitude of redeeming critique (*rettende Kritik*) with regard to the desire bound up in these images might also be made productive for contemporary theories of gender difference. For while strategies like masquerade or the parody of gender roles, such as are currently being developed on the farther side of myths of authenticity, only affect the level of performance, Benjamin's dialectical images and his body- and image-space encompass both the development and the representation of embodied ideas and of linguistic figurations.

'UNGRASPED SYMBOLISM': THE ORIGINS OF A THINKING-IN-IMAGES

We are enslaved without ceremony by a symbolism that we have not grasped. – Sometimes we remember a dream as we are just waking up. It is seldom that moments of clairvoyance thus illuminate the wreckage of our strength, past which time has flown.

(*GS* II.1, 91)

These reflections on the moment of awakening that throws light on an ungrasped symbolism are not taken, as one might think, from the material Benjamin wrote in connection with the *Passagen* project, but are to be found in the first section of a text entitled 'Conversation' (*Das Gespräch*), which he wrote in 1913 at the age of twenty-one. Among the notes which date back to the time of his student activities and his association with the Youth Movement, this is not the only image, nor the only formulation or figuration, to link his early writings to his last major project in this curious way. The concept of experience (*Erfahrung*), reflections on the structure of time, including the concept of Messianic time, closeness and distance, the movement and the look of things, the concept of revelation (*Offenbarung*), of a non-instrumental language, the connection between eroticism and cognition (*Erkenntnis*), various female figures, particularly that of the whore (*Hure*), here still consistently referred to as prostitute (*Dirne*): all of these are motifs which already characterize the structure of the early essays, articles, and notes, and which we encounter again in his writings of the 1930s. In the later texts, however, a slight, though very effective change in his mode of writing has taken place, a shift in his use of images as an aid to conceptualization and representation which turns them into dialectical images, that is, images that are read – a tiny shift which, to quote Foucault, has the effect of a 'small (and perhaps odious) piece of machinery' which enabled him 'to introduce chance, the discontinuous, and materiality at the very roots of thought' (Foucault 1981b: 69).

' Nevertheless, the relationship of conflict in which the 'I' confronts 'the fathers' in the Benjamin text quoted above, so that the first-person plural voice of the text patently identifies itself as the voice of youth, marks 'Conversation' as obviously belonging to Benjamin's early writings. Other constellations, however – ones that do not refer to the position of the writer, but are to be read as *textual* constellations – foreshadow paradigmatic thought-images of the later writings in their scenic dramaturgy and their topographical arrangement. Thus 'The Diary' (*Das Tagebuch*), for example, which was intended to form a cycle together with 'Conversation' and 'The Ball' (*Der Ball*) now known under the title 'Metaphysics of Youth' (*Metaphysik der Jugend*), anticipates a form of movement on whose philosophical and linguistic figuration Benjamin was repeatedly to work. In the 'Theologico-Political Fragment' (*c.* 1920), he tried to capture it in the conceptual image of a counter-movement of the dynamic of the profane on the one hand and of Messianic intensity on the other, two counter-directional forces which are nevertheless able to propel each other forward (*GS* II.1, 204; *OWS* 155); in the Kafka essay of 1934, the same movement appears as a figure of reversal, as the 'direction of study that transforms existence into writing' (*GS* II.2, 437; *Ill* 138, translation modified), or in the image of the cavalry attack (*Ritt*) of this study, launched against the tempest 'that blows from the land of oblivion' (*GS* II.2, 436; *Ill* 138); later, the constellation takes on shape in the historico-philosophical thought-figure on the non-synchronicity of our way of looking at the chain of events and the way the angel of history gazes upon the catastrophe and wreckage of the past – here, then, as a dialectical image.[1]

Yet it is this same movement that already structures – as a perhaps as yet 'ungrasped symbolism' – his literary text on the diary. The 'I', positioned in the midst of events happening around it, surrounded by them '*as* [by] a landscape' (*GS* II.1, 99; my emphasis), turns to face backwards; and the tempest which rages within the troubled 'I' as things move towards it engenders a 'countermovement of things in the time of the "I"' (*GS* II.1, 102). The references to time, which we felt 'flooding mightily towards us again' (*GS* II.1, 100), to the way things look which propels us into what is to come (*GS* II. 1, 99), or to the fact that, in the time of the 'I' in which things happen to us, 'all future is past' (*GS* II.1, 102) – all of these formulations topographically outline the scene of the diary which is metaphorically condensed in all its 'counter-striving disposition' (*gegenstrebige Fügung*) in the para-doxical image of the 'accession to the throne of one who abdicates' (*GS* II.1, 101). The figure of the beloved woman, however, who steps towards the 'I' out of the landscape of what is happening, or perhaps rather, who is sent to him out of it, reveals that this scene is organized in a way that is gender-specific.

The distance between this diary-landscape of the 'I' and the land-scape of collective wreckage in the ur-history of modernity – in other words, the transition from Benjamin's early writings on the self to his readings of the memory images of modernity – could not be greater. And yet its specific constellation, which stages a counter-perspective to historical time, as well as the gender dramaturgy of 'The Diary', mark a hidden link with the *Passagen* project. The figure of the beloved woman, part of a mythical scenery, for in it events are perceived as a landscape, emerges out of this scenery – sometimes quite clearly, sometimes as a shadow – to point the way through the labyrinth of texts in which that ungrasped symbolism is transformed into the great archive of a dialectical thinking-in-images. We encounter her here and everywhere in Benjamin's writings, like an Ariadne or guardian of the threshold.

And so, precisely because it has always been the image of the 'whore as an allegory of modernity', as it is met with in the Baudelaire book and in the *Passagen* project, which has been in the foreground whenever the significance of gender difference in Benjamin's work has received any attention at all, what I want to do here is to follow the traces of that Ariadne figure in order to decipher the transformation of images into dialectical images in the labyrinth of Benjamin's texts.

'HOW DID SAPPHO AND HER FRIENDS SPEAK?': LANGUAGE MAGIC AND GENDER DIFFERENCE

'Conversation' already experiments with that genre at the transition point between thinking-in-images and theoretical reflection that was to become as characteristic of 'One-Way Street' and 'Berlin Childhood Around 1900' as it was for the theses 'On the Concept of History': that is, a series of consecutive, but self-contained, short prose scenes or thought-images. The eight parts of 'Conversation' revolve around the idea of another language, here still called 'true language' (*GS* II.1, 92). This language, which is beyond a spoken language tending towards chatter (*Geschwätz*) – the speaker is described in the text as one who slanders language (*GS* II.1, 91) – is not, however, independent of conversation, but is, on the contrary, as it were made possible in and through conversation: that is, through the listener or through the silence that is produced as part of conversation – silence, then, as an 'internal limit of conversation' (*GS* 92).

These reflections were to become integrated three years later into Benjamin's elaboration of his theory of language,[2] which found its well-known programmatic formulation in a letter to Buber: in this letter Benjamin writes of leading up to 'what the word has been denied' (*das dem Wort versagte*), and of the 'unspeakable in language' towards which one must work 'within language and to this extent then through it' (Benjamin 1978: 127). What is important for my argument here is that, already in 'Conversation', the other language of which he writes is not localized as an antipole to conversation, but rather *within* it, so that the dialectical conception of Benjamin's language theory becomes apparent. This perceives the nature of language as sign as being simultaneously 'a symbol of the noncommunicable', as he formulated it in his essay 'On Language as Such and on the Language of Man' of 1916 (*GS* II.1, 156; *OWS* 123), and the semiotic in language as the vehicle of the mimetic and thus as a condition of possibility for the appearance in a flash of 'non-sensuous similitudes' (*unsinnliche Ähnlichkeiten*), as he put it in the 1933 essay 'On the Mimetic Faculty' (*GS* II.1, 213; *OWS* 162, translation modified).[3] This marks an attempt to overcome the opposition between, on the one hand, the model of arbitrariness in the 'bourgeois view of language' and, on the other, the notion in 'mystical language theory' that the word is the essence of the thing (*GS* II.1, 150; *OWS* 116).

In the 1916 essay on language, where Benjamin discusses the Adamite language of the Book of Genesis, women are completely absent. At most one might think of Eve, or women generally, when reading the passage on the other muteness and sorrow of a now named, no longer speaking Nature following the Fall of language, since women are largely to be found in the position of the named:

> In all mourning there is the deepest inclination to speechlessness, which is infinitely more than inability or disinclination to communicate. That which mourns feels itself thoroughly known by the unknowable. To be named – even when the namer is Godlike and blissful – perhaps always remains an intimation of mourning.
>
> (*GS* II.1, 155; *OWS* 121)

Whereas in Benjamin's reading of the first creation story in Genesis[4] from the point of view of a theory of language, man is situated as speaker and at the same time source of language,[5] in 'Conversation' the productivity and meaning of language originate with the listener, whose position reveals itself in due course to be a female one. For in the fourth section of the text, a significant gender change occurs amongst the text's *dramatis personae*. Here the male or gender-neutral characters of the text's literary scenery – the speaker (*der Sprechende*) and the listener (*der Hörende*) in the second section, the unproductive one (*der Unproduktive*), the chatterer (*der Schwätzer*), and the genius (*das Genie*) in the third – are replaced by a male-female couple: the *male* speaker (*der Sprechende*) and the *female* listener (*die Hörende*). This pair is carried over in the fifth section into a conversation between genius and prostitute, and in the sixth into general reflections on the difference between the sexes in language.

If the female position is here associated with silence, it is in relation to two distinct aspects. As a listener, the woman is understood as productive in terms of a 'true language' – she protects 'sense from understanding, she hinders the abuse of words and does not permit herself to be abused' (*GS* II.1, 93) – and thus she marks a position which is conceived as the female counterpart, as it were, to the (male) genius. For in this text it is 'thinkers and women' (*GS* II.1 92) who are considered agents (*Tätige*) by the author. In addition, silence is linked to the reverse side of language, to the erotic relationship between the sexes, as in the sentence: 'Silence's other conversation is sexual pleasure [*Wollust*]' (*GS* II.1, 93).

Nevertheless, the fact that Benjamin associates the female position in language with silence does not mean that he is indifferent to the issue of women's language. In the seventh and eighth sections of 'Conversation' he addresses precisely this question. Both sections open with the same words – 'How did Sappho and her friends speak?' – and deny the suitability of language for their conversation – 'For language deprives them of their souls' – in order finally to revolve around another kind of eloquence which is located between the corpus of language, the 'bodies of words', and body language. 'The language of women was left uncreated. Speaking women are possessed by a language that is mad' (*GS*II.1, 95) – a sentence with which Luce Irigaray might well find herself in agreement, coinciding as it does with her psychoanalytical description of the fact that women have no place in established discourse and, consequently, only make use of such language in the form of a distorting mimesis, that is, that women,

> as lack, deficiency, or as imitation and negative image of the subject, . . . should signify that with respect to this logic [the economy of the *logos*] a *disruptive excess* is possible on the feminine side.
>
> (Irigaray 1985: 78)

The aspect of excess so significant for Irigaray is ascribed to women in Benjamin's 'Conversation' too:

> But women are silent. In whatever direction they listen, the words are unspoken. They draw their bodies closer and caress one another. Their conversation has liberated itself from subject-matter and from language . . . Silence and sexual pleasure – eternally divided in conversation – have become one.
>
> (*GS* II.1, 95–6)

The same non-synchronicity of the discourse of language and the pleasure of the female body that structures this description is to be found in Julia Kristeva's *About Chinese Women* where – 'voice without body, body without voice' (Kristeva 1977: 15) – it is conceived from a cultural-historical perspective as a separation from and overcoming of the maternal body through the male *logos* and placed in the context of a history of monotheism, that is, of the principle of 'a symbolic, paternal order' (1977: 27) governed by the superego.

THE 'MALE FIRST-BORN OF HIS WORK': CREATION AND PROCREATION

The bodies of the Sapphic women in Benjamin's text are, however, exempt from precisely this maternal aspect, existing rather in a state of love for no specific purpose. 'The love of their bodies is without procreation, but their love is beautiful to behold' (*GS* II.1, 96). This motif of a Sapphic love without procreation, of an eroticism that is not bound to a specific purpose, anticipates a motif that will shift to the centre of attention in the *Passagen* project in the figures of the lesbian and the whore, the heroines of Baudelaire's poetic work.

As allegories of modernity, however, the lesbian and the whore in the *Passagen* project are reflected as dialectical images in so far as Benjamin also discusses the preconditions that make them objects of fascination for the modernist author who compares himself with the hero of antiquity: the rejection of nature and the natural as a reaction to technological development and to the levelling of differences between the sexes:

> It is part of the sacrificial path of male sexuality that Baudelaire must perceive pregnancy to a certain extent as unfair competition.
>
> (*GS* I.2, 670)

> Male impotence – the key figure of solitude – under its sign the standstill of productive forces is completed – an abyss separates the human being [*Mensch*] from his kind.
>
> (*GS* I.2, 679)

> Baudelaire never wrote a poem about a whore from a whore's perspective (cf. Reader for City Dwellers 5).
>
> (*GS* I.2, 672)

> Baudelaire's readers are men. It was they who earned him his fame and whom he bought off.
>
> (*GS* V.1, 419)

In this way, taking Baudelaire's poetry as an example, Benjamin places love without procreation, as this features in the imaginary self-projection of an artist, in the cultural-historical context of modernity. His readings of Baudelaire could, however, just as easily be read as comments on his own early writings. There the motif of the prostitute as well as that of non-procreation take on central significance for the figure of the genius or for the concept of intellectual creation without procreation. Many of his early texts revolve around the connection between sexuality and intellectual activity, between procreation and creation, and around the significance of gender difference for the 'community of the creative' (*GS* II.1, 84), whereby the images he uses frequently alternate between the levels of bodily and intellectual creation. While the imagery of his texts bears witness to his fascination with the transitions between the corporeal-erotic and the intellectual,[6] in his argumentation the author takes pains to prevent the two becoming intermingled or one being subjugated by the other. This is particularly emphasized in his approach to traditional and contemporary myths of intellectual creativity and to notions of the elimination of gender difference, or rather of the female as representative of the 'other' sex, as in the *topos* of the 'spiritualization of the sexual'. Thus he writes in a letter of 1913 to his friend Herbert Belmore, in which he accuses the latter of elevating the prostitute to the status of a symbol and thus of depriving thousands of women of their souls by turning them into a gallery of art-works:

> Let us be silent for a while on the subject of the spiritualization of the sexual, this precious inventory of men. And we will talk about the sexualization of the spiritual: this is the morality of the prostitute. She represents culture in Eros, Eros which is the most vehement individualist, the most hostile to culture, it, too, can be perverted, it, too, can be of service to culture.
>
> (Benjamin 1978: 67–8)

Directing his criticism at strategies instrumentalizing Eros within the intellectual sphere, as also at the elimination or incorporation of the female position in quasi gender-transcendent models (albeit represented by men) in contemporary cultural theory,[7] Benjamin accentuates – though himself not without recourse to traditional views of the gender-relationship – the other, as it were invisible productivity of women which is linked to their inaudible language and which must nevertheless be taken to be a precondition of cultural production – rather like the way Kristeva speaks of the productivity of women as an 'effect which has neither power nor a language system, but is their mute support', as a silent prop of the system which itself does not appear in it (Kristeva 1976: 167). It is in this sense that the silence of women is marked as a productive female position in 'Conversation'. And it is here that Benjamin's concept of a *different* productivity of women, which played such an important role in the texts he wrote during these years,[8] finds its expression. Admittedly, it is hardly ever described positively, and nowhere more concretely than in 'Conversation'. Rather, it appears in variations on the concept of negation – for example in the emphasis on the indispensability of this other productivity, as in Benjamin's representation of Socrates, whom he criticizes for degrading Eros to the status of a means to an end:

> In a society made up only of men, there would be no genius; genius lives through the existence of the feminine. It is true: the existence of the feminine is the guarantor of the asexuality of the intellectual in the world.
>
> (*GS* II.1, 130)

Benjamin's emphasis on this other productivity of woman could perhaps be read as a redeeming critique which serves to rescue the difference between the sexes at the moment of its historical disappearance. The problem is that women remain silent, banished to that mute region of a different productivity.

These ideas, too, are later carried over into dialectical images so that their phantasmagorical content, their cultural constructedness, and their preconditions become readable, primarily by means of a de-montage or deconstruction of the notions of genius and masterpiece. The thought-image 'After Completion' (*Nach der Vollendung*) is a demonstration of this, where Benjamin describes the masterpiece as being constituted through the consumption (*Verbrauch*) of the feminine and as the expression of the desire to overcome nature or to transcend one's own origin in the 'dark depths of the mother's womb'. In this way, the 'master' becomes the 'male first-born of the work that he once conceived' (*GS* IV.1, 438).

In fact, this thought-image directly takes up a phantasma that had been introduced in 'Conversation' two decades previously. In the earlier text the theme of 'non-procreation' is developed in the fifth section, the dialogue between the genius and the prostitute. Those who go to the prostitute are, namely, those who were not begotten by anyone and who themselves do not want to procreate – precisely the qualities which characterize the genius. The genius, however, says of himself: 'They all became mother to me. All women gave birth to me, no man was involved in my conception' (*GS* II.1, 94). This image, by virtue of the notion of a virgin mother, places the genius in the position of competing with the Son of God, thereby citing a traditional myth concerning genius.[9] But it goes further, in that the mother, too, is as it were disqualified from the competition and dis-embodied, since she appears as a woman whose births bring forth only failed intellectual products, dead poems: 'I can only think of my mother. May I tell you about her? She gave birth like you: to a hundred dead poems.'[10] If the focus here is on the genius as one who is in competition both with God and with the pregnancy of woman, and thus on a double claim to be the source of creation, in the later thought-image this notion of genius is as it were illuminated from within. In the formulation of the 'male first-born of the work that he once conceived', the process is inverted, turned on its head: for here it is not the genius who creates the work; rather, the master springs from the self-same origin as the work that fancies itself independent of nature.

Here we can observe the gradual transformation, over a period of twenty years, of an image by which the author seems fascinatedly enthralled into a dialectical image – a shift which can be understood as a dismantling of the misrecognizing, imaginary structure of the image. The operation can be compared with the way Benjamin dealt with the history of fascination that bound him to Klee's *Angelus Novus*, likewise over a period of twenty years: with the reflection on the mythical frozen posture of the image of the angel in his dialectical image of the 'angel of history' of 1940.[11] And the thirteen sentences about books and prostitutes in the section 'No. 13' of 'One-Way Street' (1928) could be understood as an intermediate station between the myth of creation-without-procreation in the conversation between genius and prostitute of 1913 and the thought-image about the master dating from the first half of the 1930s. In this text, Benjamin comments ironically on the metaphorical status of books and prostitutes which arises from the comparison of them: 'Books and prostitutes – they each have their own sort of men who live off them and by whom they are harassed. Books have critics' (*GS* IV.1, 109; *OWS* 68, translation modified).

'FOR EVERY WOMAN HAS THE PAST AND IN ANY CASE NO PRESENT': WOMEN AS GUARDIANS OF THE THRESHOLD

A further trace leads from the women in 'Conversation' to the later major projects. For at the same time as the gender change occurs amongst the characters in the fourth section of 'Conversation', the theme of present and past is introduced into the text. While the speaker is obsessed with the present, the women appear as the guardians of what is past, which makes them superior even to the genius, who is described as having cursed his recollection in the process of creation, as being poor in memory and perplexed (*GS* II.1, 93). The reverse is true for the women: 'For every woman has the past and in any case no present' (*GS* II.1, 93). Their 'past is never concluded' (*GS* II.1, 95). Instead, they live in a time structure which forms as it were an inverted counter-time to the *futur antérieur*, that 'shall have been' future historic that Lacan defined[12] as the time structure of desire and the historical time of the subject: 'The present that eternally has been shall be again' (*Die ewig gewesene Gegenwart wird wieder werden*) (*GS* II.1, 93). With regard to the past, however, the significance of gender difference becomes so dominant for Benjamin in this text that he synthesizes the two conceptually, referring to the 'female-has-been' (*Weibliches-Gewesenes*) (*GS* II.1, 95).

The interlacing of recurrence and the has-been (*Gewesenes*) – 'The present that eternally has been shall be again' – which in this early text still forms a mythical structure of the feminine will be encountered again later in a figuration of conflict (*Widerstreit*) used to describe the structure of the desire for happiness as the longing for a repetition of the never-has-been (*Noch-nie-da-gewesenes*). It is to be found in the encoded text 'Agesilaus Satander', written by Benjamin in 1933 as a birthday present for a woman with whom he was in love,[13] which links the Talmudic legend of the countless angels created anew every moment with the motif of the New Angel, the *Angelus Novus*, which is fixed to the wall:

> He wants happiness: the conflict in which the ecstasy of the unique, new, not-yet-lived meets with that bliss of the once-more, the having-again, the lived. This is why he has nothing new to hope for on any path except that of the return home when he takes a new person with him. Just as I, no sooner had I seen you for the first time, travelled back with you to where I came from.
>
> (*GS* VI, 523)

The woman is no longer situated in the past here, nor does she *have* the past; rather, she opens up the way to the past, or to the recurrence of what has been. It is in this sense that we encounter women as guardians of the past in many texts of the late 1920s and the 1930s. Yet in these texts their position has been transposed unequivocally onto the scene of writing, and becomes decipherable against the foil of a signature of the feminine in the imaginary. This is elaborated in the context of the motif of *flânerie*, which projects the 'writing' of the city as the scene of memory, as is also the case in the thought-images of 'Berlin Childhood Around 1900'. There, the structure of recollection and the significance of locations with female connotations in the imaginary were always already interconnected. And in this context, recollection appears as the Muse of *flânerie*, a process of remembering as one strolls along:

> She walks ahead on the streets, and each one is precipitous for her. She leads downwards, if not to the mothers, then at any rate into a past which can be all the more spell-binding in so far as it is not only the author's own, private one.
>
> (*GS* III, 194)[14]

By following the images and traces of recollection, Benjamin works on reconstructing the genealogy of the function of the feminine as image and sign: in 'Berlin Childhood' through a series of childhood primal scenes, and in the *Passagen* project through the reading of collective dream-images and of the ruins of a culture of modernity. In the course of this work, a semiotic of different female *loci* in writing becomes apparent: the magic function of those household spheres (sewing-box, wardrobe) associated with the feminine, for example, the subterranean or pre-symbolic areas indicated with the phrase 'the mothers', the mythical figure of Ariadne, whose image blends with that of the desired woman friend, or those allegories hewn in stone, embodiments of a recollection of myth and wilderness within the city, which Benjamin calls *Schwellenkundige*, 'those versed in thresholds', thus alluding to their function as images which fill the place of the pre-symbolic in the order of the city.

In this way the figurative function of the feminine is linked with woman's position as guardian of the past *in writing*. The reference to the 'female-has-been' thus acquires its significance not only by virtue of the fact that real women belong to the forgotten realm of culture, but also because images of the feminine, the female figures in cultural memory, predominantly represent the has-been, the forgotten, the repressed. Though they are still marked by their origins in the sphere of the forgotten, they no longer inhabit that sphere, but rather, through the figure of the return of the repressed, become embodiments of the representation of the forgotten in the image archive of modernity.

By contrast, in his essay on Kafka of 1934, Benjamin interprets the female figures in Kafka's work as figures from prehistory (*Vorweltfiguren*). This essay bears clear traces of Benjamin's reading of Bachofen at about the same time, whereby he was not so much interested in Bachofen's 'golden age' of matriarchy as in his primeval *Vorwelt* of hetaerism, that very earliest stage of the development of an 'unwedded motherhood' described in Bachofen's image of swamp vegetation (Bachofen 1948: 36).[15] Thus he describes the location of Kafka's novels:

> His novels are set in a swamp world. In his works, created things appear at the stage which Bachofen has termed the hetaeric stage. The fact that it is now forgotten does not mean that it does not extend into the present. On the contrary: it is actual by virtue of this very oblivion.
>
> (*GS* II.2, 428; *Ill* 130)

This is why Benjamin describes the female figures in Kafka's writing as swamp creatures, belonging to a sphere of 'untrammelled voluptuousness' (*regellose Üppigkeit*). If he refers in this connection to the strangeness of the 'whorelike women' in Kafka (*GS* II.2, 413; *Ill* 115), they nevertheless differ from the whores of the *Passagen* in that in their form they are not associated with the motif of the negation of procreation. Quite the contrary, for in Bachofen's prehistoric world of hetaerism the positions of whore and mother are not yet distinct. The *topos* of distortion in the Kafka essay does, however, provide a link with the whores of the Paris arcades, the allegories of modernity.

For when Benjamin makes use of the Freudian term 'distortion' (*Entstellung*) in the Kafka essay primarily as a mnemic category – distortion as the 'form things assume when they are forgotten' (*GS* II.2, 431; *Ill* 133, translation modified) – and when he, in addition, takes as his premise that what Kafka's texts are really about is forgetting and that 'everything forgotten mingles with what has been forgotten of the prehistoric world' (*GS* II.2, 430; *Ill* 131), it means that Kafka's female characters are not only creatures of this prehistoric world, but that they also have a part in the form of the distortion.

'DISTORTION INTO ALLEGORY': THE WHORE AS 'BODY- AND IMAGE-SPACE' FOR THE ALLEGORIES OF MODERNITY

Among the figures in Benjamin's imagistic archive, the whore (*Hure*) emerges ever more clearly in the course of the 1930s, more or less taking over the role played by the prostitute (*Dirne*) in his early writings.[16] While she is of great significance in the preliminary work on the 'Berlin Childhood', however, she virtually disappears from the later elaborations of this text, which becomes primarily governed by the sign of the maternal,[17] making her way instead, and then fully, into the *Passagen* project and the Baudelaire book. In the text of the 'Berlin Chronicle' (1932), whores make an appearance both as 'guardians of the past' (*GS* VI, 472; *OWS* 302) and as threshold-dwellers:

> But was it really a crossing over, is it not, rather, a wilfully voluptuous [*eigensinnig-wollüstig*] lingering on the threshold, a hesitation which has its most cogent motive in the circumstance that this threshold leads into nothingness? But the places are countless in the big cities where one stands on the threshold to nothingness, and the whores are as it were the *lares* of this cult of nothingness and stand in the doorways of the tenement blocks and on the more softly resounding asphalt of the railway platforms.
>
> (*GS* VI, 472; *OWS* 301, translation modified)

Although in this context the topography of the threshold is primarily linked to the motif of sexual awakening, the description of the scene as a cult does, nevertheless, point towards the significance of the *rites de passage* in the collective imaginary as represented in Benjamin's ur-history of modernity by the architecture of the arcades. It is in the company of the constellation of awakening as the 'textbook example of dialectical thinking' and of the conception of the dialectical image that the whore as an allegory of modernity enters onto the scene of the *Passagen* project. Here she is chiefly to be found on the threshold – she has, then, moved out of the primeval world into that sphere of the transition between dreaming and wakefulness which appears as a condition of possibility for awakening. As threshold-dwellers (*GS* V.1, 617), the whores occupy a position in Benjamin's late works to which he will return again and again in his efforts to decipher the phantasmagorias, the wish-symbols, and the materialized images of the collective.

It is not their association with the has-been or the forgotten that is of chief significance for Benjamin's interest in these women here; rather, it is the expressive character which links representations of the feminine with those of the past in the generation of the distorted representation, which Freud analysed as a structure of the language of the unconscious. 'The distortion into allegory of the world of commodities resists the deceptive transfiguration of the latter. The commodity seeks to look itself in the face. It celebrates its incarnation [*Menschwerdung*] in the whore' (*GS* I.2, 671). This incarnation of the commodity is substantiated for the purposes of Benjamin's reading of the imagistic archive of modernity above all by the fact that, in the whore, he found himself confronted by an image become flesh, so to speak: 'The form of the commodity manifests itself in Baudelaire as the social content of the form in which the allegory is perceived. Form and content become one in the prostitute as if in their synthesis' (*GS* V.1, 422). The whore is not only seller and commodity in one, she is also at one and the same time body and image. Indeed, the figuration of looking oneself in the face describes both an incarnation (*Verleiblichung*) or personification of the image and a self-reflexive relation of the image to itself or to its embodiment in real bodies. Moreover, the formulation recalls not only the famous quotation from Kraus about the word, to the effect that the more closely one looks at it, the more distantly it looks back (*GS* I.2, 647; *Ill* 202), but also Benjamin's attempts, which run like a leitmotif through his work, to make the relation between closeness and distance productive for reflection on various modes of representation – such as trace and aura, for example (see *GS* V.1, 560). The figuration also has a part in Benjamin's projection of the category of body- and image-space:

wherever an action puts forth its image and is that image, absorbing and consuming it, wherever closeness looks at itself through its own eyes, this sought-after image-space is opened up, the world of universal and integral actuality.

(GS II.1, 309; OWS 239, translation modified)

This image-space *is* body-space, since it finds representation in the form of bodily innervations, that is, through the bodies of the collective. The coming together of representation and perception in this way, and of body and image, predestines the whore to become the central figure of the *Passagen* project. For it is not only that, in her and through reflection on her, images become dialectical images and allegories become distorted representations in which the imaginary structure of figurative representation is dispersed from within. It is also through his work on the figure of the whore that Benjamin achieved the materialist reversal (*Umkehr*) in his thinking-in-images through which the first matter, the corporeality and the organic element of both human being and things, was brought into the foreground, thus forming the concept of 'body-and image-space'.

Translated by Rachel McNicholl and Georgina Paul

7 The 'other' in allegory

A prehistory of the allegory of modernity in the Baroque

THE DISAPPEARANCE OF THE 'OTHER' IN 'OTHER SPEECH'

Whenever one wishes to clarify what is meant by the term 'allegory', one inevitably meets with the formulation of the 'other speech' (*die andere Rede*). The meaning of the 'other' (*das andere*) within this paraphrase always remains curiously opaque, however. Indeed, a certain indifference as to the sense, origin, and function of this 'other' seems to suggest itself whenever the definition of allegory as 'other speech' is repeated. This is particularly noticeable at the transition to modernity where *the o/Other* in all its multilayered and iridescent meanings rises to the surface and makes its way into the foreground of literature and art. What I want to suggest is that the 'other' in the sense given to it in psychoanalysis becomes dominant in the *allegorical writing of modernity*, and that *pre-modern* allegorical techniques – such as indirect speech, pictorial representation, personification, allegorical schemata and narrative structures – go into this writing, but transformed in such a way that the 'other speech' becomes the 'speech of the Other' (*Rede des Anderen*). In this transformation, the pictorial representations metamorphose into a figurative language of the unconscious or into read images, embodiments (*Verkörperungen*) become semiotic bodies (*semiotische Körper*), body- and image-spaces for the imaginings (*Imaginationen*) of the subject, while metaphorical (literally transferred) representation[1] becomes distorted representation, or translation without an original.

These generally theoretical reflections on the changes occurring in allegorical forms and techniques at the transition into modernity are occasioned by observations made with regard to historical material on the history of the imaginative representation of the city, a history which contains as it were the building blocks of a cultural-historical genealogy for Benjamin's *Passagen* project.[2] Looking at it under this aspect, we find that the literature of modernity is dominated by texts which take up or quote the tradition of allegorical representations of the city and transform these into modes of writing which correspond in multifarious ways with the structures of the unconscious. Whether it is the case that the topography of the city becomes a form of writing which can be read as the dream-writing or allegory of the unconscious and of memory; or whether it be that the *flâneur* moves through the city as if across another scene (*ein anderer Schauplatz*) in which he follows the dictates of his curiosity (*Schaulust*, literally desire to look); or whether it be that architecture and the imagistic writing of the city are understood as the dream images of an epoch: common to all of these is the appearance of the city as the scene of a form of writing which, in an allegorical reading, points towards the o/Other or the unconscious. As far as gender relations are concerned, this change can at the same time be described as a paradigmatic shift from the allegorical personification of the city *as* woman to the representation of the city as a sexualized body (*Stadtkörper*) with feminine connotations. And the recourse to topographical structures taken from early mythical representations of the city in the writing of modernity is connected to the return of the repressed elements within those personifications.

If one allows the observations and the thesis proposed above a certain validity, the question poses itself as to what senses of the 'other' in the definition of allegory as 'other speech' have preceded this modern allegory and been subsumed into it. Since the o/Other has connotations not only of the unconscious, but also of the feminine, the question also arises as to whether the notion of allegory as 'other speech' might in any way be connected to gender relations, and thus whether – and how – the 'other' of speech has points of contact with the construction of the 'other' sex.[3] These questions have as their basis a conviction that it is only when scholarly research on allegory moves beyond the framework of the history of form-language (*Formensprache*) to take account of the different aspects of the o/Other, of gender difference, of the corporeality and materiality of signs, that this research will take on a cultural-historical dimension. As it is, research on allegory has hitherto demonstrated no interest in the significance of the 'other' in allegorical method, nor in the gender of allegorical figures.

Virtually all explanations of allegory and allegorical method are in agreement over the etymological derivation from the Greek according to which 'allegory' is construed as 'other speech': *allos* other, *agoreuein* to speak (publicly). Some are more precise in their definitions of the relationship between 'other' and 'speech', translating allegory as 'speaking other than publicly': *alläh* other than, *agoreuein* to speak in the agora or public assembly; allegory, then, as 'to speak other than comprehensibly to all'. But what precisely is meant by this 'other', what significance does it bear in this mode of speech, how and from what is it derived? These questions are seldom addressed, or else quickly disappear in what is probably the most common concretization; namely, that what is meant is a figurative form of speech. If this implicitly defines the relationship of the image or figure to the concept as one of alterity, it is nevertheless precisely in the gap between the two that the whole play of meanings is made to disappear, a play of meanings which is constituted precisely out of the heterogeneity of *logos* and *materia*, of signifier and signified, out of the most manifold and multifarious differences therefore.

On account of differing points of departure, however, concrete, visible signs are sometimes – namely, when viewed from the perspective of representation – characterized as other in relation to meaning, while elsewhere and conversely – namely, when viewed from the perspective of reading – the concrete image or literal sense of a text is seen as pointing towards another meaning. In the first case, then, the intended meaning is represented in a different, 'other' image, so that this other is what is visible, whereas in the second, what is represented contains a different, 'other' meaning which is either not visible or is encoded. Adopting a semiotic view, one might say that, on the one hand, it is the signified that is seen as other while the signifier appears to be unambiguous, proper (*eigentlich*), and original, whereas, on the other, it is the signifier that is taken as the point of departure and which, apart from its proper sense, points towards another signified. If an allegorical representation and an allegorical reading or exegesis (*Allegorese*) thus respectively situate the 'other' in the precisely converse position, within the signifier *or* within the signified, the question arises whether, for example, the attention is not in each case also being directed at something quite different.[4]

The allegorical dimension, it is said, is regulated by the relationship between 'word' and 'meaning', moreover in accordance with a definite *system*, which is as a rule one of traditional norms and ideas (Kuhn 1979: 207). The relationship of translation (*translatio*) between word or image and meaning thus has its basis in specific knowledge, which raises the problem of access to this knowledge. Academic interest in allegory is focused primarily on the way such systems are established – and, together with this, on efforts towards achieving a sufficient range of differences that constitute meaning within figurative representation[5] – or, alternatively, on the reconstruction of historical keys and codes.

This means that scholarship on allegory is very largely characterized by an encyclopaedic approach. The question concerning the significance of the 'other' in the allegorical dimension has, in the meantime, been for the most part forgotten. And yet experience shows that many allegorical paintings, regardless of what they are supposed to portray and independently of the search for their unknown meaning – that is, quite apart from the knowledge or decodability of the intended meaning – exercise a strange fascination. And in the case of many images one is tempted to ask whether the allegorical meaning did not simply provide the (moral) occasion for an artistic representation, and whether the desire of artist and viewer is not primarily directed towards this *other representation* – for desire is always the desire for the other. Quite apart from the question of *access* to a knowledge-system which regulates the allegorical relationship between text and meaning, allegories permit different readings in which either the system of translation or the concrete representation may provide the central focus.

EMBODIMENT AND DISEMBODIMENT

This tendency to forget the circumstance that in the case of allegory one has to do with translation into *another* language corresponds with an approach that is primarily interested in *one* side alone in the constitution of allegorical meaning – namely, in the illustration or symbolization of abstract, conceptual notions, which may also be understood as an embodiment of immaterial ideas. In the meantime, the reverse side of this process remains outside the field of vision: namely, disembodiment, such as takes place in respect of the material and of the images which are used – and consumed – in the allegorical representation. In this approach, too, then, a certain indifference is expressed towards the other in 'other speech'.

Taking the example of Baroque *Trauerspiel*, Benjamin elaborated precisely this tendency towards the devaluation of things material which, in the allegorical representation, always become 'something other'.[6] For him, there was a connection between allegory and practices of stripping naked sensuous things (*Entblößung der sinnlichen Dinge*) (*GS* I, 360; see *OGT* 185), of rigidification, dismemberment, and deprivation of life:

> Allegorical personification has always concealed the fact that its function is not the personification of things [*Dinghaftes*], but rather to give the concrete [*das Dingliche*] a more imposing form by getting it up as a person.
>
> (*GS* I, 362; *OGT* 187)

There is not the faintest glimmer of any spiritualization of the physical. The whole of nature is personalized, not so as to be made more inward, but, on the contrary – so as to be deprived of soul.

(*GS* I, 363; *OGT* 187)[7]

Benjamin shows this tendency as coming to a head, at the point where allegory and emblem use the human body as their material, in his thesis of the 'pious mortification of the flesh' (*GS* I, 396; *OGT* 222):

> the human body could be no exception to the commandment which ordered the destruction of the organic so that the true meaning, as it was written and ordained [*fixiert*], might be picked up from its fragments. . . . the allegorization of the physis can only be carried through in all its vigour in respect of the corpse. And the characters of the *Trauerspiel* die, because it is only thus, as corpses, that they can enter into the homeland of allegory.
>
> (*GS* I, 391–2; *OGT* 216–17)

This devaluating tendency in allegorical representation has its counterpart, too, in allegorical exegesis. For the genesis of allegorical reading – whether in the debate concerning allegorical interpretation of myth, sparked off in relation to Homeric epic, or in the allegorical extrapolation of certain passages in Holy Scripture – lies in the assumption of another sense, an assumption which has its basis in the rejection of the literal meaning of the textual passages in question – the story of Lot and his daughters, for example, or the story of Susanna, or the Song of Songs.[8] The establishment of an allegorical interpretation of texts is thus accompanied at its origin by a devaluation of literal sense and therefore also by an act of repression.

KNOWLEDGE AND ABYSS: THE CHARACTER OF ALLEGORY AS A FORM OF WRITING

On the other hand, there is constituted out of the difference between text or image and meaning, out of the gap between literal and allegorical reading, a field of interpretation which is bound up in the history of power-knowledge-systems, both in their establishment and in their dissolution. In this respect, precisely this field of allegorical interpretation is one in which an explicit or hidden battle for control over knowledge is fought out, a knowledge which, with the aid of the structures of the imaginary and through the interpretation of all forms of imagistic perception, becomes inscribed in the experience and everyday life of individuals. It is for this reason that allegory plays such an important role in the tradition of cultural memory, and not only in that trace of tradition to which Frances A. Yates has called attention in her examination of the specific connections between the *ars memoria* and the allegorical paintings of the Renaissance (Yates 1966: 91ff.). Rather, wherever they form a repertoire of established *topoi* which structures memory and experience, allegorical images and schemata become building blocks in the archive of cultural memory. 'It [allegory] is a schema; and as a schema it is an object of knowledge, but it is not securely possessed until it is a fixed schema: at one and the same time a fixed image and a fixing sign' (*GS* I, 359; *OGT* 184). It is in this way, too, that the fact that images and bodies of women became the privileged material of allegorical personifications – as they did in direct proportion to the disappearance of mythical figures out of the repertoire of personification – had its effect on the symbolic construction of the 'other sex'. In the allegorical personification, the fixing of the 'other speech' and the consolidation of the notion of the 'other sex' coincide.[9]

However, precisely the fact that fixations of this kind are not constant for all time, that the gap between text and meaning cannot be lastingly safeguarded by a coherent knowledge-system, but is rather ever open to question, leads to the repeated renewal of allegorical activity. When, for example, Benjamin describes, in his book on the Baroque *Trauerspiel*, the place of allegorical immersion as the 'abyss which separates imagistic being and meaning' (*Abgrund zwischen bildlichem Sein und Bedeuten*) (*GS* I, 342; *OGT* 165, translation modified), this presupposes, on the one hand, the loss of an unequivocal and universally valid interpretative system. But at the same time, this loss is, in terms of the history of signs, part of the process described by Foucault as the loss of similitude at the transition from the Renaissance to what he terms the Classical age: as the transition, then, from a more complex ternary sign system to a binary one, a system of representative signs which Foucault defines as 'the connection of a significant and a signified' (Foucault 1970: 42).[10]

The ternary sign system, which is both uniform *and* threefold, implies 'three quite distinct elements: that which was marked, that which did the marking, and that which made it possible to see in the first the mark of the second' (1970: 64). Foucault grasps the experience of language as the dissolution of these three elements contained in a single figure into: (1) the existence of 'the simple, material form of writing, a stigma upon things', (2) 'above it, . . . commentary, which recasts the given signs to serve a new purpose', and (3) 'below it, the text, whose primacy is presupposed by the commentary to exist hidden beneath the marks visible to all. Hence there are three levels of language, all based upon the single being of the written word' (1970: 42). And it is precisely this kind of *writing* which loses its dominant role at the inception of the Classical age (according to Foucault, in the seventeenth century). Under the dominance of similitude and writing, therefore, a *gap* between signifier and signified was held open across which thought was required to weave its way in, as Foucault puts it, 'an endless zigzag course from the resemblance to what resembles it' (1970: 30). And I think that it is this gap which describes the field of the other, that same field in which 'the other speech' is constituted: as regulative speech about the other, and also as the speech of the Other which challenges that regulation.

If Benjamin lays such a strong emphasis on the *character of allegory as a form of writing* in *The Origin of German Tragic Drama*, this gives expression to his method of redeeming criticism which is already being practised there. According to Benjamin, the allegorical gaze transforms 'things and works into excitatory writing [*erregende Schrift*]' (*GS* I, 352; *OGT* 176, translation modified). In an historical constellation in which it is suppressed by the general domination of representative signs, writing (in the above-mentioned Foucauldian sense) has migrated into or is recuperated in the literary allegory, the 'character of allegory as a form of writing' (*GS* I 359; *OGT* 184). Thus the allegory provides a memory trace for a similitude which has been lost, a trace for that literature with which Foucault associates a kind of counter-discourse, a recollection and – with modernity – reappearance of lost similitude. Seen in this light, allegory would be a field within writing in which – under the sign of representation – a memory trace of the ternary system of language and of the gap held open between image or text and meaning as contained within that system are discernible, a memory trace, then, of the repressed gap which returns in the literature of modernity, not infrequently to be perceived as an abyss (*Abgrund*), as Benjamin remarks in his notes for the *Passagen*:

> The 'abysmal' sense [*der abgründige Sinn*] is to be defined as 'meaning' [*Bedeutung*]. It is always an allegorical one.
>
> (*GS* V.1, 347)

> Baudelaire's abyss is . . . a secularized one: the abyss of knowledge and of meanings. What constitutes his historical index?
>
> (*GS* V.1, 348)

This memory trace in allegorical method is, however, repeatedly concealed, covered up by the prescriptions of the *translatio*, whereby the allegory, with its tendency towards the schematic, repeatedly takes on the form of fixed knowledge.

In his [the allegorist's] hands the thing becomes something other; through it he speaks to something other and for him it becomes a key to the realm of hidden knowledge; and he reveres it as the emblem of this. This is what determines the character of allegory as a form of writing. It is a schema; and as a schema [. . . continuation as above].

(*GS* I, 359; *OGT* 184)

And if the allegorist and his activity play such an important role in Benjamin's analysis – as opposed to the schema and key of the *translatio* – so that the *subject* takes the place of interpretative authority, the established regulative system of allegorical relations,[11] then it is here that that moment of the allegorical writing of modernity is heralded in which the subject is situated entirely in the 'abyss which separates imagistic being and meaning'.[12]

THE MODERN ALLEGORY AND THE STRUCTURE OF THE UNCONSCIOUS

For, on the one hand, the allegories of modernity contribute towards the recuperation of the character of language as writing, while on the other, they radically discharge the subject into the uncertain relation between text or image and meaning. Traces of a prehistory of this allegory of modernity are to be found wherever allegorical *reading* – not a learned, typologically ordered, or systematically regulated exegesis – permits the images or texts to become writing, the deciphering of which is passed into the responsibility of the subject. That is, the allegory of modernity is constituted through the practice of reading, through the observation of texts and images *as writing*. It is in this sense that Benjamin also speaks of 'read images' and of the 'critical, dangerous moment which is at the basis of all reading' (*GS* V.1, 578; see *N* 50–1). The allegorical method devised by Benjamin in the *Passagen* project, which has visible links with the model of the 'dialectical image' and with the historico-theoretical conception of the 'Now of cognizability' (*Jetzt der Erkennbarkeit*) – that is, the second stage of Benjamin's theory of allegory which was developed in the context of his work on modernity – is, moreover, grounded in a psychoanalytical re-reading of the character of allegory as writing.

Thus it is that in Benjamin it is the allegorist's gaze that allows things to become writing, in that he reads in the 'book of what has happened' (*Buch des Geschehenen*) (*GS* V.1, 580; see *N* 52) as in a 'waking man's Egyptian dream-book' (*ägyptischen Traumbuch des Wachenden*)

(*GS* III, 198). And conversely: in the deciphering of the picture-puzzles (*Vexierbilder*) of modernity, the relationship of the picture-puzzle to the literal text is described in analogy to allegorical method, with the literal text as 'the sole repository in which the picture-puzzle can form itself' (*GS* II.1, 208–9; *DS* 68, translation modified). It is, however, not only the quoted image of hieroglyphics ('Egyptian dream-book') that points towards allegorical representations of the unconscious in psychoanalysis. All of his reflections take as their basis an existing affinity between allegory and the conception of the unconscious in psychoanalysis.

For Freud very frequently avails himself of allegorical methods in order to make the processes of the psychic apparatus representable, first and foremost for the reason that he rejects the localization of psychic processes in the body in favour of seeing the body as a scene (*Schauplatz*) in which psychic disturbances manifest themselves (Starobinski 1991: 26). The functions and structures of the invisible primary processes are often explained by him in terms of allegorical descriptions, which are nevertheless at the same time also a reflection on these representational methods. Whether the functioning of memory is conceived according to the model of the 'mystic writing-pad' (*Wunderblock*), or whether the language of the dream is analysed as figurative writing and compared with a rebus or with hieroglyphics; whether he has recourse to a topological schema in order to differentiate between the varying systems of the psychic apparatus, or whether the unconscious in general appears as the scene of a form of writing, Freud's descriptions of the structures of the unconscious always make use of allegorical representation. And since Freud does not only *represent* the structures of the unconscious allegorically, but also, in his analysis of the articulations of the unconscious, reads the images produced by the subject as allegories – as 'other speech', so to speak – that is, as a different representation whose proper (*eigentlich*) thought, the so-called dream thought, remains unindicated, as translations without an original, then – *his* own texts are as it were second-degree allegories.

The regulative system of translation between manifest and latent (dream-) text cannot, according to Freud, be reconstructed in the form of a code, but can only be described in terms of the way it works (the means of dream-work: condensation [*Verdichtung*], displacement [*Verschiebung*], the considerations of representability [*Rücksicht auf Darstellbarkeit*]), all of which means produce a *distorted* representation. And distortion (*Entstellung*) is then one of the psychoanalytical terms which Benjamin takes up explicitly in his works on modernity: both in the Kafka essay, in which he designates the gestures and figures in Kafka's texts as distorted, bringing them into association with the forgotten (*GS* II.2, 431ff.; *Ill* 133ff.), and in that he speaks in 'Central Park' (*Zentralpark*) of a 'distortion into allegory': 'The distortion into allegory of the world of commodities resists the deceptive transfiguration of the latter. The commodity seeks to look itself in the face. It celebrates its incarnation in the whore' (*GS* I.2, 671).

Just as second-degree allegories are at work in Freud's texts, so, too, is the allegory of modernity in Benjamin a second-degree allegory: for it is both allegory and at the same time a dispersal of allegorical idea and representation – that is, of the imaginary structure which bridges the gap between image and meaning. If, for example, the destruction of organic connections or the devaluation of the world of things through the commodity recalls the allegorical intention, then their aura, their appearance of naturalness is dispersed under the allegorist's gaze. And then allegorical personifications have also, in the figure of the prostitutes from Baudelaire's poetry, found their successors in Benjamin's 'ur-history of modernity', albeit no longer as the embodiments of an idea, but as 'the commodity which most completely fulfils allegorical perception', in which fulfilment the dispersal of allegorical appearance (*Schein*) is contained as a potential, as Benjamin indicated in a letter to Horkheimer of 1938 (Benjamin 1978: 752; see Benjamin 1995: 556).

This reading is, however, only made possible by a text which reads the metropolitan experience of modernity as allegorical writing, whereby the arcades of Paris are *the* paradigmatic locations, because it is with respect to them that the writing of the city (architecture and topography) and the experiences of the subject intersect in the most manifold ways, producing the most complex multiplicity of meanings: they are *rites de passage*, dream-places, threshold, and transition point. Here, as in many texts by other authors, topographical schemata dominate the image-writing (*Bilderschrift*) of modernity. In them, topographical models from myths make their reappearance, whereby these can be understood as quasi pre-allegorical image-writing. In representing the movements of inclusion and exclusion in a single text, topographical structures open up for the subject's Other a body- and image-space in writing and seem, then, pre-eminently suited to transforming 'other speech' into the speech of the Other. Yet in so doing, the allegory in modernity as it were dissolves into a form of writing which opens up a space for the structures of the unconscious. The memory trace of the gap between image or text and meaning which is marked by the 'other speech' of

Classical allegory, a hidden trace, on which Benjamin had his eye with the character of allegory as writing in the *Trauerspiel* book, comes to the surface of writing in modernity as the speech of the o/Other, as the language of the unconscious, and, in Benjamin's 'ur-history of modernity', is deciphered as the dream-writing of the collective.

Memory and writing

'Images that we never saw until we remembered them.'

'To be past, to be no longer works passionately on things.'

8   From topography to writing
Benjamin's concept of memory

THE SCENE OF MEMORY BETWEEN ARCHAEOLOGY AND WRITING

When in Benjamin's last completed text, the thought-images (*Denk-bilder*) 'On the Concept of History', historiography and recollection are presented as structurally analogous activities and the images of the has-been (*das Gewesene*) are described as mnemic images (*Erinner-ungsbilder*), this marks the culmination of a long preoccupation with the concepts of memory (*Gedächtnis*) and recollection (*Erinnerung*), in the course of which Benjamin's concept of images – or, more specifically, of their cognizability and readability – found a basis in a theory of memory. The text 'On Some Motifs in Baudelaire' (1939), and here above all the sections I to IV, marks the point in Benjamin's writings at which he explicitly discusses different models of memory, whereby section III, in which he enters into a consideration of Freud's concept of shock or impact (*Chock*), comes closest in character to a *theoretical* exposition. Yet the traces of his work on a concept of memory go much further back, attaining a particular concentration above all between the first phase of work on the *Passagen* (1927–29) and his resumption of the project from 1934 onwards. It could be said that those writings which Benjamin himself attributed to his 'more recent physiognomy' and which he saw as beginning with 'One-Way Street' (Benjamin 1978: 416; see Benjamin 1995: 293), following the completion of the 'production complex on German literature' and the break that he considered the 'revolutionary turn' in his thought (1978: 659), that those writings, then, which were composed under the sign of modernity and which were all more or less directly related to the *Passagen* project, are in large part concerned with problems of memory.

Many of the texts within the radius of the *Passagen* contain reflections or single thought-images on the complex of recollection and

memory, and may be seen as testing out different models and possibilities for representing this complex. In them, Benjamin experiments
with a variety of different registers – with notions from archaeology
and from optics, for example, but above all with topographical representations – in order to illustrate the attitude of the subject towards the
traces and images of history, an attitude which, in the course of the
development of his theoretical reflections, takes on ever clearer profile
in terms of a specific model of reading. Within this model, the reading
of the traces and images of history is located in the scene (*Schauplatz*)
of individual and collective memory (which are regarded as being
analogous in structure) and understood as a perceptual activity on the
threshold between receptivity and action, between revelation and
historiography, between dreaming and philosophizing.

As his thoughts develop, a clear paradigm shift becomes evident from
a topographical-spatial model of memory, such as is characteristic of
the first phase of the *Passagen* project, to a scripto-topographical
concept of memory, bearing the imprint of psychoanalytical thinking,
such as structures the work of the 1930s on the *Passagen*. The notes
and thought-images of 'A Berlin Chronicle' (1932) can be taken as the
site in his writing (*Schrift-Ort*) in which this paradigm shift can be most
clearly observed; it will then find a theoretical grounding with Benjamin's psychoanalytical reformulation of his theory of language in the
two short essays 'On the Mimetic Faculty' and 'The Doctrine of the
Similar' of 1933 and with the category of 'non-sensuous similitude'
(*unsinnliche Ähnlichkeit*) set out there.[1]

In the 'Berlin Chronicle', the imagery of the section on memory
derives, for example, from the register of *archaeology*; here Benjamin
emphasizes the relevance of the place and precise spot (*Ort und Stelle*)
in which things are recovered or found and which may have a significant
bearing on their readability or on the relationship between traces
(*Spuren*) and remains (*Reste*). The 'attitude of genuine recollections'
(*Haltung echter Erinnerungen*) is described in this context in the image
of excavation as an archaeological activity, in which it is not what is
found, but rather the way in which the search is carried out that is of
chief importance. And in that it says that recollection should not be
afraid to 'return again and again to the same matter [*denselben
Sachverhalt*]', the figure of a repetition is simultaneously inscribed into
the activity of recollection, albeit a repetition which with the characterization 'the same' ('the same matter') has not yet identified its object,
but so far only the point of departure for its movement:

> For the matters themselves are only deposits, strata, which yield only
> to the most meticulous examination what constitutes the real assets

[*Werte*] hidden within the earth: the images which, severed from all earlier contexts, stand as precious objects [*Kostbarkeiten*] – like ruins [*Trümmer*] or torsos in the collector's gallery – in the prosaic rooms of our later understanding.

(*GS* VI, 486; *OWS* 314, translation modified)

If the images severed from their earlier contexts are here at first, through the comparison with precious collector's pieces, rated as coveted or cult objects of memory – as meaningful remains, so to speak – which the movement of the search is intended to bring to light, their value is relativized in what follows:

> and it is to cheat oneself of the richest prize to preserve as a record [*Niederschrift*] merely the inventory of one's discoveries, and not this dark joy of the place [*Ort und Stelle*] of the finding itself. Fruitless searching is as much a part of this as succeeding, and consequently remembrance [*Erinnerung*] must not proceed in the manner of a narrative or still less that of a report, but must, in the strictest epic and rhapsodic manner, assay its spade in ever new places, and in the old ones delve to ever deeper layers.

(*GS* VI, 486; *OWS* 314)

Under the heading of memory as a scene, this attempt at representation, taking as its starting point a narrative structure (the repeated return to the same), and leading on from here to the movements of excavation which are on the trail of meaningful individual pieces, culminates in a catalogue of the places where the findings are made or even of the vain search. This catalogue – in that it is distinguished from the *inventory* of retrieved objects – appears as it were as a different form of *written* record (*Niederschrift*), in relation to which the movement of the search is now also described in terms of a different form of repetition: in ever new places and at ever deeper levels. Thus in this representation of the memory-scene – a thought-image *par excellence* – a model of writing is superimposed upon an archaeological allegory. And if the archaeological allegory introduces the association of a model of levels, the model of writing is like that proposed by Freud in his topographical concept of memory in which memory is described as a different, or other, scene (*ein anderer Schauplatz*).

The 'Berlin Chronicle', a preliminary study for Benjamin's 'Berlin Childhood Around 1900' (composed from 1933 on), is the work of the author's in which he works most intensively on *his* model for representing memory. Here he tests out a variety of different representational allegories, not only that of excavation, but also, for example, that of the family tree and the labyrinth. This undertaking, which was the result of a commission for a series of glosses on Berlin in 'loosely subjective form' (*GS* VI, 476; *OWS* 305), had been preceded by the first drafts and sketches for the *Passagen* project in which the Paris arcades were to be examined as paradigms of a 'past become space' (*eine raumgewordene Vergangenheit*) (*GS* V.2, 1041). In these initial sketches, the topography and architecture of the city are regarded as the memory-space (*Gedächtnisraum*) of the collective, so that already here we find a materialized memory-topography, in which the external topography, the city of modernity, and the topographical representation of memory in psychoanalysis converge. It is a mode of observation, however, that was only to take on a more differentiated form via the detour of the mnemic images of the 'Berlin Childhood' and other works composed in the late 1920s and early 1930s. And the aim in what follows is to reconstruct the development of this Benjaminian model of memory.

THE TOPOGRAPHY OF DREAM AND WAKING

In the early sketches for the *Passagen*, Benjamin works at a dialectical mode of observation which he himself terms a 'Copernican turning point in the perception of history' (*kopernikanische Wendung in der historischen Anschauung*) (*GS* V.2, 1057) and which he discovers, in connection with the relation between dream and consciousness, in the constellation of awakening: on the threshold, then, between dream and waking. The turning point in the perception of history[2] of which Benjamin speaks here is to be understood thus: that awakening, characterized as the 'exemplary case of recollection' (*exemplarischer Fall des Erinnerns*) (*GS* V.2, 1057), gives access to a different kind of knowledge of things past, to 'a not yet conscious knowledge of the has-been' (*GS* V.2, 1014) or to the dream form of the past which has left its traces in the present, even if Benjamin does not yet use the term 'trace' (*Spur*) here:

There is an absolutely singular experience of dialectic. The compelling, the drastic experience, giving the lie to all 'gradualness of becoming' [*Allgemach des Werdens*] and revealing all apparent 'development' [*Entwicklung*] to be an eminent, highly sophisticated, sudden dialectical transformation [*Umschlag*], is that of awakening from a dream ... And with this we present the new, the dialectical historical method: to go through the has-been with the intensity of a dream in order to experience the present as the waking world to which the dream is related! (And every dream is related to the waking world. *Everything* previous must be penetrated historically.)

(*GS* V.2, 1006)

It is not only in contradistinction to the conception of linear time and developmental models of history that the relationship between the has-been and the present is disallowed any kind of temporal status here. For it is thought of rather in terms of a relationship between dream and waking world and ultimately – since this in turn is represented in the topography of the city – seen as a spatial relationship. Yet the topography of the city does not serve to *represent* the dream-world and the world of waking consciousness in the way that Freud, for example, used the 'mystic writing-pad' (*Wunderblock*) as an allegory to represent the interplay of the two distinct systems of the psychic apparatus, perception-consciousness (*Wahrnehmung-Bewußtsein*) on the one hand, and the unconscious (*Unbewußtes*) on the other. It is rather the case that Benjamin compares certain phenomena, figures, and locations in the real topography of the city with dream and consciousness. He thus *rediscovers* the relationship between dream and consciousness in material form in the topography of the city – a mode of observation which anticipates the concept of 'correspondences' (*Korrespondenzen*), which he did not develop until rather later, and here describes correspondences between myth, the city, and the relationship between dream and waking:

> In ancient Greece places [*Stellen*] were shown from which paths led down into the underworld. Our waking existence is also a country in which there are hidden places which lead down into the underworld, a country full of inconspicuous locations where dreams open out onto the world. During the day we go past them unsuspectingly, but scarcely are we asleep than we feel our way back to them with rapid hand-movements and lose ourselves in dark passageways. In bright daylight the labyrinth of houses in the city is like consciousness; during the day the arcades (these are the galleries which lead into [the city's] past existence) open out unnoticed onto the street. But åt night, beneath the dark mass of the houses, their more compact darkness leaps out terrifyingly; and the late passer-by hurries on past them, unless, that is, we have encouraged him to take a journey through that narrow passage.

(*GS* V.2, 1046)

When Benjamin writes here of places (*Stellen*) where dreams open out onto waking existence or the arcades onto the street, he is already giving emphasis to location, as again in the archaeological image quoted from the 'Berlin Chronicle' above: not in this case the location where things are found or looked for, but the location of the transition point, the threshold which marks the access to the past. In another passage he characterizes the houses and the labyrinth they form as dream formations (*Traumgebilde*), that is, dreams of the ancients that have taken on shape and become stone; and these in turn have entered into language via the street-names:

> The most concealed aspect of the big cities: this historical object of the modern city, with its uniform streets and incalculable rows of houses, has realized the architectural structures dreamt of by the ancients: the labyrinths . . .
>
> What the city of the modern epoch has made of the ancient conception of the labyrinth. It has, through the street-names, raised it to the sphere of language, out of the network of streets into the (x) called (x) within language (x).[3]

(GS V, 1007)

This attention to the sphere of language gives an early hint at a perspective which will become more central in his subsequent investigations. For it is striking that, in this first phase of his work on the *Passagen* project, Benjamin does not yet make use of the term or the concept of the unconscious. Rather, he refers to the relationship between dream and waking or dream and consciousness, and projects this onto space. It is true that in doing so he makes explicit reference to psychoanalytical theory, albeit to the notion of a 'fluctuating state of a consciousness divided at all times and in multiple ways between waking and sleeping', a notion which he proposes to transfer from the individual to the collective (*GS* V, 1012). If, then, the topographical scene of memory which Benjamin discovers in the city of modernity is compared with the conception of memory in Freud, there are at this stage, at the end of the 1920s, both similarities and differences to be observed.

READING TRACES VERSUS SECURING CLUES

A reading of Freud's topographical model of memory as set out in 'Beyond the Pleasure Principle' (1923) and the 'Note upon the "Mystic Writing-Pad"'[4] (1925) reveals several characteristics relevant to our considerations here. First, the *distinction* he draws between the two, in terms of the way they function, incompatible systems of the psychic apparatus, of which the unconscious (*das Unbewußte*) serves the unlimited reception of permanent traces (*Dauerspuren*) and recorded excitations (*aufgezeichnete Erregungen*), whereas the system perception-consciousness or *Pcpt.-Cs.* (*Wahrnehmung-Bewußtsein* or *W-Bw*) is ever ready to receive new stimuli (*Reize*) or perceptions (*Wahrnehmungen*), but also takes on the task of a protective shield (*Reizschutz*). Of fundamental significance is, however, secondly, the *relation* between the two systems, which may be described as dialectical in so far as Freud writes that 'consciousness arises in place of a memory trace' (*Bewußtsein entstehe an Stelle der Erinnerungsspur*) (Freud 1969: III, 235) whereby 'in place of' (*an Stelle*) has the meaning 'instead of' as well as 'at the site of';[5] this occurs in that consciousness flickers up (*aufleuchtet*) and passes away again in the moment that, as a result of discontinuous cathexis in the system, a connection is established between perception and permanent trace. In describing permanent traces as 'the foundation of memory' and linking their readability to certain preconditions, Freud here promotes the view that memory traces are a form of writing – albeit a form of writing which is never readable as such and in its entirety. For its *readability* is structured by the dialectic of consciousness and mnemic traces, and described in terms of a momentary flickering-up or becoming visible.

As far as the *deciphering* (*Entzifferung*) of this writing is concerned, one must turn to other texts of Freud's: to *The Interpretation of Dreams* (1900), for example, where he – bearing in mind 'considerations of representability' (*Rücksicht auf Darstellbarkeit*) – examines the dream's mode of represention as an image-writing (*Bilderschrift*) and takes as his premise that this writing corresponds to the form of a distorted representation. Thirdly, this aspect of *distortion* (*Entstellung*) is characteristic of the structure of the unconscious in Freud, and also becomes significant for other phenomena apart from the dream, for other languages of the unconscious – as when Freud sees the hysterical or corporeal symptom as a mnemic symbol, a bodily memory trace, then, which cannot be interpreted as an engram or imprint (*Abdruck*).

In semiotic terms, it is these three characteristics – the figuration 'in place of' in the relationship between consciousness and permanent traces, the readability bound to the momentary flickering-up or *Aufleuchten*, and the phenomenon of distorted representation in the visible or readable signs of the memory traces – which mark the specificity of Freud's concept of memory. It is these, too, which distinguish his notion of traces (*Spuren*) from the evidential paradigm whose history Carlo Ginzburg has set out in his essay 'Clues: Roots of an Evidential Paradigm' (Ginzburg 1990: 96–125).[6] It is true that the medical and criminological forms of deciphering clues, traces, and symptoms described by Ginzburg did indeed have a part in the prehistory and development of Freudian psychoanalysis, forms which Ginzburg, taking the examples of the Morelli method (for identifying the authorship of paintings),[7] of detection, physiognomy, graphology, and fingerprinting, places in the larger context of a whole history of the interpretation of signs and describes in turn as a 'venatic, divinatory, conjectural, or semiotic' paradigm (1990: 117).

Yet the caesura between Freudian theory and Ginzburg's evidential paradigm is to be found in the fact that all of Ginzburg's examples are concerned with establishing identity. The *symptoms* which Ginzburg, together with *clues* (in Sherlock Holmes) and pictorial *marks* (in Morelli), considers under the category of *traces* (1990: 101) are in Freud's work to be distinguished from signs in a system of circumstantial evidence. For symptoms are understood by Freud as signs for a return of the repressed and thus described as the results of a psychic process (*Bearbeitung*) which is thought of as analogous in structure to distortion in dream-work. That is, they serve as indicators of a past that has left its traces in the unconscious, but traces which only become readable in the form of symptoms – signs of a *distorted* representation in the visible. Symptoms are thus mnemic *symbols*. When it comes to deciphering the various traces of the past – remains, ruins, fragments, testimonies, and so on – it is, then, a matter of some importance whether they are interpreted as being clues in the context of an evidential paradigm or whether they are read as visible mnemic symbols in the reformulated model of memory traces in psychoanalysis: that is, as visible representatives of otherwise unreadable permanent traces.

In the case of Benjamin, it may be contended that there is a clear affinity between the development of his theory of memory and the Freudian conception. His attentiveness to topographical correspondences and to the significance of (transitional) places is concentrated in thought-figures which can be seen as offering the preconditions for an assimilation of the Freudian topography of memory. It is, however, more difficult to reconstruct exactly Benjamin's reading of Freud's work, since he only seldom makes any explicit reference to it – and is perhaps inclined to do so least where the traces of Freudian thought-figures are most influential in his work.

There are, for example, indications of his reading of Freud[8] in the context of his university studies (in 1918 he attended Paul Häberlein's seminar on Freud in Bern),[9] then references to Freud's 'doctrine of the unconscious' (*Lehre vom Unbewußten*) in his discussion of a children's primer in the *Frankfurter Zeitung* of 13 December 1930 under the title 'Chichleuchlauchra' (*GS* III, 271) and to 'Freud's study of narcissism' in his review 'Colonial Pedagogy' (*Kolonialpädagogik*) in the same newspaper the following week (*GS* III, 273).[10] Apart from this, he himself reports on his reading of Freud's essay on 'Psychoanalysis and Telepathy' (1934) in a 1935 letter to Gretel Adorno (Benjamin 1979: 28), and speaks highly of the 'Freudian School' in his Bachofen essay of the same year (*GS* II.3, 953). Also in 1935, he writes to Adorno that he wants to 'take on' reading Freud in the near future (*GS* V.2, 1121), as if he were not 'conscious' of how strongly his writings had long been corresponding with Freudian theory. This remark to Adorno could, however, be taken as an indication that Benjamin's interest in Freud was at this time taking on a more systematic character or yielding conceptual features for his theory of memory as is also suggested by a number of entries in the *Passagen*. For example, in *Konvolut* K (*Traumstadt und Traumhaus*, 'dream-city and dream-house'), we find noted under the heading 'On the psychoanalytical theory of recollection' (*Zur psychoanalytischen Theorie der Erinnerung*) the quotation from Reik which will reappear in the section on theories of memory in 'Baudelaire' and in which Reik discusses his reading of Freud with reference to the relation between memory (*Gedächtnis*) and recollection (*Erinnerung*). This entry, then, can be seen as belonging to a preliminary stage[11] leading up to the already mentioned central placing of 'Beyond the Pleasure Principle' and the Freudian *Chock* theory in the Baudelaire essay of 1939, in which Benjamin discusses Freud in relation to other authors (Bergson, Reik, Proust). It is here that he cites the central premise of Freud's concept of memory, namely the 'assumption that "consciousness comes into being in the place [*an der Stelle*] of the memory trace"' (*GS* I.2, 612; *Ill* 162, translation modified).

Since Benjamin here quotes Freud's essay 'Beyond the Pleasure Principle' in distorted form – *an der Stelle* instead of *an Stelle* – it may be assumed that, despite the fact that he gives date and page reference to the third edition of the text (Vienna, 1923: 31), he was in fact quoting from his own notes made at the time of an earlier, perhaps even considerably earlier, reading. What I would like to suggest is that, between the second, major phase of work on the *Passagen* project (1939–40), in which Benjamin quite consciously and systematically worked on the 'psychoanalytical theory of memory', by which is meant that he *studied* it, 'took on' Freud, and the working phase on the first drafts (1927–29), an in all probability less systematic and conscious, but for all that no less intensive reception of Freudian methods of observation and terminology took place, a different kind of *reading* of Freud, then, which nevertheless left clear traces. In what follows, I propose to substantiate this thesis by following some of the traces of this reading – quite in the spirit of philological clue-gathering – via Benjamin's use of various Freudian terms – such as facilitation (*Bahnung*), the unconscious (*Unbewußtes*), repression (*Verdrängung*), innervations (*Innervationen*), distortion (*Entstellung*) – whose appearance can be observed in the texts Benjamin wrote in the period mentioned without there being any explicit discussion of Freudian theory such as we find in the Baudelaire essay. Of more fundamental importance than the retracing of his reading of Freud, however, is the reconstruction of Benjamin's work on his own theory of memory which forms the basis of the *Passagen* texts of the 1930s and the thought-figures and representational images developed there. Before embarking on the securing of clues of Benjamin's reading of Freud, then, let us turn first to this latter aspect.

THE *PASSAGEN*: READING COLLECTIVE MEMORY TRACES

Whereas in the early sketches for the *Passagen*, as already shown, the paradigm of dream and waking, but *not yet* the concept of the unconscious, structures the representation, and the houses of the city are at certain points described as dream formations, in his 1935 exposé 'Paris – the Capital of the Nineteenth Century' Benjamin now speaks of the unconscious of the collective:[12]

> In the dream in which every epoch sees in images the epoch which is to succeed it, the latter appears coupled with elements of prehistory – that is to say of a classless society. The experiences of this society, which have their store-place in the *unconscious of the collective*, interact with the new to give birth to the utopias which leave their *traces* in a thousand configurations of life, from permanent buildings to ephemeral fashions.
>
> (*GS* V.1, 47; *CB* 159, translation modified; my emphasis)

If the dream is in this text brought into association with the Freudian motif of the wish-symbol, the traces made visible in the city are the results of a process in which past and present enter into a relationship with each other. The stone remains – Benjamin speaks of the monuments of the bourgeoisie in ruins (*GS* V.1, 59; *CB* 176) – become, in the context of a topographical collective memory, a form of writing whose decipherability and readability follows the Freudian model of memory:

> The development of the forces of production had laid the wish-symbols of the previous century in ruins, even before the monuments

which represented them had crumbled . . . From this epoch spring
the arcades and the interiors, the exhibition halls and the dioramas.
They are residues of a dream world. The evaluation (*Verwertung*) of
dream-elements upon awakening is the textbook example of dialectical thought. Hence dialectical thought is the organ of historical
awakening.[13]

(*GS* V.1, 59; *CB* 176, translation modified)

In the way that he associates ruins, wish-symbols, and monuments
Benjamin sets out a mode of historical perception which takes the form
of a reading of the signs of preceding representations. The act of
deciphering within the present does not, however, stand in mirror-
relation to this representation, and is not, then, to be understood as a
deciphering of clues or method of de- or encoding, but rather as a
reading of memory traces and distorted representations. The topography
of the city is thus here no longer simply the past become space or stone,
but is also readable as the topography of a collective memory in which
mnemic symbols and traces reveal themselves to reading. And the dream
is no longer seen as a sphere separated from waking (as space, layer, or
the like), but as a form of representation or language of the unconscious.

Moreover, in Benjamin's reflections on the theory and conceptuality
of his project, we encounter precisely those aspects which characterize
the topographical model of memory in Freud. The *readability* of the
memory traces, bound, in Freud, to the flickering-up and passing away
of consciousness in apperception, in analogy to a kind of writing
becoming visible and disappearing again (Freud 1969: III, 368),[14] is
applied by Benjamin to the images of what has been. The readability
of the images is termed their 'historical index',[15] and the historical
index, or readability of the image, bears the stamp of the Now of
cognizability:

What distinguishes images from the 'essences' of phenomenology is
their historical index. . . . For the historical index of images does
not simply say that they belong to a specific time, it says above all
that they only arrive at readability at a specific time. And indeed, this
'arriving at readability' constitutes a specific critical point of the
movement contained within them. Every present is determined by
those images that are synchronic with it: every Now is the Now of a
specific cognizability [*das Jetzt einer bestimmten Erkennbarkeit*].

(*GS* V.1, 577–8; *N* 50, translation modified)

Here, the connection between past and present is conceptualized in
analogy to the process of cathexis which regulates the connection

between the different systems of the psychic apparatus in Freud. Furthermore, the connection is understood by Benjamin as an imagistic relation, not a temporal one: 'an image is that in which the has-been comes together in a flash with the Now to form a constellation.' And this coming together in a flash takes place, as he adds, in language: 'Only dialectical images are genuine (i.e., not archaic) images; and the place one meets with them is language' (*GS* V.1, 576–7; see *N* 49).

The dismissal of archaic images is evidence of the distance between Benjamin and Jung, with whose model of the 'collective unconscious' Benjamin's talk of the 'unconscious of the collective' has nothing to do. Even if Benjamin's model of historical perception as reading has as its chief focus the *images* of the has-been, his premise is a model which posits memory traces as writing – as is indicated, for example, by his description of the dialectical image as the image that is read (*GS* V.1, 578; *N* 50) or also as a dream image (*GS* V.1, 55; *CB* 171). For his reading of images corresponds to the model which sees the image-writing of the dream as a language, and which in the *Passagen* project is related to the permanent and ephemeral 'configurations of life' (*GS* V.1, 47; *CB* 159) in which the dream-work of the collective has left its traces. Moreover, the concept of the trace makes a connection between the creation in the past of a written record (*Niederschrift*), the leaving of traces, and the present practice of deciphering that writing, the Now of cognizability. So we find in the well-known passage which sets out trace and aura as counter-striving concepts:

> Trace and aura. The trace is the appearance of a closeness, however distant whatever left it may be. Aura is the appearance of a distance, however close whatever gives rise to it may be. In the trace we take possession of a thing, in aura it overpowers us.
>
> (*GS* V.1, 560)

Of course, the process of taking possession of a thing, which is made possible by the trace, has features of an activity in that it is described as an act of deciphering; and in this it bears a similarity to a being-on-the-trail-of (*ein Auf-der-Spur-sein*), an approach drawn from psychoanalysis which Benjamin transfers onto the language of things or the picture-puzzles of the banal.

> It is easier to penetrate to the heart of obsolete things in order to decipher as picture-puzzles [*Vexierbilder*] the contours of the banal. . . . Psychoanalysis has long since exposed picture-puzzles as schematisms of dream-work. We, however, are with such certainty *less on*

the trail of the soul than of things. It is the totem
we look for in the thicket of primeval history.

(GS V.1, 28

Less on the trail of the soul than of things! Here the ps.
method of deciphering the image-writing of the dream
transferred onto things and the contours of the banal, whicl
it is, bearing in mind the considerations of represental   of a
language of the unconscious of *the collective* or of collective memory,
re-materialized and transposed as it were onto the cultural plane. In the
process, a method of reading learned from psychoanalysis becomes the
model for historical perception and the matrix for a dialectical
historiography. At the same time, this passage bears witness to
Benjamin's reading of Freud's 'Dream-Work' (1900) and 'Totem and
Taboo' (1912–13).

SECURING THE CLUES OF A READING OF FREUD

On the whole, though, the traces of psychoanalytic thought-figures in
Benjamin's texts serve not so much as evidence of his reception of
individual works of Freud's as indications of the way he developed his
thought in relation to particular Freudian concepts.

If, in the early sketches for the *Passagen*, the motif of forgetting
already makes an appearance (see, for example, *GS* V.2, 1031), it is
only a short while later that the focus of interest shifts increasingly to
the dialectic of remembering and forgetting, as in the Proust essay of
1929, in which Benjamin establishes a connection between the 'weav-
ing of memory' and the 'ornaments of forgetting' (*GS* II.1, 311; *Ill* 204).

In the context of his reflections on collective memory, however, the
concepts of the unconscious and of *repression* now take centre stage.
Thus Benjamin refers explicitly to the 'law of repression' as he
discusses the lacunae in the interpretative possibilities offered by
Marxism. This occurs in his 1930 review of Siegfried Kracauer's book
on white-collar workers, where Benjamin, as it were in passing, sets out
his perspective of a theoretical superimposition of the paradigms of
being–consciousness (from Marxism) on the one hand, and consciousness–unconscious (from psychoanalysis) on the other. Taking as his
starting point the 'production of false consciousness' – a category
which will thereafter disappear from his texts – he proposes seeing this
as the production of images which should be investigated according to
the law of repression: 'The productions of false consciousness are like
picture-puzzles in which the essential matter [*Hauptsache*] only just

out from between clouds, foliage, and shadows' (*GS* III, 223). The attempt, which will be one of the leitmotifs of the *Passagen* project, at reformulating problems derived from Marxism with the aid of a way of looking at things that has been through the school of psychoanalysis appears here in connection with journalistic publications from the period around 1930 in which Benjamin, on the eve of National Socialism, was working on a programme towards the politicization of intellectuals.

Further evidence of this, apart from the Kracauer review, can be found, for example, in the essay on Surrealism of 1929, in which – in proximity to body- and image-space – the term 'innervations' is used. In Freud, the term refers to recordings of excitations (*Erregungs-aufzeichnungen*); its matrix is to be found in the genesis of his theory of the nerve tracts (*Nervenbahnen*) in the early, neurologically orientated 'Project for a Scientific Psychology' (*Entwurf einer Psychologie*) (Freud 1987); later it was then transferred to the facilitations (*Bahnungen*) or permanent traces (*Dauerspuren*) in the unconscious. In Benjamin's formulation, the term is as it were restored to its corporeal matrix, as when he writes of the 'bodily innervations of the collective' and their revolutionary discharge (*Entladung*). The older, neurological variant of psychoanalysis, in which bodily processes were attributed greater significance, evidently played a role in Benjamin's earliest studies of Freud during his university years in Bern, as the notes on anthropology composed at this time demonstrate.[16] From here, the term 'innervation'[17] can be traced through to his later readings of Freud, where his foremost interest is now in the language of the unconscious, whereby the connection between excitations or innervations and the production of images is a central focus, as it is in Freud himself. Thus in a passage on images in the mind or pictorial imagination in 'One-Way Street', we find the phrase: 'No imagination without innervation' (*GS* IV.1, 116; *OWS* 75).

The character of allegory as a form of writing in the *Trauerspiel* book was evidently not arrived at either without *excitation* (*Erregung*), as Benjamin writes there that the allegorical gaze transforms 'things and works into excitatory writing [*erregende Schrift*]' (*GS* I, 352; *OGT* 176, translation modified). And then, in the context of a passage concerning the recollections of the individual in 'A Berlin Chronicle', the term *facilitation* (*Bahnung*) occurs. This was the text in which Benjamin tested out a range of different images for representing the processes of recollection and in the course of so doing also proposed a topographical model for the individual[18] in contradistinction to autobiographical models bound to such concepts as origin, sequence, continuous flow of life, and so on. Just as, in the passage discussed at the beginning of this chapter, the archaeological allegory employed to represent memory as a scene culminates in the notion of a different form of (written) record, in this part of the text the labyrinth undergoes a transformation into a topographical image of memory in accordance with the model of facilitations in the psychic apparatus.

The passage on the labyrinth opens with the observation that images of scenes and locations frequently overlie the images of people in the memory. An attempt is made to counter this forgetting of persons with a graphic diagram of life in which the significance of people for a life history is as it were to be retained in written form. The representation of this diagram, however, undergoes a transformation from a series of family trees to a labyrinth. Here the labyrinth no longer appears, as in the early sketches for the *Passagen*, as the past become stone – and not even as the realization of 'the architectural structures dreamt of by the ancients' (*GS* V.2, 1007) – but as an image in which the history of the individual becomes representable in a mnemonic figure; and yet it is again the entrances which lead into the interior which are noted first, to be followed by observations concerning the cross-connections and pathways/facilitations (*Bahnungen*). Here, then, the entrances take on significance, no longer in terms of the access they provide to the interior, but in terms of the intertwinements proceeding from them.

> I should, rather, speak of a labyrinth. I am not concerned here with what is installed in the chamber at its enigmatic centre, ego or fate, but all the more with the many entrances leading into the interior. These entrances I call primal acquaintances. . . . But since most of them [the primal acquaintances] – at least those that remain in our memory – for their part open up new acquaintances, relations to new people, after some time they branch off these corridors (the male may be drawn to the right, female to the left). Whether cross-connections are finally established [*sich bahnen*, literally 'forge a path'] between these systems also depends on the intertwinements of our path through life [*Verflechtungen unseres Lebenslaufes*].
>
> (*GS* VI, 491; *OWS* 319)

In the attempt at representing memory in an archaeological image, a transition took place from a notion of levels or layers to one of writing; here, the labyrinth provides the medium in which a genealogical image, recalling representations related to origin and provenance, undergoes a shift into a model of pathways/facilitations and their intertwinements as memory traces. In this way, 'A Berlin Chronicle' becomes readable as the text in which the traces of the change from a spatial-topographical to a scripto-topographical memory-scene can be most clearly identified.

There are a number of passages from Benjamin's work which can be cited to illustrate the increasing importance of the concept of *distortion* (*Entstellung*) in this connection. Distortion is described as the 'form things assume when they are forgotten' in the Kafka essay of 1934, in which Benjamin discusses the significance of gestures in Kafka's writing and regards the body, 'the most forgotten alien land' (*GS* II.2, 431; *Ill* 132), as it were as the material and matrix of a representation of the forgotten which here – in that it mingles with the forgotten of the primeval world – points into a mythical distance. Whether the forgotten is loaded onto the body or inscribed in it, its wordless signs are readable as a language of memory. In 'Franz Kafka: Building the Wall of China' (*Franz Kafka: Beim Bau der Chinesischen Mauer*) (1931), the short text that preceded the Kafka essay, Benjamin describes Kafka's distortions as the representation of 'signs, indications, and symptoms of displacements' (*GS* II.2, 678) seen as deriving from a connection between forgetting and guilt (*GS* II.2, 682). This serves as evidence that the use of the term 'distortion' in the later essay does indeed refer to the Freudian term.

By contrast, in the context of reflections on the functioning of individual reminiscences in literature, Benjamin links the concept of distortion with the figure of resemblance (*Ähnlichkeit*). Already in his essay on Proust of 1929, we come across the formulation concerning 'the world distorted in the state of resemblance' with which Benjamin suggests that those resemblances which structure the traces of memory in Proust's *Recherche* always have an aspect of distortion inscribed into them, that is, of dream-work.

> The similarity of one thing to another which we are used to, which occupies us in a wakeful state, is a suggestion merely of the *deeper* resemblances of the dream world in which everything that happens appears not in identical, but in similar guise, opaquely similar to itself . . . so Proust could not get his fill of emptying at a single stroke the display dummy, the ego, in order to bring in that third, the image, with which his curiosity, no, his homesickness was assuaged. He lay on his bed racked with homesickness, homesick for the *world distorted in the state of resemblance*, a world in which the true surrealist face of existence breaks through. To this world belongs . . .: the image.
>
> (*GS* II.1, 314; *Ill* 206–7, translation modified; my emphasis)

On the one hand, the connection made here between image and (distorted) resemblance is of significance for Benjamin's concept of images.[19] But the Proust essay is also of interest with regard to the model of memory set out there and its chronological proximity to the early work on the *Passagen* project. A link between the two can be found in the notion of the spatial depth of the dream. For if the metaphor of depth in the Proust essay still largely follows Proust's own representation, when the figuration of *entstellte Ähnlichkeit*, distorted resemblance or similitude, is taken up again a few years later in the mnemic images of Benjamin's own *Recherche*, his 'Berlin Childhood Around 1900' – 'I was distorted by resemblance' (*Ich war entstellt von Ähnlichkeit*) (Benjamin 1987: 59) – it has in the meantime passed through a reformulation of the concept of distortion in relation to a theory of language on which Benjamin had been working in the interim.

DISTORTED SIMILITUDE: THE LANGUAGE OF MEMORY AND THE MEMORY OF LANGUAGE

The mnemic images of the 'Berlin Childhood' are composed throughout in such a way that they redraw memory traces by reconstructing chains of association formed from the links between various images, scenes, words, and names. These then take on the status as it were of representatives, in the medium of language, of recorded excitations or the status of mnemic symbols. But their meaning is not disclosed through the question, like that posed by the teacher Knoche in the section entitled 'Two Cryptic Images' (*Zwei Rätselbilder*), of *what* they are supposed to mean. Rather, the traces can only be understood by following the chains of association; and these are wrought out of a multitude of resemblances, albeit resemblances which do not so much become visible to sensuous perception or in objective, concrete form as cognizable in constellations and figurations.

It is these constellations which form that 'archive of non-sensuous similitudes'[20] which Benjamin perceives as existing in language and writing and into which, in the course of history, man's mimetic faculty has passed (*GS* II.1, 209; *OWS* 163), as he writes in the two short essays on language theory, 'The Doctrine of the Similar' and 'On the Mimetic Faculty', composed in 1933 in the context of his work on the mnemic images of the 'Berlin Childhood'. The manner in which Benjamin describes the perception of resemblances in these essays corresponds very precisely to the constellation of readability such as is structured by the dialectic of consciousness and the unconscious: for the perception of resemblance or similarity

> is in every case bound to an instantaneous flash [*ist an ein Aufblitzen gebunden*]. It slips past, can possibly be regained, but cannot really

be held fast, unlike other perceptions. It offers itself to the eye as fleetingly and transitorily as a constellation of stars. The perception of similarities thus seems to be bound to a time-moment (*Zeit-moment*).

(GS II.1, 206–7; DS 66)

The perception of resemblances thus refers precisely to the instant of the readability of memory traces which Freud described as the flickering-up (*Aufleuchten*) of consciousness in apperception. If perception in the present moment thus entertains a correspondence with facilitations in the memory, the connection is produced through a cathectic or excitatory resemblance which cannot be reproduced in permanent form or in an identical re-presentation, but can, as Benjamin shows, become cognizable in non-sensuous similitudes. This term, like the formulation 'distorted similitude', can therefore be taken as an attempt to describe the way that similitudes or resemblances work in the medium of a language of the unconscious, which means in the medium of a distorted representation. And Freud had incidentally also attributed a central role in dream-work to relations of resemblance.[21]

In Benjamin, the ability to recognize resemblances is situated within a history of the mimetic faculty and considered as a rudiment of the lost ability to become *like* – an ability for which he cites examples from the sphere of the cult and the occult. His proposal that 'the perceived world (*Merkwelt*) of modern human beings seems to contain infinitely fewer of those magical correspondences' (*GS* II.1, 206; *DS* 66) calls to mind (and called to his mind also)[22] his work on a philosophy of language magic which he wrote in 1916. The immediacy described there in the translation of the mute language of nature into the sonic language of humans, an immediacy inherent in the lost language of paradise, can now be understood in terms of a mimetic faculty which has disappeared, but which has passed into writing and language.

> Rather, everything mimetic in language is an intention with an established basis which can only appear at all in connection with something alien, namely the semiotic or communicative element of language as its repository [*Fundus*]. Thus the literal text of writing is the sole repository in which the picture-puzzle can form itself.
>
> (GS II.1, 208–9; DS 68, translation modified)[23]

In this conceptualization of the relation between the semiotic function of language and the resemblances which appear in connection with it, reflections on the language of memory intersect with those on the memory of language. For since the picture-puzzles – the distortions –

are here not only read as signs of a form of writing that flashes
of the traces of memory, but also and at the same time recall a lost s
of language, the archive of non-sensuous similitudes that is languag
provides a language-memory that can be made productive for the
deciphering of memory traces in modernity.

It may be said, then, that the picture-puzzles, as which Benjamin
reads the contours of the banal in the city-topography of modernity (*GS*
V.1, 281), constitute a *writing of things* (*eine Schrift der Dinge*) or,
alternatively, of the configurations of life, a writing which is radically
different from the *language of things* (*Sprache der Dinge*) or of *nature*
in the immediacy of language magic such as Benjamin had described
in relation to the language of paradise – historically different and
theoretically distinct.[24]

However, the perception or readability of the picture-puzzles and the
similitudes that appear in an instantaneous flash activates an old ability
which was still required during the age of the ternary sign system, an
ability which Benjamin, in the *Origin of German Tragic Drama*, had
rescued in the very moment of its disappearance in the form of an
'excitatory writing' called forth with the aid of the allegorical gaze: the
ability to read images as writing, which comes to the aid of the mimetic
faculty of human beings. A reading of this kind, which is adept at
deciphering non-sensuous similitudes and distorted representations and
in which language-memory and memory-language converge, constitutes, then, the attitude through which remains, images, things, words,
gestures, and graphic images become readable and cognizable as traces.
And this is, as Benjamin says, the 'attitude of genuine recollection'.

ading that takes the place
slation

hoanalytical reformulation of
ory of language magic

THE WRITING OF EXISTENCE

'Reversal [*Umkehr*] is the direction of study [*die Richtung des Studiums*] which transforms existence into writing' (*GS* II.2, 437; *Ill* 138, translation modified). The transformation of existence into writing of which Benjamin writes in his essay on Kafka can be understood as a kind of *translation* brought about through the figure of reversal. If existence only becomes readable when it is seen *as* writing, that is, when it has become writing or is perceived as such, its transformation into writing and the study of it as writing nevertheless depend on a certain figuration. Reversal, characterized as the direction of study, denotes an attitude of reading (*Lektüre-Haltung*) towards the has-been (*das Gewesene*), an attitude intimately connected to the concept of memory which forms the basis of Benjamin's works within the radius of the *Passagen* project[1] and which took on full theoretical shape in his writings of the early 1930s. The transformation perfected here in relation to 'existence' in order that it become writing is the effect of an attitude which arises solely out of the activity of deciphering on the part of the observer or student, who looks on the images and traces of the has-been, the permanent and ephemeral configurations of life – gestures and words, things and events – *as* a form of writing, and thus reads them.[2] It is precisely that attitude of reading which is directed in the *Passagen* towards the topography of the city and the 'picture-puzzles of the banal' in modernity, whereby the readability and decipherability of this writing are conceptualized in analogy to the language of the unconscious as conceived in psychoanalysis.

This model of writing corresponds to a topographical concept of memory which sees the visible signs as mnemic symbols, as the products of a psychic process (*Bearbeitung*), and as distorted representations – as a form of writing, then, in which the memory traces are never visible unmediatedly and in their entirety. Such a model of a writing of the language of the unconscious (of the collective) underlies the *Passagen* project in its second, longer, phase from 1934 onwards, whereas in the first phase of work on the project (1927–29), Benjamin had proceeded from a spatial-topographical model in which the spheres of dream and waking appear as opposing spaces, as it were duplicated in the topography of the city. The intervening period – that is, the years from around 1927 to 1934 – was a time spent in elaborating his specific conception of memory, thus a time spent in theoretical work on the representation, functioning, and language of memory, which may be reconstructed on the basis of the essays, reviews, and sketches he wrote during this period and in which clear signs of a reading of Freud can be discerned.[3]

In working out in this context a theory of reading, with the aid of which the picture-puzzles of the banal and the images of the has-been might be deciphered, he was focusing on a *writing of things* (*Schrift der Dinge*) quite radically different from that *language of things* (*Sprache der Dinge*) or of nature of which he had written in his early theory of language magic: a mute language which revealed itself immediately – that is, without mediation – to translation into the language of humans: 'The translation of the language of things into that of man is not only the translation of the mute into the sonic; it is also a translation of the nameless into name' (*GS* II.1, 151; *OWS* 117).

Since Benjamin founds the concept of translation here, in his 1916 reading of the Book of Genesis in the context of an elaboration of his theory of language, 'at the deepest level of linguistic theory' (*GS* II.1, 151; *OWS* 117) and returns to it in 'The Task of the Translator' (1921), it is apparent that the notion of a mute language of things is an essential component in his concept of translation. And the shift of the focus of his interest from this *language* of things to a *writing* of things or of existence in his late writings must surely also bear consequences for his concept of translation as formulated in the 1921 essay. And with this observation in mind, the purpose in what follows is to set out a hypothesis concerning the provisional nature of his concept of translation of 1921 within the framework of the genesis of Benjaminian theory, or, more precisely, concerning the transformation of his concept of translation and the substitution for it of the model of reading in his work of the 1930s.

It is far from coincidental that it was precisely in the context of his studies on modernity that Benjamin came back to reflections on a theory of language and, in his work on the two short essays 'The Doctrine of the Similar' and 'On the Mimetic Faculty' (1933), found himself reminded of his elaborations on language magic of seventeen years previously. In the two essays of 1933 he develops his concept of 'non-sensuous similitude' (*unsinnliche Ähnlichkeit*),[4] a term that marks very precisely the vanishing point at which the lines of a language of the unconscious and those of language magic converge in his theoretical considerations. This term 'non-sensuous similitude' – in other texts he writes also of 'distorted similitude' (*entstellte Ähnlichkeit*) – marks the location within his writings at which a reformulation of the language of the unconscious in terms of a philosophy of language and, *vice versa*, a psychoanalytical re-reading of his theory of language magic take place.

At the same time, the formulation 'distorted similitudes' contains the shibboleth that calls the difference by its name: the difference between a language of things, proposed in the 1916 essay 'On Language as Such and on the Language of Man' as a paradisiac language, and the language of things in modernity, which are to be read as picture-puzzles and mnemic symbols. For *distortion* (*Entstellung*) marks that irreversible caesura which differentiates and divides the existence that is readable as writing in the 'ur-history of modernity' from the 'unspoken word in the existence of things' (*GS* II.1, 152; *OWS* 118) in the myth of a creation out of the word. It is distortion that has as it were interrupted, come between the immediacy in the revelations of the mute, the immediacy of the 'translation of the language of things into that of man' (*GS* II.1, 150; *OWS* 117). But this caesura is not to be confused with the one already discussed in the early essay on language.

In respect of that (first) caesura referred to by Benjamin as the 'Fall of language-mind' (*der Sündenfall des Sprachgeistes*), a caesura which is interpreted as the origin of the character of language as sign, of abstraction, and of the proliferation of tongues, this *second* caesura bears the features of a subsequent elaboration, both in terms of its theoretical status as also within the genesis of Benjaminian figures of thought. Its consequence for Benjamin's theory of translation is that, with this (second) caesura, reading takes the place of translation, both in theoretical significance and with regard to the relation to Baudelaire's texts. For if the essay on the 'Task of the Translator' was composed in the context of Benjamin's translations of the *Tableaux Parisiens*, these same texts now become, no longer a model for the work of translation, but the paradigm for a reading of modernity in which things are seen as writing.

THE TWOFOLD FOREIGNNESS OF LANGUAGE

The 'translation of the language of things into that of man' or, alternatively, of 'the mute into the sonic' or 'the nameless into name'

(*GS* II.1, 150– 1; *OWS* 117) was bound to the aspect of immediacy. And it is this notion of translation that took on exemplary status for Benjamin's theory of translation as set out in the essay 'The Task of the Translator' (1921). This is made explicit in the orientation of the translation towards the non-communicable (*das Nicht-Mitteilbare*), 'that very nucleus of pure language' (*GS* IV.1, 19; *Ill* 79). At the same time, though, the loss of immediacy which accompanied the 'Fall of language-mind' and in the wake of which came – so to speak as a secondary phenomenon resulting from the Fall – the proliferation of languages and confusion of tongues – this loss of immediacy, then, is the precondition which dictates the need for a different kind of translation, a translation from one language into another. This is the kind of translation which is treated in Benjamin's theory of translation.

> After the Fall, which, in making language mediate, laid the foundation for its multiplicity, it could only be a step to linguistic confusion. Since men had injured the purity of name, the turning away from that contemplation of things in which their language passes into man needed only to be completed in order to deprive men of the common foundation of an already shaken language-mind. *Signs* must become confused where things are entangled. The enslavement of language in prattle [*Geschwätz*] is joined by the enslavement of things in folly almost as its inevitable consequence. In this turning away from things, which was enslavement, the plan for the tower of Babel came into being, and linguistic confusion with it.
>
> (*GS* II.1, 154; *OWS* 120– 1)

Besides the threefold significance which Benjamin ascribes to the 'Fall of language-mind' – the inception of the character of language as sign (that is, its mediacy), the emergence of a new magic, that of judgement, and the birth of abstraction, the classification of good and evil – it is in addition the confusion of signs and tongues which marks the caesura that severs language from its Adamite state of immediacy, a state *prior to* history. If it is this caesura that makes a theory of translation necessary, it is at the same time the retrospective look, the look *back* to the caesura that determines the direction of the study of it.

In placing his theory of translation in relation to 'the eternally prolonged life of the works', Benjamin from the start sites translation *within* history, that is, after the Fall. The 'foreignness of languages' of which he writes in the essay on translation (*GS* IV.1, 14; *Ill* 75) and which has arisen because of their multiplicity is thus evaluated above all according to the measure of their remoteness from revelation (*Entfernung von der Offenbarung*), their distance, then, from paradisiac language. This explains why Benjamin can speak in the same breath, on the one hand, of the 'foreignness of languages', and, on the other, of the fact that 'languages are not strangers to one another' (*GS* IV.1, 12; *Ill* 72), for they are related in 'suprahistorical kinship' (*GS* IV.1, 13; *Ill* 74) and in a kind of virtual communion to pure language. The foreignness of languages in history thus corresponds to a kinship of languages prior to history. Within this constellation, translation has the task, *not* to bridge the foreignness nor to reverse the caesura, but rather to emphasize the knowledge of the remoteness from revelation, or to put this knowledge to the test:

> If, however, these languages carry on growing in this manner until the Messianic end of history, it is translation which catches fire on the eternally prolonged life [*das ewige Fortleben*] of the works and the perpetual renewal of language. Translation keeps putting the hallowed growth of languages to the test: How far removed is their hidden aspect [*ihr Verborgenes*] from revelation, how present [*gegenwärtig*] can it become by the knowledge of this remoteness?
>
> (*GS* IV.1, 14; *Ill* 74–5, translation modified)

Following the caesura through which immediacy was lost, in the state in which language has become mediate, a medium of communication, translation has the task of orientating itself towards the non-communicable, a task which Benjamin brings into the proximity of redemption (*Erlösung*): 'It is the task of the translator to *redeem* [*erlösen*] in his own language that pure language which lies spellbound in foreign ones, to liberate the language imprisoned in a work in his re-creation of that work' (*GS* IV.1, 19; *Ill* 80, translation modified; my emphasis).

Now when Benjamin writes in this essay that 'all translation is only a somewhat provisional way of coming to terms with the foreignness of languages' (*GS* IV.1, 14; *Ill* 75), it is presumably not only for the reason that this redemption can never fully be attained. His talk of provisionality may also be taken as an indication of the provisional nature of his concept of translation. For the foreignness of language does not only consist of the foreignness of the different languages to one another; each single tongue is also characterized by foreignness, and moreover a foreignness which cannot be circumvented with translation. This is a different kind of foreignness, one recalling that confusion of signs of which Benjamin wrote at the end of the essay on language and which was in part responsible for the caesura he describes there, although it did not attain any real significance for the theory of translation that Benjamin developed subsequent to that earlier essay.

Yet when linguistic praxis, when communication, comprehension, and reading are confronted, not only with the foreignness of languages, but also with the confusion and enigmas of their signs and symbols, the possibilities of the concept of translation elaborated by Benjamin in 1921 have perhaps come up against their limit. And this limit relates to what I have called the second caesura; it has to do, not with the problem of translating an original, but with translations without an original or, alternatively, with the disappearance of the original.

In 'The Task of the Translator', Benjamin describes the act of translation in an image: to translate means to produce the echo of the original in the language into which one is translating:

> Translation . . . calls the original into it [i.e. into the language forest or *Bergwald der Sprache*], and into it at that single spot where in each case the echo is able to give in its own language the resonance of the work in the foreign one.
>
> (*GS* IV.1, 16; *Ill* 76, translation modified)[5]

To continue this metaphor, one might say that the limit of the concept of translation set out here becomes visible at the point where now only the echo is apprehended, while the perception of the call has been removed beyond the range of the senses; where, then, the echo alone, as the memory trace of the call, can be perceived, and the connection to the original has been lost. Precisely this possibility is already contained in the image of the echo, for the echo has always symbolized a different return – just like the language of the unconscious, which can be understood as a translation without an original.

It is possible, namely, to perceive an analogy between the provisionality of 'translation' in Benjamin's work and the provisionality of the concept of translation in Freud's *Interpretation of Dreams* (1900), where the relationship between dream-thought and dream-content is compared with that of original and translation (Freud 1969: II, 280; see 1953: IV, 277). However, the notion of the original in Freud's book becomes ever harder to discern as the concentration on the image-writing of the dream as a specific and always already distorted manner of representation and the conceptualization of this as the language of the unconscious takes over. Thus, the metaphor of translation in the text of the *Interpretation of Dreams* itself bears features of a distortion – a distortion which is only really put to rights in the reformulation of the language of the unconscious as being a 'translation without an original'. (Lacan).

In the face of a translation without an original, however – and the picture-puzzles of modernity may be understood in this way also – there is only one approach to be adopted that has any sense: that of reading. But if reading is thus to be comprehended as an approach arising out of a concept of translation from which the notion of the original has vanished, then, as the theory of reading *takes the place of* the theory of translation, the significance of the original disappears too, and with it all ideas orientated towards the question of 'the way it really was'. In this way, translation has not disappeared so much as it has passed into reading in precisely the same manner as, according to Benjamin, the mimetic gift of humans has 'found its way into language and writing' and created for itself there 'the most perfect archive of non-sensuous similitudes' (*GS* II.1, 209; *DS* 68, translation modified). Reading would thus be the very form which translation has taken on in a 'world distorted in the state of resemblance' (*GS* II.1, 314; *Ill* 207).

THE RETURN OF THE FORGOTTEN MIMESIS

In this sense, the concept of 'non-sensuous similitude' can also be read as a figure for the return of the repressed. In his early language theory, Benjamin had taken as his premise above all the irreconcilable opposition between the paradigm of arbitrariness in the 'bourgeois view of language' and the view that the word is the essence of the thing in 'mystical linguistic theory' (*GS* II.1, 150; *OWS* 116–17), in order then to dissolve this opposition into an historical dialectic. In his description of the state of affairs *after* the Fall, though, the aspect of the mimetic has for the time being disappeared from his own text. Instead, he emphasizes, as already mentioned, the overnaming and the muteness of nature, and in addition, with reference to the myth of the Tower of Babel, the confusion of tongues, which becomes the linking motif for his theory of translation. Neither does the mimetic have much significance in the essay on 'The Task of the Translator'. The concept of resemblance has no clear profile here, and its significance is dismissed in favour of the notion of kinship (*Verwandtschaft*) (*GS* IV.1, 13; *Ill* 72–3). For through the innermost, concealed kinship of the languages, through their participation, founded in the aspect of the non-communicable, in 'pure language', the many languages remain orientated towards a common, but never realizable ideal, towards that 'interlinear version of the Scriptures' which is described as the 'prototype or ideal of all translation' (*GS* IV.1, 21; *Ill* 82). It is only at a stratum of language in which 'all information [*Mitteilung*], all sense, and all intention . . . are destined to be extinguished' (*GS* IV.1, 19; *Ill* 80) that a new immediacy appears which now becomes the criterion of translatability: 'Where a text belongs immediately, without the mediation of meaning, and in its literalness, to true language, truth, or doctrine, then it becomes unconditionally translatable' (*GS* IV.1, 21; *Ill* 82, translation modified). It is, then, above all through the aspect of the non-communicable that the connection is here established to revelation, to paradisiac language or language magic. Already in Benjamin's attempt, at the end of the essay on language, at finding a formulation with which to grasp the dialectic of a language *after* the Fall and of that function of language which is lost, repressed, and which yet remains present in and in relation to language, he focuses the lost aspects of language in the concept of the non-communicable, without mentioning resemblance, the mimetic, and magic: 'For language is in every case not only communication of the communicable but also, at the same time, a symbol of the noncommunicable. This symbolic side of language is connected to its relation to signs' (*GS* II.1, 156; *OWS* 123).

When he returns to this figuration in the text on the 'Doctrine of the Similar' seventeen years later, in which he develops the model of 'nonsensuous similitude', magic and mimesis have returned to the dialectic.

This, if you will, magical side of both language and writing does not, however, merely run parallel, without relation to the other, the semiotic side. Rather, everything mimetic in language is an intention with an established basis [*eine fundierte Intention*] which can only appear at all in connection with something alien, namely the semiotic or communicative element of language as its repository [*Fundus*]. Thus the literal text of writing is the sole repository in which the picture-puzzle can form itself. Thus the nexus of meaning implicit in the sounds of the sentence is the repository from which similitude can instantaneously, in a flash, from out of the tone [*Klang*], become apparent. Since this non-sensuous similitude has its effect on all reading, however, access is opened up, at this deep level, to the peculiar ambiguity of the word 'reading' in both its profane and magical senses.

(*GS* II.1, 208–9; *DS* 68, translation modified)[6]

Yet this is not only to be read as the return of aspects of mimesis into Benjamin's reflections on a theory of language following his elaboration of a model of memory: starting with topographical figures, as in the early sketches for the *Passagen*, proceeding to the scene of memory as a different form of written record (*Niederschrift*) in the 'Berlin Chronicle', and culminating in the readable traces (*Spuren*) of the unconscious of the collective in the city-topography of modernity. The passage quoted can also be read as a representation of the return of the forgotten mimesis, made possible through the concept of distortion (as a language of the unconscious). Distortion is thus *the* form in which lost similitude is both concealed and yet at one and the same time becomes perceivable.

The distorted representations can be read, then, not just – in the sense of a return of the repressed – as the signs of a form of writing that flickers up out of mnemic traces, but they also themselves recall a lost state of language. An historical reference point for Benjamin's concept of non-sensuous similitude can be found in the 'writing of things' and the ternary sign system whose disappearance at the transition into the Classical age, the age of representation, has been analysed by Michel Foucault.[7] The recollection of this lost similitude in the medium of the language of literature (as a kind of counter-discourse) and its re-emergence in modernity – as a second caesura, so to speak – does not, however, reinstate the similitude that has been lost or magical immediacy. Rather, the figure of distortion is inscribed into the return of resemblance, so that it returns as distorted or non-sensuous similitude.[8]

The theoretical enterprise of psychoanalysis is above all directed towards this second caesura, and it is psychoanalysis, too, which marks the difference between Benjamin's linguistic theory of the 1930s and his earlier theory of language magic. If the two short essays of 1933 are read simply as a supplement or continuation of the essay 'On Language' of 1916, as is usually the case, then it is at the cost of overlooking precisely the aspect that can be grasped as Benjamin's psychoanalytical reformulation of his theory of language. For in the concept of distorted similitude, two traces within his theoretical undertaking intersect: on the one hand, the reflections on language magic which can be traced back to his reading of the Book of Genesis and which attach to the concept of similitude, and, on the other, the concept of a language of the unconscious bound to the term 'distortion', which Benjamin arrived at through his studies on memory. The writing of existence (*Schrift des Daseins*) and the writing of things (*Schrift der Dinge*) in the topography of modernity are thus not only separated by the first caesura from the language of things in language magic, but in addition by a second caesura related to the figure of distortion. What is at stake here is, then, the return of a distorted writing of things whose resemblances flash up within the visible.

BABEL AND LABYRINTH

In the course of the elucidation of his theory of language, which emphasizes the character of all that is perceived as writing, reading, then, has taken the place of translation. The thought-image (*Denkbild*) under whose sign this substitution and transformation takes place is that of the labyrinth. Proceeding from a confusion of languages (*Sprachverwirrung*) described under the name 'Babel' – and the name already signals the state of language represented here: the Hebrew *balal* translates as 'confusion' (*Verwirrung*) – this shift leads in Benjamin's theoretical contemplations to the figure of *straying* (*Sich-Verirren*), an activity described in the image of the labyrinth. The labyrinth can thus be taken as the allegory of his work on the concept of memory in so far as it is in this image that the traces of the superimpositions and displacements taking place in connection with his efforts at finding a way of representing recollection(s) can be read most clearly: take the labyrinth of the houses in the city, for example, which is compared in the early sketches for the *Passagen* with a topography of dream and waking (*GS* V.2, 1046) and interpreted as the realized dreams of antiquity (*GS* V.2, 1007); or the labyrinth as a notional image (*Vorstellungsbild*) in 'A Berlin Chronicle', in the course of reflection on which the representation of recollection is transformed from the figure of the family tree to a system of pathways/facilitations (*Bahnungen*), that is, to a form of mnemic writing. The labyrinth thus is a dialectical image *par excellence*. In the medium of recollection – in the retrospective view of the has-been, in reversal as the direction of study – the transformation of existence into writing is accomplished.

In a thought-image from the 'Berlin Childhood' entitled 'Tiergarten' (a large public park in the centre of Berlin and the name of the district in which it is located), the labyrinth appears as a place of skilful straying:

Not to be able to find one's way in a city doesn't mean much. To stray in a city as one strays in a forest, however, requires training. The street-names must speak to the strayer like the snapping of dry twigs, and the little streets in the heart of the city reflect the times of day to him as clearly as does a hollow on a mountainside. I learned this art late; it fulfilled the dream of which the first traces were labyrinths scrawled on the blotting paper of my notebooks. No not the first, for before them came the certain thing that has outlasted them. The path into this labyrinth, which was not without its Ariadne, led over the Bendler Bridge, whose gentle camber became for me the first flank of the hillside. Not far from its foot lay the goal: Friedrich Wilhelm and Queen Luise. On rounded pedestals they rose out of the flower-beds, as if spellbound by the magical curves inscribed by a watercourse before them in the sand. But rather than to the rulers, I turned to their pedestals, since what went on on them, albeit if unclear in its connection, was closer in space.

(Benjamin 1987: 23)

In the midst of the topography of the city, the labyrinth here, through the art of straying that does not follow the index-bound order of the city map, becomes a mnemic image of a language-magical trace which points towards the mute language of nature, from whose ground the symbols of a collective memory rise up as monuments become stone. The same applies to them as what Benjamin will write of the 'ruins of the bourgeoisie' in his exposé 'Paris – the Capital of the Nineteenth Century': that the wish-symbols of the previous century are laid in ruins even before the monuments which represented them had crumbled (*GS* V.1, 59; *CB* 176).

By contrast, the labyrinthine traces on the blotting paper stand for the traces of those distortions which have come about through the overlay of numerous past and inverted (*ver-kehrt*) writings; and they point towards the picture-puzzles that become visible in the graphic image (*Schriftbild*). The deciphering of these likewise requires an art of straying, not now straying within the city, though, but within writing – an art, then, which bears the name 'reading'. This constitutes the attitude to writing and language which no longer stands under the sign of Babylon, but under the sign of the labyrinth.

From Babylon to the labyrinth: *verwirren–verirren*. The space opened up by the missing 'w' within this shift had already signalled itself towards the close of the essay on translation: as an abyss – namely, the abyss of Hölderlin's translations: 'in them meaning plunges from abyss to abyss until it threatens *to become lost* in the bottomless depths of language' (*GS* IV.1, 21; *Ill* 82; my emphasis).

The becoming lost evidently forms a link between translation and reading. But in the transition from the notion of layers or depths of language and recollection to a topographical model of memory, it has undergone a transformation from something dangerous to something that is trained, a skilful activity. This skill contributes to an attitude of reading through which existence is transformed into writing. Earlier, Benjamin had ascribed to translation the task of testing, under conditions of linguistic confusion: 'How far removed is their [the languages'] hidden aspect from revelation, how present can it become by the knowledge of this remoteness?' (*GS* IV.1, 14; *Ill* 74–5). Corresponding to this, one could see the skilful straying in the labyrinth of the city as putting to the test the presence of the forgotten and the has-been within the knowledge of the world as distorted in the state of resemblance – an attitude of genuine reading.

THE REVERSAL OF REVELATION INTO THE MESSIANIC

In the essay on translation, however, the possibility of being 'saved' from the plunge into the abyss of meaning is addressed, a possibility bound to the figure of a *hold* (*ein Halten*); and this is presented with a linguistic gesture bearing the features of a certain confidence: 'But there is a hold' (*Aber es gibt ein Halten*).[9] If the prerequisite for the necessity and possibility of translation is the remoteness from revelation, here nevertheless the figure of a bridging of this distance is suggested, even if it remains ultimately unattainable. For if the remoteness from revelation provides the criterion for the theory of translation, it is nevertheless the case that this theory still contains the weak idea of a prototype (*Urbild*), and thus the idea of an original, or at any rate of the one ideal to which the hidden content of all individual translations is related: 'But there is a hold. No text guarantees it, however, apart from Holy Writ, in which meaning has ceased to be the watershed for the flow of language and the flow of revelation' (*GS* IV.1, 21; *Ill* 82, translation modified).

'Hold' (*ein Halten*) in this context means having something to hold onto which prevents one from losing oneself in the abyss of the 'bottomless depths of language' in that it allows that immediacy lost in the Fall of language-mind to shine through once more, an immediacy whose return within the text, following the collapse of meaning, becomes the criterion of translatability: 'Where a text belongs *immediately*, without the mediation of meaning, and in its literalness, to true language, truth, or doctrine, then it becomes unconditionally translatable' (*GS* IV.1, 21; *Ill* 82, translation modified; my emphasis). But if 'hold' means something to hold onto, something which holds one from losing oneself, in the Kafka essay, written more than ten years later, the figure of the 'hold' has intensified into a counter-movement and is transformed into a cavalry attack (*Ritt*) launched against the storm.

For when it says at one point in this essay that there is a tempest 'that blows from the land of oblivion [*aus dem Vergessen herweht*], and study is a cavalry attack against it' (*GS* II.2, 436; *Ill* 138, translation modified), and when at another point distortion is described as a form which 'things assume when they are forgotten' (*GS* II.2, 431; *Ill* 133, translation modified), then it seems that, with the concept of distortion, the remoteness from revelation has changed radically. As has also the notion, linked to it, of danger, for here the danger is not that of plunging into the depths, but that of being swept away by the storm. In this situation, finding a hold is no longer of any use; the only help is to be found in a counter-movement, a confrontation, a *launching out against it*: the act of studying that – if it is to confront the storm that blows from oblivion, from forgetfulness – can only adopt the figure of a reversal, a turning back (*Umkehr*). 'Reversal is the direction of study which transforms existence into writing' (*GS* II.2, 437; *Ill* 138, translation modified).

This figure of reversal in the Kafka essay can also be read as a shibboleth, as a sign by which a displaced recollection of the essay on translation may be recognized, and also a sign for the replacement of thought-figures that were dominant there with others. 'Reversal' in the Kafka essay stands namely in the place of an author name not explicitly mentioned, but which in the essay on 'The Task of the Translator' was invoked as the creator of prototypes (*Urbilder*) of translation: 'Hölderlin's translations are prototypes of their kind' (*GS* IV.1, 21; *Ill* 81). For it is from Hölderlin's poetics that the figure of reversal derives, as a 'reversal of all kinds of ideas and forms' (*Umkehr aller Vorstellungsarten und Formen*) (Hölderlin 1992: II, 375).[10] For him, in his translations of Greek tragedies, reversal had the function of giving a stronger accentuation to the 'Oriental element' (*das Orientalische*) that had disappeared in them (1992: II, 925). And to speak in the terms used by Benjamin in 'The Task of the Translator', Hölderlin's concern in his translations of Sophocles was not only to 'Greekify' the German, but beyond this – as if to include a preceding layer of transformation – to 'orientalize' the Greek.

In the essay on translation, however, reversal is not explicitly mentioned; rather, it remains concealed within the reference to Hölderlin's translation work. Instead, the text itself follows a figure of reversal. It takes up, as already discussed, the closing formula of the essay 'On Language' and the concept of the non-communicable set out there, and makes this latter the central term in a theory of translation in which the remoteness from revelation and the figure of redemption can coincide. By the close of the essay, however, the concept of the non-communicable is itself cancelled out in the movement towards the prototype and ideal of all translation, the 'interlinear version of the Scriptures' (*GS* IV.1, 21; *Ill* 82). In the very same moment as all informative content (*Mitteilung*) and all meaning is extinguished, the remoteness from revelation reverses into a Messianic figure: into redemption. But this becomes perceivable, precisely not in the look *forward* to the 'Messianic end of history', but only in the look *backward* to revelation and the knowledge of remoteness from it, in the look, namely, towards that text which is simultaneously prototype and ideal, and which represents both the lost and the unattainable form of writing:

the interlinear version of Holy Scripture. Perhaps one has to imagine the lost Adamite language, the translation of the divine creation into words, as *one* possible variant of such an interlinear version – and as such as the lost variant.

Within 'The Task of the Translator', Hölderlin's translations of Sophocles do not only conceal the figure of reversal, however. They also mark, within the movement of Benjamin's text, the limit beyond which there is only the plunge into silence, the 'hold' in the face of the abyss, and the transition to Holy Scripture: 'But there is a hold. No text guarantees it, however, apart from Holy Writ.' The figure of reversal which then appears unconcealed in the Kafka essay becomes in this latter context a figure through which a *different* translation, the transformation of existence into writing, is arrived at. But since it must confront a storm, the 'hold' holds out no promise any longer, for with it the possibility of launching out against the storm would be eliminated.

With the knowledge that the remoteness from revelation is not just determined by distance, but also by distortions, redemption changes too: not appearing now as the extinguishing of meaning, but in the righting of distortions, for which latter, in both Kafka and Benjamin, the 'hunchback' provides the form of a prototype:

> This little man is the inmate of distorted life; he will disappear with the coming of the Messiah, of whom a great rabbi once said that he would not wish to change the world by force, but would put it to rights in slight ways. . . . No one says that the distortions, to set aright which the Messiah will one day appear, are those of our space alone. They are also certainly those of our time.
>
> (*GS* II.2, 432–3; *Ill* 134–5, translation modified)

If the putting to rights is related here to the distortions of the body and of time and space, this embraces all the dimensions of reading and of a mnemic writing into which – following the return of the forgotten mimetic – the Messianic too has now passed. In the concept of distortion in the Kafka essay, a psychoanalytically reformulated theory of language *and* the Messianic aspect of Benjamin's theory of history meet, for it is distortion that marks both the distance from the vanished original in dream-work and the remoteness from revelation *and* redemption. Within the genesis of his theoretical work, the concept of redemption in the theory of translation has the task of carrying the Messianic – taken up into and replaced by the theory of reading – into the writing of the late texts. And the reading that has taken the place of translation continues to bear its traces.

DE MAN'S REJECTION OF THE MESSIANIC

It is precisely the aspect of the Messianic against which de Man's attempt at a – to this extent then dubious – recuperation of Benjamin's theory of translation is directed.[11] The disturbance which the Messianic in Benjamin's texts represents for de Man is presumably not only connected to the fact that he (mis)reads into the term a colloquial, mythical meaning – namely, the sense of a myth of genius and creativity which casts the poet as an as it were holy figure (his example is George: de Man 1986: 77). The Messianic must presumably also be eliminated in order to achieve in his reading of Benjamin his own norm of a strict division between poetic and sacred language. For his irritation concerning the Messianic in the opening of his essay is taken up, by its close, into the attempt at eliminating this aspect from Benjamin's theory of translation – moreover, by appealing to Benjamin himself. For this purpose, de Man turns his attention to another text, the 'Theologico-Political Fragment', quoting it in a wrong translation and supplementing this with his own interpretation. This is particularly remarkable, since his essay has otherwise become known for the precision of its linguistic observations and its criticism of misunderstandable translations of Benjamin's essay on the 'Task of the Translator'.

The 'Theologico-Political Fragment', probably written around 1920–21 and thus indeed in the chronological context of the essay on translation, serves the purpose for de Man of underpinning his thesis concerning the rigorous separation of poetic and pure language (*reine Sprache*):

> History, as Benjamin conceives it, is certainly not messianic, since it consists in the rigorous separation and the acting out of the separation of the sacred from the poetic, the separation of the *reine Sprache* from poetic language. *Reine Sprache*, the sacred language, has *nothing in common* with poetic language; poetic language *does not* resemble it, poetic language *does not* depend on it, poetic language has *nothing to do with it*.
>
> (1986: 92; my emphases)

Quite apart from the strikingly forced rhetoric of denial which lends expression to de Man's own concern here, the dialectic in Benjamin's language theory, in which the relation of pure and poetic language is conceived in a much more complex way, is lost. In addition, his theory is not about separation, but about distance and remoteness. De Man continues:

It is within this negative knowledge of its relation to the language of the sacred that poetic language initiates. It is, if you want, a necessarily nihilistic moment that is necessary in any understanding of history.

Benjamin said this in the clearest of terms, not in this essay but in another text called 'Theological and Political Fragment', from which I will quote a short passage in conclusion.

In the Benjamin fragment de Man goes on to quote, however, the issue is not, as de Man maintains, a separation between the historical and the Messianic, but their dialectic: that is, the end of everything historical *in* the Messianic. The consummation (*Vollendung*) of all history (*alles historische Geschehen*) through the Messiah is introduced in the text in a figure which describes the simultaneous redemption, completion, and creation of the relation between the historical and the Messianic: 'Only the Messiah himself consummates all history, in the sense that he alone redeems [*erlöst*], completes [*vollendet*], creates [*schafft*] its relation to the Messianic' (*GS* II.1, 203; *OWS* 155).

In de Man's translation (1) 'completes' becomes 'puts an end to'; (2) 'redeems' becomes 'frees'; (3) 'he' ('the Messiah') becomes 'it' ('the end'); and (4) the creation gets lost altogether: 'Only the messiah himself puts an end to history, in the sense that it frees, completely fulfills the relationship of history to the messianic' (de Man 1986: 93).

When, in what follows, Benjamin says that the Kingdom of God is not the *telos*, not the goal, but the end of the historical, and when he denies that theocracy has a political meaning, it is in order to go on to discuss instead the complex relation between the two by representing – as 'one of the essential teachings of the philosophy of history' (*eines der wesentlichen Lehrstücke der Geschichtsphilosophie*) – the relation of the profane to the Messianic in an image – namely the constellation of a counter-striving disposition (*gegenstrebige Fügung*).[12] The relation between the dynamic of the profane and Messianic intensity is represented in this image as the movement of two forces which, while moving in opposite directions, nevertheless propel each other forward – a figure which will reappear in the Kafka essay in the image of the cavalry attack against the storm.

In order further to assert his thesis concerning non-Messianic history, de Man continues his interpretative translation, this time in the form of an addition. Where Benjamin writes 'To have repudiated with utmost vehemence [*mit aller Intensität*] the political significance of theocracy is the cardinal merit of Bloch's *Spirit of Utopia*', de Man's English translation of the quotation reads:

To have denied the political significance of theocracy <, to have denied the political significance of the religious, messianic view, to have denied this > with all < desirable > intensity is the great merit of Bloch's book *The Spirit of Utopia*.

(de Man 1986: 93; my brackets indicate the passages added)[13]

In his additional commentary, de Man equates theocracy, the Kingdom of God, with the Messianic view (*der messianische Blick*), while Benjamin criticizes the confusion and reconciliation of politics and religion precisely in order to work on the relation between the historical and the Messianic. And it is precisely the political significance of the Messianic view which will bear paramount importance for his work on a site in and opposed to history, as becomes evident in his theses on the concept of history, in which he develops further the complex relation between the Messianic and the historical.

Since de Man's text is the transcription of a lecture, it may be that he indicated by modulations of the voice that the changes made to the quotation from Benjamin's text were additions of his own, while those responsible for the publication of the text failed to check the quotation and to distinguish between quotation and commentary. However, my concern is not to prove a falsification, but rather to discuss a mis-recognition of Benjamin's work on the relation between the Messianic and the historical. In this respect, the interpretative additions to Benjamin's text can be read as symptoms of an interpretation which rejects the Messianic element in his theory. Since it disturbs, it is to be done away with, in order to assimilate Benjamin's writings into de Man's own theory of rhetoric:

Since we saw that what is here called political and historical is due to purely linguistic reasons, we can in this passage replace 'political' by 'poetical', in the sense of a poetics. For we now see that the nonmessianic, nonsacred, that is the political aspect of history is the result of a poetical structure of language, so that the political and poetical here are substituted, in opposition to the notion of the sacred. To the extent that such a poetics, such a history, is nonmessianic, not a theocracy but a rhetoric, it has no room for certain historical notions such as the notion of modernity, which is always a dialectical, that is to say an essentially theological notion.

(1986: 93)

With the driving out from Benjamin's theory not only of the Messianic, but also of the dialectic along with it here, it may be regarded as an irony of the afterlife of Benjamin's writings that de Man's re-interpretation, although coming from the diametrically opposed camp in the academy, here meets with the re-interpretation by Habermas which was discussed at the beginning of this book. They are united in their resistance to Benjamin's work on and with the Messianic, and both equate the political and the poetic, which in Habermas – in the context of a communication-theoretical social philosophy – is evaluated negatively and in de Man – in the project of a deconstructive rhetoric – is rated positively. In any case, however, Benjamin's thinking-in-images (*Bilddenken*), read by the former as metaphor and by the latter as trope, is deprived of its genuine significance for his theory.

10 Readability

Benjamin's place in contemporary theoretical
approaches to pictorial and corporeal memory

The last few years have seen a marked vogue in the publication of
studies on memory within the field of cultural studies theory (at any
rate in the German-language work in this field), and for this reason the
concern in what follows is to situate Benjamin's work on the concept
and significance of memory within the field of differing perspectives in
the contemporary discourse of memory and its prehistory.

MEMORY AND WRITING

> For your invention [i.e. that of writing, *grammata*] will produce
> forgetfulness in the souls of those who have learned it, through lack
> of practice at using their memory, as through reliance on writing they
> are reminded from outside by alien marks, not from inside, them-
> selves by themselves: you have discovered an elixir not of memory
> [*mneme*] but of reminding [*hypomnesis*]. To your students you give
> an appearance of wisdom, not the reality of it.
>
> (Plato, *Phaedrus* 275a)[1]

Socrates' reservations about writing as recorded by Plato are today to
be encountered everywhere in the wealth of recent research on the
themes of *memory* and *writing*.[2] In a situation lamented by many, on
account of the increasing significance of the electronic media, as
heralding the end of written culture – the end, that is, of a culture in
which writing has been regarded as the dominant and most reliable
medium of transmission – it is as if the impulse to look back to the
originary myth of writing is at one with the impulse once more to call
to mind the history of this medium. For in this recent research, Socrates'
reservations, and the opposition he perceives between the alien marks
of writing and the 'living and animate speech of the one who knows'
(276a), are presented primarily because they are seen as a vestige of a
consciousness of a pre-writing culture.[3] The as it were paradoxical

constellation of the look backward to a transition (that from speech to
writing) in Plato is already established through the form in which it is
transmitted: Plato *relates* in his *text* a *dialogue* in which Socrates in
turn *reports* a *conversation* between the Egyptians Thamus and Theuth
of which he has *heard* and whose subject was the invention of *writing*.
Taking this myth as its starting point, recent research has been
concerned above all with the history of the complex connection between
writing and memory, in the course of which the two terms have become
partially interchangeable: writing has come to be regarded as a form of
cultural memory, while memory is described as a form of writing or as
the 'scene of writing'.[4] In the series of metaphors arising out of the
repeated attempt to engage with the immateriality, intelligibility, and
invisibility of human memory – from the seal in wax (Aristotle) and the
wax tablet of the soul (Plato), via temple, library, treasure-house, book,
palimpsest, storehouse, archive, building, space, theatre, labyrinth, and
topography, to trace, 'mystic writing-pad', and writing – in this series,
then, writing has come to be the dominant metaphor ever since the time
that, with the advent of psychoanalysis, the interest in memory became
focused on the unconscious and the language of the dream. With the
triumphal rise of electronic data-processing, the 'new media', this
has all changed, however. For, simultaneously with its significance
as the most important medium of transmission, writing is also being
challenged in its function as a metaphor for memory: in its place
comes the computer memory (in German *Speicher*, meaning literally
'storage-place').

And with that we seem to be right back at the beginning. For Socrates
by all means conceded to writing the function of storing information;
not, however, the function of re-*mind*-ing. And is it not the case that,
given a change in the terms ('writing' instead of 'speech', 'computer'
instead of 'writing'), his words could today once more lend expression
to fears in the face of a new invention: namely, that this invention will
rather inspire forgetfulness and a neglect of writing among those who
learn, since they, in relying on the computer, will only remember with
the aid of external, alien signs, and no longer by and of themselves?[5]
And so the vogue in studies on memory within contemporary research
in the humanities may be seen also as a recollection of, and self-
reassurance with regard to, an ability and skill which cannot be
subsumed into the function simply of storing information.

For most of the numerous essay collections and monographs on
memory which have appeared in the last few years have focused on
techniques of so-called artificial memory – mnemotechnics, for example, or the *ars memoria*: the art of memory and the arts as memory.

Apart from the effort to come to grips with materialized and institutionalized forms within culture, *cultural memory* in the form of rites, living
habits, images, texts, tools, monuments, cities, landscapes, and so on,[6]
a particular concern has namely been with the scholarly, and in part also
hermetic, traditions of mnemonic art, that is, with fundamentally *literary*
traditions.[7] With the paradigmatic shift from the discourse of recollection (*Erinnerungsdiskurs*) to the discourse of memory (*Gedächtnis-
diskurs*) which has taken place within this current research, the focus of
interest also shifts from individual to collective memory, to memory as
culture and the culture of memory. And here there appears to be a
repetition of that paradoxical constellation of transition (this time not
from speech to writing, but from the cultural to the technical). In the face
of the computer which in terms of its storage capacity is unsurpassable,
the skill and scholarship of a tradition of memory which is linked to
writing is being called to mind. And yet, in the focus on mnemotechnics,
it is precisely the functions of 'recall' and 'memory-store' that are being
accentuated, albeit with an eye not to the quantity involved, but the skill
– a kind of displacement within this constellation of competition.

IMAGES IN MNEMONIC ART

In this mnemonic art, *images* play a central role, as mental images and
as images used in figurative speech, rhetoric, emblematics, and allegory, but also as materialized images, that is, in painting and sculpture.
Proceeding from Aristotle's assertion that there is no thought without
a (mental) image and that recollection means to perceive something as
an image (Aristotle 1984), the concern of the art of memory, of
mnemotechnics, is the regulative systems for the voluntary production
of such images. The creation of mnemotechnical images, the so-called
imagines agentes, and the depositing of these images at points within
an imaginary building follows, on the one hand, the principle of
conspicuousness, of particularity, unusualness, and vividness, in order
that their active aspect be guaranteed, but also, on the other, the
principle of onomatopoeia, of phonetic or semantic association. Whatever else, though, it follows the principle of arbitrary encoding in order
that the image's representative function for the thing or word to be
recalled be fulfilled.

The reverse side of the mnemonic function of such images, in so far
as they are recorded at all, is, however, their indecipherability for those
who do not know the code or key. The writing of the *ars memoria* and
the graphic mnemonic images that have been handed down to us thus
also remain – just like speech – intrinsically bound to their author. In

this sense, *memoria*, which has always been understood as the first virtue on the path to wisdom (*prudentia*), also participates, through its links with the authorization and institutionalization of mnemonic activity, in the history of power-knowledge-discourses. As an art of encoding, the *ars memoria* tends far from coincidentally to become a component part of an hermetic knowledge.

In examining the after-history (*Nachgeschichte*) of mnemotechnics in the art of the Middle Ages and the Renaissance in her study of 'mnemonics from Aristotle to Shakespeare'[8] (mnemotechnics, for example, as a key to categorizing the allegorical paintings of the Renaissance), Frances Yates once more accentuated the significance of mnemotechnics for art history. And through the demonstration of the connection between the *imagines agentes*, often described as corporeal images or similitudes (*Gleichnisse*), and figurative modes of speech, the former are also discovered, or rediscovered, as origins of rhetoric and metaphor, for we first hear of *memoria* as an aid to rhetoric. In the studies on memory that have followed those of Yates, the analysis of the forms and images employed in figurative speech, based on examples taken from European literature, as well as the identification of mnemo-technical methods in the various arts up to and including modernist literature,[9] has played a central role.

Corporeal memory has, by contrast, played a strikingly marginal role within this discussion. On the other hand, the central significance of images within this context may be a reason why the continuation of the text from the *Phaedrus* which was quoted to begin with is more seldom to be encountered. Here, in order to underpin his reservations concerning writing, Socrates compares writing with painting. The former is, he says, like the latter, for 'the offspring of painting stand there as if alive, but if you ask them something they preserve a solemn silence' (275d). What Socrates seems to be chiefly concerned about here is the comprehensibility of writing and painting, the fact that they need to be explained. But as we read on, it becomes clear that what is at stake is rather the existence of the individual words or images once they have moved beyond the reach of their creator and thus slipped, so to speak, out of his interpretative control over them: 'Besides, once a thing is committed to writing it circulates equally among those who understand the subject and those who have no business with it' (275d).[10]

READABILITY

If this is so, then what is at stake is the comprehensibility and *readability* of individual texts, the danger of an un-*author*-ized reading (the danger, that is, from the perspective of the speaker, Socrates), or of a reading beyond, and perhaps far removed from, the *intentio* of the author. But when this inference is approached in reverse, writing now appears as the precondition for the possibility of different and alterable readings, for the decipherability and readability even of apocryphal or corrupt texts, or of fragments of text preserved out of context.

It is in this sense – that is, in the tradition of a method of reading demanded by such signs and tested out in relation to them – that text and writing have become for today's cultural anthropologists and cultural semioticians paradigms for the reading of distant and foreign cultures. Clifford Geertz has compared the readability of these latter with

> trying to read (in the sense of 'construct a reading of') a manuscript
> – foreign, faded, full of ellipses, incoherencies, suspicious emenda-
> tions, and tendentious commentaries, but written not in conventional-
> ized graphs of sound but in transient examples of shaped behaviour.
>
> (Geertz 1973: 10)

A reading of this kind has nothing to do with arbitrary individual interpretation, but requires a well-founded methodological approach, for its goal is the deciphering of the cultural construction of meaning, of linguistic and pictorial signs, as also physical gestures and behavi-oural patterns, which now come to be regarded as an 'ensemble of texts'. Readability is achieved through an approach which Geertz has called 'thick description', a way of looking at things based on ex-periences gained in the encounter with symbolic languages. The ability to 'read' in a practised and systematic manner is then transferred onto so-called cultural 'texts', and may be applied to cultures both chrono-logically and geographically at some remove, as to the cultural memory of both European and other, non-European cultures.

THE PICTURE-ATLAS OF EXPRESSIVE GESTURES: ABY WARBURG

The work of Aby Warburg, founder of the *Kulturwissenschaftliche Bibliothek*,[11] and of the Warburg Institute towards deciphering the *pictorial memory* of European art history could also be described as an endeavour aimed at achieving readability. Warburg's starting point was the attempt to understand and interpret the revival of the language of images of antiquity in the art of the Renaissance – the point of his enterprise was, then, 'to make an image that is no longer *directly* intelligible *communicate its meaning*' (Wind 1983: 25; my emphasis).

This led him to approach images (in painting) from the perspective of the work of recollection taking place within them. The processes through which an ancient language of forms and symbols was quoted, appropriated, and recast – today this would be termed 'intertextuality' – were understood by Warburg as a form of recollection of pre-existing forms and of the experiences deposited within them.

In particular with respect to his picture-atlas *Mnemosyne*, a sequence of plates on which were collected together related or similar expressive gestures (*Ausdrucksgebärden*) from different pictorial representations of various periods and genres,[12] this pictorial memory becomes recognizable as a memory of the languages of gesture and of the body. The gesture – or, more precisely, the gesture as represented in the image – is here understood as a symbolic form, the significance of which is not disclosed through translation into language, but only through the recollection of the form and experience actualized within it. The fact that an image in the form of a bodily expressive gesture becomes engraved in memory, the so-called 'pathos formula' (*Pathosformel*), is attributed to an excitation and compared with the leaving of a trace; that is, entirely analogous with the psychoanalytical description of the mnemic or memory trace (see Wind 1983: 30–1). The project of setting out the pathos formulae in a picture-atlas, arranged in groups according to particular forms of bodily expressive gesture, does not, then, result in an encyclopaedic classification of knowledge after the pattern of a taxonomy[13] so much as in a (re)construction of mnemic traces in which each repetition also includes a variation.[14]

Even when gestures are read as embodiments of passions and suffering, this approach to reading *corporeal memory* does not follow the phantasm of the interpretations characteristic of physiognomy which deem themselves able to read the inner workings of the mind from external bodily signs. Efforts of this kind to overcome the enigma of the invisible or intangible aspects of the subject, whether these be called soul, inwardness, or mind, with the aid of an interpretation of features of the image of the body have a long tradition. It is very clear from the work of one of the classic physiognomists, Johann Caspar Lavater, that this interpretative effort is based on a concept of corporeal memory in which memory appears as an engram, as a kind of mirror-image imprint of internal processes. The individual characteristics and abilities of the human subject are here seen as having engraved themselves on the body – for example, on the features of the face – so that they become comprehensible as unambiguous signs. In its focus on the static image of the body, on measurable and categorizable aspects of the physique and countenance, Lavater's interpretative method has a place in the history of criminal identification.

The relation between language and body is here particularly problematical, since the image of the body is understood on the one hand as a language, but at the same time put into a position of exclusivity in that this language is situated beyond symbolic language and understood as an identical representation of something immaterial. The interpretative variation adopted in physiognomy thus projects the myth of an (other) language which offers a way of overcoming the uncertainty attaching to the comprehensibility and truth of written and spoken language once the relationship between word and meaning has become open to question.

CORPOREAL AND PICTORIAL MEMORY IN PSYCHOANALYSIS

There are also certain fields within contemporary discourse on the body where this myth of a language of the body that speaks true is virulent, albeit that it is here applied not to features of the physiognomy, but primarily to symptoms of illness. In the history of theoretical reflections on the body as an expressive medium, however, it was at the latest with Freud's psychoanalysis that a break was made *vis-à-vis* the idea of an absolute interpretability of and resemblance between physical and psychological processes.[15] This is to be attributed above all to the fact that in Freud the relation between body and language, of *soma* and *sema*, is conceptualized in the context of a complex concept of memory. Together with the idea of the outward representation of inward processes, Freud also rejects the localization of notions of the mental within the physical, proposing instead that the psychological process runs parallel to the physical, but is not based on a relation of resemblance to it.[16] At the same time, physiological modification which is caused by excitation (*Erregung*) is seen as a possible indication of recollection, that is, as a possible indication of the return of an idea associated with the excitation. In this manner the hysterical symptom, for example, is understood by Freud as a mnemic symbol.

Symptoms, as indeed the articulations of the body generally, are part of a language of the unconscious, and to this extent follow the structure of a *distorted representation* (*entstellte Darstellung*), a translation without an original, as paradigmatically described by Freud in relation to dream language. This language presents both those who produce it and those who apprehend it with the task of deciphering it, with the problem of its readability, then, whereby it takes on the features of a language whose authorship has become problematical. In *The Inter-pretation of Dreams* (1900), the significance of the body as the source of the dream or of other psychic processes recedes also, to be replaced by its importance as the scene in which these processes manifest themselves:[17] the body, then, as the site in which inner conflicts are fought out and as a field of symbolization.

According to this conception, it is not that the body *has* a memory – just as we do not *have* a body – nor that the body represents memory. Rather, memory is inscribed into the body in the form of permanent traces which structure, in response to certain perceptions, the repetition of affects and mental images associated with them, whereby this repetition is never the repetition of the same, but always an 'other' return, the return of the Other. Of course, this applies only to the permanent traces in the unconscious, which are to be distinguished from conscious notions, in accordance with Freud's dictum that 'con-sciousness and memory are mutually exclusive' (letter to Fliess dated 6 December 1896: Freud 1986: 217; see 1953: I, 234). Later he will concretize this relationship as an incompatibility in the functioning of the two systems and reformulate it as a dialectical one with the assertion that consciousness arises in place of the memory trace (Freud 1969: III, 235; see 1953: XVIII, 25).

Pictorial and corporeal memory are here very closely linked, and both participate in the dialectic of consciousness and the unconscious, to whose two mutually exclusive systems they cannot be schematically allocated. And in taking up this psychoanalytical conception, the chief concern would be, not so much to distinguish between the conscious and unconscious elements of memory, as rather to bring to the project of reading pictorial and corporeal memory the insights gained into the analogies between language and the structure of the unconscious.

These considerations are not only of significance for individual memory. As a site in which inner conflicts are fought out and as a field of symbolization, the body, for example, also plays a central role in *cultural memory*. Nietzsche characterized pain, above all in relation to the sacrificial structure (*Opferstruktur*) of the history of civilization, as the 'most powerful aid to mnemonics' and spoke of the fact that 'whenever mankind has found it necessary to make a memory for itself, it has never come off without blood, torment, sacrifice' (Nietzsche 1980: IV, 802). His talk of burning into (*einbrennen*) or engraving upon (*einprägen*) the memory presumably concerns that process generally described today as *inscribing*, and thus applies to cruelty as 'the movement of culture that is realized in bodies and inscribed on them, belaboring them' (Deleuze and Guattari 1984: 145).

This is most strikingly represented in the image of the apparatus which inscribes the laws of the colonial masters on the back of the native prisoner in Kafka's 'Penal Colony'. The work of the machine is organized in such a way that the condemned man's deciphering of the writing from his own wounds accompanies his death throes, a process whose completion is at one with his death.

> In the *Penal Colony* those in power use an archaic apparatus which engraves ornate letters on the backs of guilty men, multiplying the cuts and increasing the ornamentation to the point where the back of the guilty man becomes clairvoyant, able itself to decipher the writing from whose letters it must learn the name of its unknown guilt. It is, then, the back upon which this is incumbent.
>
> (*GS* II.2, 432; *Ill* 133, translation modified)

Thus Walter Benjamin in his essay on Kafka.

DISTORTIONS, DIALECTICAL IMAGES, AND REDEMPTION

In this essay, in which Benjamin examines the gestures and also a number of the figures from Kafka's writing as distortions, at the same time proposing distortion to be 'the form things assume when they are forgotten' (*GS* II.2, 431; *Ill* 133, translation modified) and taking as his premise that everything that is forgotten mingles with the forgotten of prehistory, it is above all the body that appears as the medium of distortion. As a result the body has, he says, become alien to the human being, an alien territory to him although his own, so that – as is indicated by the term 'distortion', as a form of expression, as a language – in this text, too, a psychoanalytical reading has superseded a concept otherwise associated with ideology critique such as 'alienation'.[18]

This approach to reading body language could be compared with the project of Warburg's picture-atlas, with its concentration on expressive gestures within the concept of pictorial memory, whereby Benjamin's material is taken from *literary* texts and his method of reading has passed through the school of Freud. For in the Kafka essay Benjamin discusses gesture not only in terms of the aspect of forgetting, and thus of memory, but also as an aspect of a distorted representation. Of course, if one were to read the movement of garments as apprehended by Warburg in his model of pictorial memory as symptoms and, further, compare these with the bodily symptom in Freud, the proximity between Warburg's and Benjamin's conceptions would seem all the greater. But it is precisely on this point – namely, the understanding of the specific symbolic character of the pathos formulae, that opinion in Warburg reception is divided. Either way, there are clear differences between Warburg's explicit, and in his terminology particular evident, affiliation to humanist traditions and Benjamin's break with a progressive history, as also between Warburg's search for a figure in which the tension in the middle, 'provisionalizing' (*vorbehaltend*) level of the symbol takes on form and Benjamin's dialectical image or his allegorical method which has as its basis the breaking of an image out of the continuum.

The Messianism in Benjaminian thought expresses itself in the Kafka essay in that Benjamin here evaluates *distortion* as marking at the same time a *difference* in relation to redemption (*Erlösung*) or to the forgotten origin. According to Benjamin, Kafka's figures have lost the access to writing, the study of which holds out the promise of redemption. If distortion in Freud is a translation without an original, from which the attempt is derived to paraphrase this original through association, in Benjamin distortion also means the remoteness from a lost and unreachable place towards which he turns in the figure of reversal. 'Reversal is the direction of study which transforms existence into writing.' (*GS* II.2, 437; *Ill* 138, translation modified). Existence *as* writing (and it has the reversal, the attitude of the one recalling, to thank for its becoming this) makes – in the hope of redemption – the distortions cognizable.[19]

Benjamin elaborated his theory of readability very much more differentiatedly in relation to pictorial memory than to corporeal memory, notably in the *Passagen* project and the historico-theoretical theses. His theory of the *dialectical image* stresses the praxis of reading, as it is only reading that constitutes the has-been (*das Gewesene*) in the first place by producing it as an image. Here, the concern is no longer a memory *of* images, nor a practice of recollection in, in relation to, and with the aid of images. Rather, the structure of recollection itself is transposed into an image-space (*Bildraum*), has an imagistic character. Thus the relation between the has-been and the Now is itself described as imagistic, as dialectical. Whereby the dialectical image is for Benjamin not really a variant of the image, but the image in itself:

> an image is that in which the has-been comes together in a flash with the Now to form a constellation. . . . The read image, by which is meant the image in the Now of cognizability, bears to the highest degree the stamp of the critical, dangerous moment which is at the basis of all reading.
>
> (*GS* V.1, 578; see *N* 50–1)

In this model of readability, in accordance with Jewish traditions (see Yerushalmi 1988), the qualitative difference between memory and historiography is eliminated, and the construction of history becomes analogous to the structure of recollection, whereby the incompatibility of philosophy of history and Messianism is stressed.[20] The image of the has-been is an effect of recollection, as formulated in the often quoted sentence: 'To articulate the past historically . . . means to seize hold of a memory' (*GS* I.2, 695; *Ill* 257). At the same time, this model enacts a final, radical break with the *intentio*. Here, that which creates the conditions of possibility for the Now of cognizability – Benjamin speaks of it in metaphors of illumination, explosive charge, or also the development of a photograph – that, then, which produces the cognizability and visibility of the images takes on central significance. 'For the historical index of images does not simply say that they belong to a specific time, it says above all that they only arrive at readability at a specific time' (*GS* V.1, 577; see *N* 50). What becomes decipherable in this process is not so much the knowledge and intentions of past ages, but rather the 'residues of a dream-world', the wish-symbols of an epoch which are laid in ruins 'even before the monuments which represented them had crumbled' (*GS* V.1, 59; *CB* 176).

Already in Benjamin's terminology, Messianic and psychoanalytical perspectives are superimposed upon one another – and not only in the Kafka essay, where distortion and redemption are brought into immediate association with each other. Through the 'Now of cognizability', the dialectical image, too, has become related to redemption, as is visible in the *Passagen* and the reflections on the concept of history. When Benjamin calls now-time (*Jetztzeit*), whose perceptual structure corresponds to the psychoanalytic model of the readability of memory traces, the 'model of Messianic time' (*GS* I.2, 703; *Ill* 265), this means that the perspective of redemption always has a part in the readability, the historical index of the images of the has-been: not as its goal, but in the immediacy of each moment, just as Scholem characterized Messianic time as the 'divine immediacy of each day' (*Gottesunmittelbarkeit eines jeden Tages*) (Scholem 1963: 26). And in the sketches for 'On the Concept of History', we find the sentence: 'The dialectical image is to be defined as the involuntary recollection of redeemed mankind' (*GS* I.3, 1233). Benjamin adopted into his thought-images, which he also did not yet think ripe for publication, the variant that 'only for a redeemed mankind has its past become citable in all its moments' (*GS* I.2, 694; *Ill* 256), a sentence that conceals more effectively the scandalous connection made between psychoanalysis and Messianism. In his treatise 'Understanding the Messianic idea in Judaism' ('Zum Verständnis der messianischen Idee im Judentum'), Scholem stresses the worldliness of Jewish Messianism in contrast to the inwardness of the Christian concept of redemption (Scholem 1963).

He explores the way it connects catastrophe and redemption, restoration and utopia, ur-time and the end of time, horror and consolation as expressive variations in the history of Messianic ideas and movements.

But the claim to worldliness on the one hand and on the other the 'absence of any transition between history and redemption', which means that there can be 'no progress towards redemption in history', but, rather, a 'radical difference between the unredeemed world of history and that of Messianic redemption' (1963: 36), produces an aporetic constellation. Scholem indicates this under the heading 'The price of Messianism': 'The greatness of the Messianic idea corresponds to the endless weakness of Jewish history which in exile was not prepared to engage on the historical plane' (1963: 73). The difficult historico-philosophical status of Messianism in modernity, grasped as the 'crisis of the Messianic claim' (1963: 74), must then remain unresolved in Scholem's account. He examines this claim in relation to its consequences for the individual, because of the problematical idea of living in hope as 'life in deferral' (1963: 73).

From the perspective of modern theories of the subject, in particular the psychoanalytic positioning of the subject, life is, however, always already determined as life in deferral: in terms of the figure of desire, longing, wishing, and expectation. Walter Benjamin's version of reference to the Messianic, his concept of 'Messianic intensity' with which he describes the position and attitude of the subject in history, can be understood against this background. Thus, for Benjamin, waiting can become an experience of profane illumination, alongside reading, thinking, strolling (*Flanieren*), and solitude. In this he in some senses radicalizes the insight that the coming of the Messiah coincides with the end of history and wins from the non-synchronicity of history and redemption a third site: his concept of 'now-time' (*Jetzeit*), a structure of time which is blasted out of the continuum and which places the subject in an attitude of Messianic intensity, in the midst of the unredeemed world, in the midst of the order of the profane. At any rate, the non-synchronicity between Messianic time and the philosophy of history, a problematic which Benjamin had for the first time explicitly set out around 1920 (in the 'Theologico-Political Fragment'), had now, twenty years later, found form in a psychoanalytical mnemonic figure – not a figure of sublation, but an image for the representation of non-synchronicity, as the reading of the 'angel of history' as a dialectical image demonstrates.[21]

11 Non-philosophical amazement – writing in amazement

Benjamin's position in the aftermath of the holocaust

BENJAMIN'S AMAZEMENT AS AN HISTORICO-PHILOSOPHICAL BOUNDARY CASE

Walter Benjamin's remark on amazement in view of contemporary events as contained in his theses 'On the Concept of History',[1] written shortly before his unsuccessful attempt to flee France and his death, is one of the most frequently cited passages from his writings: 'The current amazement that the things we are experiencing are "still" possible in the twentieth century is *not* philosophical' (*GS* I.2, 697; *Ill* 259).

This sentence is usually quoted in order to emphasize how normal and everyday violence, annihilation, and destruction have become in contemporary life – that is, in order to counter a stance of amazement, astonishment, or horror. In so doing, the intention is to give the numerous phenomena of man-made disasters a place in the logic of historical development, a logic that is always grasped in negatively charged concepts, even if they differ according to the commentator's particular attitude.[2] In other words, a negative course of history or a history of catastrophes is taken as the norm, and by this Benjamin's critique of the concept of progress is, in the final instance, re-forged in the shape of a negative teleology of history.

A more precise reading of the sentence on amazement clearly shows that Benjamin by no means attacked amazement *per se*, but instead rejected the philosophical status given it. He emphasizes two words in the sentence: by placing the word 'still' in quotation marks he frames it as if it were a quoted commonplace, an *on dit* that becomes a sign of a 'notion of progress' which is the basis of and thus implicit to a specific form of amazement – namely, at that which is still possible. And by italicizing the word 'not', Benjamin strongly negates the philosophical status of amazement. This means that he does not reject amazement itself, but rather makes it the precondition for the sole form of cognition possible, as is shown by the very next sentence in Thesis VIII: 'This amazement is not at the beginning of a cognition – unless it is the cognition that the view of history which gives rise to it is untenable' (*GS* I.2, 697; *Ill* 259, translation modified).[3]

Here, amazement stands at the possible beginning of a cognition of an untenable notion of the history that engendered it and at the same time marks the end of precisely that notion of history. Amazement is thus described as a boundary case (*Grenzfall*). Considered *not* philosophical, it pinpoints the caesura *vis-à-vis* a concept of history which describes contemporary events as inadequate or retrogressive parts of the course of history or the historical progression. And given that it is not philosophical, it is at the same time the condition of possibility for a different type of perception.

The meaning Benjamin gives amazement here, as a boundary case, corresponds to the way he uses the notion of a 'state of emergency' (*Ausnahmezustand*). At the beginning of Thesis VIII he states that the intention must be to arrive at a notion of history that corresponds to the doctrine 'that the "state of emergency" in which we live is not the exception but the rule' (*GS* I.2, 697; *Ill* 259). The words 'state of emergency' are again placed in quotation marks to show that they are a quotation of a widespread notion, from which Benjamin proceeds to set off his own concept of a 'real state of emergency' in what then follows.

If events which common sense must regard as constituting a state of emergency (such as those taking place under fascism) become the rule, then what Benjamin is interested in bringing about as a 'real state of emergency' is intended to break with this rule. This break does not involve a simple transformation of a progressive teleology of history into a negative variant; just as the well-known phrase from the *Passagen* project – namely, 'that things "just keep on going" *is* the catastrophe' (*GS* V.1, 592; *N* 64) does not imply that the catastrophe is considered to be normal. For the opposite is true: here, it is the norm which is the catastrophe. This is the other side to the fact that all those phenomena which people like to term 'states of emergency' follow the rule or the order of things. 'Bringing about a real state of emergency' in Benjamin's sense thus requires a break with that concept of history which is based on a notion of progress as the rule and therefore regards everything that does not fit in with the rule as an exception, a relapse, barbarism, irrationality, or something similar.

This 'real state of emergency' refers rather more to Carl Schmitt than to a negative teleology of history or a history as based on catastrophes.

For Carl Schmitt also believed that the state of emergency was linked to a boundary concept and a boundary case. He stated:

> He so ever is sovereign who defines what a state of emergency is. Only a concept of sovereignty as a boundary concept can do justice to this definition. For a boundary concept does not mean an obscure concept, such as in the murky terminology of popular literature, but rather a concept of the outermost sphere. This accords with the fact that the definition in question cannot take up normal cases but only boundary cases.
>
> (Schmitt 1988: 5)

Schmitt thus understands the state of emergency as a 'universal concept of political science [*Staatslehre*]', and Benjamin adopts his explanation in the context of a boundary case, but at the same time deviates from it by deploying the concept in the field of philosophy of history. And in the form of the concept of amazement, which pinpoints the boundary in *this* historico-philosophical terrain, Benjamin's thought enters a sphere which can no longer be brought into harmony with Carl Schmitt's *Politische Theologie* (*Political Theology*). For in Benjamin's exposition on the state of emergency, amazement is introduced at precisely that point where, in Schmitt's thought, the moment of decision-making comes to bear. Schmitt avers: 'The decision on the emergency is a decision in an emphatic sense' (1988: 5). In Benjamin's thought, by contrast, bringing about a real state of emergency is linked to an epistemological caesura, for it rests on a notion of history which is rendered possible by non-philosophical amazement, and at the same time distinguishes amazement at what we have experienced in the twentieth century from the figure of what is 'still' possible.

With regard to the concept of history, this argumentation highlights two things: (1) a break with the synthesis of amazement and a philosophical discourse, and (2) a caesura with the traditional philosophy of history.

If amazement was at the root of all philosophy, then it was swiftly incorporated into *logos* by philosophy as a discipline and subjected to the rules of a rational and logical discourse. The need to find an explanation for enigmatic phenomena tended to strip these of any fear they might instil in the beholder. *To tambos* – that is to say amazement, fright, and horror – was incorporated in a discourse which in the interests of knowledge, explanation, and truth worked away at integrating the amazing into an order accessible to reason and thus, in the final instance, sublating its enigmatic elements. If, therefore, *after* the enlightenment of amazement, amazement occurs again, then it is a different type of amazement; namely, amazement at the deviation from reason that was assumed to be the rule or from the rule which was construed as reasonable. To this extent, amazement, having once been a stance that prompted philosophy, has now become a *non*-philosophical attitude that is an effect of and a residue after the history of philosophy. Only by then taking this latter form of amazement seriously and understanding it as marking the boundaries of traditional philosophy can a different form of conception emerge. This does not involve a return to some 'original', quasi pre-philosophical amazement, but instead a negation of philosophical amazement in order to make amazement the beginning of a different mode of cognition.

At the same time, Benjamin is thus suggesting that precisely that philosophy of history is untenable which is bound up with notions of totality, development, and meaningfulness.[4] Benjamin's phrase concerning the untenability of a specific 'view of history' not only pinpoints the limits of a concrete concept of history – for example, a concept of progress – but at the same time points up the limitations of any fundamental conception of 'history' as a meaningful process that unfolds over time, that is, a conception on which all such philosophies of history are based that construe the cognizability of reason in history as the precondition for finding a philosophical meaning in history – be it the Christian doctrine of salvation, or Kant, Hegel, Marx, or Löwith.[5] The critique of progress and of reason being innate to the course of history itself – that is, the critique of those phenomena which Horkheimer and Adorno, taking up Benjamin's theses, termed the 'dialectic of enlightenment' – involves reason in such contradictions, which can no longer be grasped in terms of an historico-philosophical discourse.

In Thesis XIII Benjamin explicitly states that he is not just interested in a critique of the 'conception of progress' (*Fortschritt*), but that such a critique must rest on a critique of the conception of historical progression, or going on (*Fortgang*) (*GS* I.2, 701; *Ill* 262–3). In other words, his theses focus on questions of how we construe history – that is, the 'concept of history' – which is why the title Adorno and Horkheimer gave the theses, namely *Geschichtsphilosophische Thesen* (literally, 'Historico-Philosophical Theses'), obscures the radical epistemological position the text contains. For Benjamin here precisely does not develop historico-philosophical theses as such, but rather theses *on* the philosophy of history (to this extent, the English title is more accurate) which expose its limits and constitute it as it were as a boundary case. Therefore the distorted title which affects the central argument is one of the preconditions for the lasting misrecognition of Benjamin's reflections on the concept of history.

In the passage that immediately precedes the thesis on non-philosophical amazement – namely, in the well-known Thesis IX about the 'angel of history' – Benjamin attempted to present this epistemological boundary case in terms of a thought-image (*Denkbild*). Neither the first angel from Gershom Scholem's poem, who formulates the desire for a return based in a negative teleology of history, nor the *Angelus Novus* frozen with its open mouth and wide-opened eyes – a mythical image that stresses the aspect of fear in amazement – engender a different notion of history. It is only with the figure of a counterstriving disposition (*gegenstrebige Fügung*) – in which the gaze of the frightened angel, who is being driven into the future by the storm of progress without being able to look the latter in the face, is positioned non-synchronously in relation to the chain of events we see – it is only with this constellation, then, that this different notion of history is presented. Wherever we see that 'things keep going on', the angel's gaze, and only his, sees a catastrophe. The catastrophe is therefore no exception, but rather is simply inaccessible to our gaze, which is trained only to see continual progression. It is the *other* gaze which is the condition of possibility for perceiving the catastrophe in history.

Benjamin's way of thinking and writing in this passage is the fruit of non- or post-philosophical amazement, and takes the shape of presenting concepts via thought-images or dialectical images;[6] it is inseparably bound up with the specific constellation involved here – namely, the tension and incompatibility of a philosophy of history and Jewish Messianism.[7] Amazement as a boundary case thus also leads to the limits of philosophical discourse; that is, to the end of philosophy as a meta-discourse and to the beginning of a different way of writing. The different mode of cognition also calls for a different mode of writing, which can no longer be described in terms of form. In Benjamin's work this mode is not only shaped by his textual use of thought-images, but also by his transgression of the boundaries between the genres and disciplines – that is, the boundaries between literature, philosophy, and historiography – in his theoretically informed attempt to render the most diverse phenomena, things, and writings 'readable' as images of history.

THE LIMITS OF PHILOSOPHY AFTER AUSCHWITZ: ADORNO

In part, the *Dialectic of Enlightenment*, which was written ensuing upon and taking up Benjamin's theses – and in particular the chapter on Ulysses, in which a reading of primal scenes in mythology[8] corresponds as a textual approach to the transition from myth to enlightenment presented there – is also shaped by the demands made by a different mode of cognition. However, the authors shy back from the radicality with which Benjamin breaks thought-images out of the continuum of philosophical discourse: 'It [our conception of history] is a critique of philosophy, and therefore refuses to abandon philosophy,' write Horkheimer and Adorno in the foreword to the 1969 edition of the book (Horkheimer and Adorno 1973: x). Adorno's 'reflections on a damaged life', which he wrote immediately after completing the first version of *Dialectic of Enlightenment* in 1944 and thereafter, and then published as *Minima Moralia*, are certainly the text in his overall *oeuvre* which most departs from the methods of a coherent philosophical discourse. However, Adorno commented on this by stating that 'the parts do not altogether satisfy the demands of philosophy of which they are nevertheless a part' (Adorno 1974: 18), and then goes on to justify their inability to stand that test with the fact that they are imbued with subjective elements.

The 'dedication' written for the 1951 book version could be read as a commentary which critically reflects, from the perspective of renewed emigration, this time to Frankfurt in post-war Germany – that is, from a distance in both time and space – on the previous position of writing in exile. While it was from the position of the 'intellectual in emigration' (1974: 18) that Adorno's notes reflected historical movements which 'consist so far only in the dissolution of the subject, without yet giving rise to a new one' (1974: 16), by dint of the fact that Adorno penned his aphorisms at the same time as Auschwitz was happening,[9] that historical movement is now (that is, looking back in 1951) placed in a different, completely incomparable historical context, which Adorno endeavoured after the event to inscribe in his work by pointing to 'the nullity demonstrated to the subject by the concentration camp' (1974: 16).

The experience of the damaged life in Adorno's notes in exile was predominantly one shaped by the emigrants' injured cultural memory:

> The past life of the emigrés is, as we know, annulled. . . . To complete its violation, life is dragged along on the triumphal automobile of the united statisticians, and even the past is no longer safe from the present, whose remembrance of it consigns it a second time to oblivion.
>
> (1974: 46–7)[10]

Following re-emigration and with the gradual and certain knowledge of the extent to which European Jewry had been annihilated, Adorno now reflects on the place of this experience in terms of guilt:

The major part of this book was written during the war, under conditions enforcing contemplation. The violence that expelled me thereby denied me full knowledge of it. I did not yet admit to myself the complicity that enfolds all those who, in face of unspeakable collective events, speak of individual matters at all.

(1974: 18)

The bias in his own knowledge, which he diagnoses after the event, is virulent above all in *Minima Moralia* to the extent that there the concrete references to National Socialism rest on a knowledge of the concentration camps, but not a knowledge of the 'final solution' and the extermination camps. This viewpoint is symptomatic for the perspective of the emigrant, as is, for example, expressed in Hannah Arendt's essay 'We Refugees', written in 1943: 'Clearly no one wishes to know that contemporary history has spawned a new species of human being – people who were thrown into concentration camps by the enemies and into internment camps by their friends' (Arendt 1986: 9). This statement, though exposing a repressed knowledge, is not yet touched by the notion of the extermination of (specified groups of) the 'human species', that incomprehensible experience which can never be brought to rest by an explanation being produced for it and which informs the writings of the survivors, such as those of Primo Levi. Even the *Dialectic of Enlightenment*, whose central thesis concerning the relapse of enlightenment into mythology was elaborated between 1942 and 1944 above all in the face of National Socialism, does not yet appear to be marked by traces of a knowledge of the 'final solution'. Indeed, the appended 'Elements of Anti-Semitism', which stem from a wide-ranging research project conducted by the group of emigrants in California, sketch out a 'philosophical prehistory of anti-Semitism' (Horkheimer and Adorno 1973: xvii) which is as it were located in a thinking *before* Auschwitz, prior to a knowledge of the systematic destruction of the Jews with means based on an organized division of labour.[11]

The 'final solution' as an objective historical caesura that, as far as historical data are concerned, comes between Benjamin's last text and the *Dialectic of Enlightenment*, to begin with at least left no obvious epistemological caesura in its wake. Conversely, Benjamin's text, which is characterized by a way of thinking that is closer to the danger (possibly owing to Benjamin's having written it in greater proximity to factual persecution), seems to reflect on an epistemological boundary case which, as a condition of possibility, provides the means for approaching the caesura in question retrospectively. Thought *after*

Auschwitz will, at any rate, not be able to circumvent that amazement or horror to which Benjamin did full justice both as a boundary case and as the beginning of a new mode of cognition. This necessarily has consequences for the philosophical discourse after the Shoah.[12]

By contrast, Adorno's critical reflections on his own position and on the consequences which the name 'Auschwitz' had for thought for a long time take up the question of how we can speak when faced with the unspeakable, and discuss the paradigm of 'speaking after Auschwitz', frequently in relation to specific genres or disciplines. What strikes the eye is that Adorno did not extend the radical end he postulated for certain literary genres as such in the aftermath of Auschwitz – for poetry and satire, for example[13] – to philosophy. Now Adorno's sentence on poetry after Auschwitz, in contrast to the trivializing history of its reception, which has tended to take it out of context, is not a postulate, but describes a cultural-critical constellation which can clearly be read as a boundary case. The suggestion that 'it is barbaric to write a poem after Auschwitz' follows after a colon – thus earmarking a situation which cultural critique must address and which Adorno terms 'the final stage of the dialectic of culture and barbarism' ('Cultural Critique and Society' [1949]: Adorno 1981: 34). The latter, he says, even whittles away that 'knowledge, which expresses why it has become impossible to write poems today'.

Yet many years were to pass before he wrote a similarly radical sentence about philosophy. Rather, his writings, which debate fundamental issues in the relationship between literature and philosophy – such as the 1957 essay on the 'Essay as Form' – and on whether philosophy can continue to exist – such as 'Why Philosophy Still', written in 1962 – remain strangely nearly immune to traces of thought after Auschwitz. Although the metaphor of the yellow star (*der gelbe Fleck*) in 'Essay as Form', for example, clearly makes reference to the persecution of the Jews under National Socialism, the connection remains metaphorical to the extent that it is the essay that is here described as 'impure' (*unrein*) and excluded from the 'guild as philosophy' (*Zunft als Philosophie*), that is, from demands concerning system, truth, unity of origin, and so on. The essay is thus associated metaphorically with the image of the Jew in the discourse of anti-Semitism.[14] Arguing against the 'guild as philosophy' here, Adorno does not turn his reflections into an argument against philosophy as a guild. It is not until 1966 that the 'final stage of the dialectic', as formulated in 'Cultural Critique and Society' in 1949, or rather the boundary case of cultural critique which he postulates there, becomes embedded in a central philosophical constellation and thus transformed into a 'negative dialectics'.

In the famous third chapter of Part Three, the figure of 'After Auschwitz' becomes one of the models of negative dialectics, even if the form of the text in question, its textual shape, keeps open the heterogeneity between philosophical discourse and the site named as 'after Auschwitz'. As a running head – not a title – 'After Auschwitz' seems to be a name that cannot be integrated into the philosophical text and therefore is strangely at loggerheads with the chapter title 'Meditations on Metaphysics'. Perhaps this constellation *literally* reflects the concept of thought thinking-versus-itself, as is postulated at the end of the first section.

Here, the motif of guilt which emerged fifteen years before in the dedication of *Minima Moralia* is taken up again and now positioned as the starting point of a *different* philosophy. It is the position of someone who has remained unscathed, who has managed to get away, of someone 'guilty solely by being alive': it is this that now becomes one of the necessary conditions of philosophy, indeed of a philosophy that is always already suspicious of itself.

> The guilt of life, which purely as a fact will strangle another life, according to statistics that eke out an overwhelming number of killed with a minimal number of rescued, as if this were provided in the theory of probabilities – this guilt is irreconcilable with living. And the guilt does not cease to reproduce itself, because not for an instant can it be made fully, presently conscious [*weil sie dem Bewußtsein in keinem Augenblick ganz gegenwärtig sein kann*]. This, nothing else, is what compels us to philosophize. And in philosophy we experience a shock [*diese erfährt dabei den Schock*, literally 'philosophy experiences the shock']: the deeper, the more vigorous its penetration, the greater our [the] suspicion that philosophy removes us [*sie entferne sich*, literally that it, i.e. philosophy, is becoming removed] from things as they are.
>
> (Adorno 1973: 364)

Even if in *Negative Dialectics* the figure of enlightenment's reflection on itself, a figure from the *Dialectic of Enlightenment*, is given a more radical form as the 'self-reflection of thinking', or a form of thought that 'must also be a thinking against itself' (1973: 365), there is still a residue left that is not conceptualized. If the only compulsion to engage in philosophy is the fact that the guilt cannot be completely present in consciousness at one single moment, then the question arises as to what form those elements of guilt which are *not present in our consciousness* take, what status they must be accorded, what form of knowledge they engender, how we can address them. Since the figure of a guilt which in no single moment can be fully present in conciousness precisely corresponds to the way in which Freud describes the trauma, these elements constitute the respective *Other* of consciousness; they are thus only readable in mnemic signs, symptoms, and other modes of the language of the unconscious. To justify the necessity of philosophy by referring to this guilt is at the same time to mark the limits of philosophy – that is, unless it incorporates theorems from psychoanalysis and other forms of reading the language of the unconscious. But that would bring a quite different form of philosophizing and quite different figures of thought into play. Adorno, by pointing to the non-presence of guilt as a whole, put his finger on a central problem, however. Yet it is also remarkable that he, in the very moment that he represses the cognition of the psychoanalytical structure of his own figure, displaces the shock from the survivors to philosophy: for in his words, it is philosophy that experiences the shock.

The various signs of a return of that guilt which is not integrated into consciousness strongly determined the shape that the further aftermath of National Socialism took, something that can be seen not least from the fact that as of the 1970s the paradigm of traumatization[15] has emerged ever further into the foreground of discussion. The *topos* of 'speaking after Auschwitz' for a long time informed cultural discourse in post-1945 Germany and clearly contributed to a more radical confrontation with the central problems of 'thought after Auschwitz' being skirted in the form of a figure of speech which, with its use of universal categories such as the ineffable (*das Unaussprechliche*), repeatedly diverted attention away from the specificities of the Shoah. It was not until the follow-up to the *Historikerstreit* that these central problems came more clearly into focus. On the one hand, we have to do with the irreconcilability of the different positions in the aftermath of National Socialism, that is, with the fact that the memories of the survivors and of the subsequent descendants of the victims cannot be reconciled with the memories of the descendants of the collective of perpetrators to create one coherent image of history.[16] On the other, we are faced with attempts to present the politics of extermination in an historical form, a project that constantly comes up against an intractable contradiction that can no longer be described in terms of a critique of instrumental reason or the dialectic of enlightenment – namely, the simultaneity of the rationality with which the annihilation was perpetrated, on the one side, and the irrationality and incomprehensibility of the motives and justifications given for it, on the other. If the historico-philosophical 'connections among an assumption of rationality, ability to understand, and the meaningful reconstruction' (Diner 1992: 142)[17] is fundamentally shattered by the Shoah, then it is, in the final instance, the inability to 'think Auschwitz' which prevents 'thought after Auschwitz' from ever coming to rest, an ability, moreover, which cannot be overcome in any discourse, be it philosophical, historiographical, or literary. Which is why George Steiner shifted the terrain in which the singularity of the Shoah is discussed away from its historicization in the direction of its comprehension, and why he attacks attempts to integrate it into 'normal human history' and thereby normalize understanding (Steiner 1987: 57).

Now, the problematics and reflective figures towards which 'thought after Auschwitz' has been moving via all these detours are linked by the impossibility of integrating the events into the existing notion of history with a stance that could well be described in terms of Benjamin's negation of philosophical amazement. In other words, they are moving towards the site of that boundary case which he had already described in Thesis VIII.

BACHMANN'S 'WRITING IN AMAZEMENT' AS A LITERARY BOUNDARY CASE

The inability to integrate the events into consciousness and the traces of traumatization in the aftermath of National Socialism structure the dream sequence chapter in Ingeborg Bachmann's novel *Malina*, which she published in 1971. In the text the obverse of 'negative dialectics' is thus articulated, for the chapter records those traces and symptoms which have been created by the fact that the guilt in its entirety is not present to our consciousness.[18] The dream sequence chapter is marked above all by symptoms of the return of the repressed totalitarianism. In the dream images, scenes emerge which allude to a complete break of civilization in the relations between the sexes and to female desire being caught up in guilt. Through the various stereotypical elements of a petrified symbolic language of destruction (such as gas chambers, rails, hoses, and so on) that are quoted here and there in the dream images, the scenery becomes readable as the scene of 'memory after Auschwitz', without the novel thereby containing a discourse *on* Auschwitz. It is precisely those aspects which stand counter to any attempt at historicization, the blanks in consciousness and the symptoms and mnemic symbols, that give the text its historical position.

In one of the dream scenes, in which she appears as an author (albeit one who is imprisoned and forbidden to write), the female dreamer endeavours to write down the 'sentence on reason' (*Satz vom Grund*); however, instead of appearing on the paper, the sentence becomes incorporated within her and illegible, while three stones appear next to her, thrown down 'by the highest authority' (Bachmann 1978: 3, 230). The meaning of the first stone is to 'live with amazement' (*staunend leben*), that of the second 'writing in amazement' (*Schreiben im Staunen*), and of the third we were told that she will hear the final message only after she has been freed. This scene, which quotes Benjamin's amazement, can clearly be read as an allegory for Bachmann's writing, which here – with the *Satz vom Grund*, a title of Heidegger's – takes up a motif that she had developed twenty years earlier at the beginning of her own literary work – namely, the motif of a critique of reason and/or rationality. And when in the scene in *Malina* the sentence about 'writing in amazement' takes the place of the 'sentence on reason', then this is, on the one hand, a cipher for the fact that Benjamin finally has displaced the secret fascination for Heideggerian figures – such as that of fear (*Angst*) – in Bachmann's writing. On the other hand, it is not only to be understood as a definitive rejection of Heidegger, but also as a commentary on her own earlier critique of reason, whereby we should read in the latter the impact of her reading of the *Dialectic of Enlightenment*.

In 1949, Bachmann, then a twenty-three-year-old student of philosophy, had while working on her PhD thesis on the reception of Heidegger published a short story in the *Wiener Tageszeitung* called 'The Sphinx's Smile' (*Das Lächeln der Sphinx*). The story focuses on the transformation of enlightenment into mythology and on the destructive character of a form of rationality that regards itself as absolute. Following the interpretative patterns of the *Dialectic of Enlightenment* as it does, Bachmann's text is situated within the sphere of impact of Horkheimer's and Adorno's programmatic cultural-theoretical work which, written in the face of National Socialism, was published in 1947 by Querido in Amsterdam. In a manner similar to Horkheimer's and Adorno's chapter on Ulysses, Bachmann's text presents a reading of a mythical scene, not in the form of historico-philosophical commentary, however, but as a narrative, the structure of which itself makes reference to mythical elements and in the final instance leads to a re-writing of the myth.

Bachmann's story takes up the famous founding myth of the Sphinx in which the monster lodges outside the gates of the city, appearing both as riddle-spinner and as devouring dragon, while the victory of the hero over the Sphinx is achieved through knowledge. In Bachmann's text, the place of Oedipus is taken by the 'ruler of a country', a country which is not situated historically. Rather, the text presents a paradigmatic constellation, as the beginning of the story makes clear: 'At a time in which all governments were threatened' (Bachmann 1978: 2, 19). The ruler, with his restlessness and fear of a threat which he cannot place, but which does not come from below, rather from 'demands and instructions that had not been stated but which he believed he had to obey and which he did not know', appears to embody that 'fear of the just son of modern civilization' mentioned in the foreword of *Dialectic of Enlightenment*.

The changes to the myth that Bachmann makes in 'The Sphinx's Smile', in which the ruler is defeated, do not involve a figure of simple reversal (*Umkehr*), but are readable as an inversion of the myth, for now the ruler is as it were vanquished by his own means – namely, the weaponry of rationality, weapons that transpire to be deadly. For the point of departure here is his fear and his desire to disenchant the world, and it is these which cause the Sphinx to appear in the first place – in line with a psychoanalytical interpretation of mythical monsters as projections. Bachmann writes 'that he had to call up the shadow, which perhaps concealed the threat, and had to force it into life, in order to do battle with it'. When Bachmann writes that the ruler has to challenge the Sphinx to challenge him, it becomes abundantly clear that the questions the Sphinx now asks him emerge from his own will to knowledge. In the course of the three tasks she then sets him, his will to disenchant the world emerges as a desire to expose everything hidden from his gaze, to grasp, register, and control it, whereby rationality functions as a method of putting this desire into practice, even if the price is death. The work of the scientists and their research teams trying to find answers is thus increasingly understandable as the mimesis of death (Horkheimer and Adorno 1973: 180–6), and in the course of the third task their practices finally become those of the machinery of death:

> A little later the order sent the people in groups to places where highly specialized guillotines had been set up; with painstaking care, each was individually called up and then expedited from life into death.
>
> (Bachmann 1978: 2, 21–2)

This scene of irrationally motivated, but rationally executed extermination, above all with its elements of the killing of groups and at places specially equipped for this purpose, as well as the description of killing as work, calls to mind associations of the 'final solution'. In the spirit of perfection and completeness, so we read, the ruler hands even those who had helped him with the organization over to the machines. Thus far, Bachmann's story, which can no doubt best be read as a critique of civilization in literary form, presents an enlightenment of enlightenment. Written four years after the end of the war, it refers more concretely than its philosophical model to National Socialism. However, the text at the same time generates a symbolic language that was to be symptomatic of the way mass destruction was mentioned in literature after Auschwitz: namely, the tendency to resort to universal metaphors of death and images of horror. Bachmann's own poems are themselves part of the metaphorical shape given to speech about Auschwitz: in her poem 'Early Midday' (*Früher Mittag*) of 1952 she writes: *Sieben Jahre später, / in einem Totenhaus, / trinken die Henker von gestern / den goldenen Becher aus / Die Augen täten dir sinken* ('Seven years later, / in a house of death, / yesterday's hangmen / drain the golden cup / Enough to make you lower your gaze') (Bachmann 1978: 1, 44). The combination of a precise historical reference (seven years later, that is, seven years after 1945) on the one hand, and an unspecific, metaphorical scenery of horror (*Henker, Totenhaus*) on the other, is characteristic for the problem of working through the past in lyrical form in Bachmann's poems. This played a substantial part in her decision at the end of the 1950s to abandon poetry and concentrate on prose.

With the end of her story 'The Sphinx's Smile', Bachmann clearly, in relation to the philosophical model, embarks on a path of her own, one that wins a new position from the representation of the moment of enlightenment's transformation back into mythology. To begin with, the effect of the execution of the third task is termed a 'revelation, which came out of this procedure'. In this the story goes beyond being a mere parable, since the parable does not engender knowledge. Moreover, the Sphinx does not appear as victor, but as a shadow which prevents the dead from becoming an occasion for messages and the object of a new enlightenment. In a similar sense to that of an essay she never completed entitled 'No one may appeal to the victims' (*Auf das Opfer darf sich keiner berufen*) (Bachmann 1978: 4, 335), she writes in the story: 'He saw her shadow spreading itself out like a coat over the dead, who now no longer stated what was to be said, because the shadow now lay over them in order to preserve them.'

This gesture, which preserves the corpses of the dead from being used as a 'moral to the story' or translated into a statement, also functions to preserve a residue which is inaccessible to reason. Thus the story not only presents the transformation of enlightenment back into mythology, but also a piece of unsuccessful enlightenment – unsuccessful not in a negative sense, but rather in the sense of its marking the limits of enlightenment *and* of the critique of enlightenment. For this residue results from the enlightenment of enlightenment, and it is from this that those elements of Bachmann's story arise which are not accessible to reason. The 'wave, thrown up by a sea of secrets' written across the Sphinx's face, her smile, and her disappearance beyond the bounds of the ruler's realm, which mark the end of the story, become the signs of a different, *other* position in which that upon which the desire for disenchantment sets its sights receives an intrinsic meaning of its own. The constellation of ruler and Sphinx, on the one hand, expresses that will for knowledge which is meant to banish the fear of the Sphinx's shadow, but the riddle-spinner at the end herself remains enigmatic, part of the non-cognizable, the inexplicable. She is an image of the Other of Reason, to which rationality has no access and which here functions as a shelter over the dead – that is, a shadow which does not precede Reason, but is an effect of and residue after the history of enlightenment. The Sphinx's smile at the end of the story can be read as a sort of commentary on the parabolic critique of civilization that comes before it. And thus, in the final image of the story, there is an anticipation of the mode of writing Bachmann will develop in the prose written subsequent to her poetry – for example, in the volume *The Thirtieth Year* (*Das dreißigste Jahr*) (1960). The constitution of a literary position through traversing philosophical paradigms, which she will practise there *vis-à-vis* Wittgenstein, is here already tested out *vis-à-vis* the historico-philosophical reflections of 'Critical Theory'. And thus, in her early short story, Bachmann arrives at a stance (*Haltung*) very close to that of Benjamin's version of non-philosophical amazement. Although Bachmann will only come to know Benjamin's thought later, after the publication of the first edition of his writings in 1955, her text 'The Sphinx's Smile' can be read as demonstrating the preconditions of her later close interest in his work.

If we follow this reading, the story can then be considered an early monad of Bachmann's project *Ways of Death* (*Todesarten*), in which, however, through the introduction of a female subject position, the relations between Reason and the Other have been multiplied.[19] However, before the student of philosophy became the writer who created a poetics of 'writing in amazement', Bachmann was first to embark on numerous attempts along a path that took many detours – and according to Benjamin, 'method is detour' – through the terrain of philosophy and literature. If we take a closer look, then her well-known switch from writing poetry to writing prose is far more complex than it initially seemed. For Bachmann's prose, her new stance and way of writing, stems from the previous positioning of philosophical discourse and poetry alongside each other. Her commitment, on the one hand, to

Wittgenstein's critique of language and his postulate that the logical structure of language forms the boundaries to our world, and her involvement, on the other, in a poetic field beyond that structure – namely, that of a poetically metaphorical language – complemented each other. We can compare them with the interplay between the theme of the ineffable and the creation of metaphors when addressing Auschwitz in post-1945 literature.

It was prose that first enabled Bachmann to overcome this contradiction and to address in quite concrete manner the contemporaneity (*Gegenwärtigkeit*) of the past, the memory traces, and the problems of representation in the aftermath of National Socialism. Although some of her stories in the first prose volume *The Thirtieth Year* deconstruct several philosophical theorems in Wittgensteinian manner, her literary involvement – and here I part company with received academic opinion – centred on a stronger reference to Critical Theory, in particular the *Dialectic of Enlightenment* and Benjamin's work,[20] than to Wittgenstein. However, she was not working on philosophical prose, but on a literary form of creating thought-images and symbols of memory which refer to those fragments of guilt that were excluded from presence in our consciousness: hers was a literature in the shadow of a 'negative dialectics', a form of writing that attempted to move into the blind spot of such dialectics.

In this sense, one of her early prose works, 'The Sphinx's Smile', and one of her latest, the novel *Malina*, are connected by communicating tubes: the first one standing in relation to Horkheimer's and Adorno's critique of rationality, the latter to Benjamin's negation of the philosophical status of amazement in the face of historical events. In *Malina*, written under the motto of 'writing in amazement', there are a number of references to amazement. In the well-known episode concerning the postman Kranewitzer, for example, Bachmann once again, this time ironically, takes up the motif of amazement. With the story of this 'postman by vocation', who, reflecting on the letter secret (*Briefgeheimnis*) and the 'problem of the post' (*das Problem der Post*), falls into amazement and thus cannot deliver his post any longer, Bachmann comments upon the founding myth of philosophy. And in the numerous different connotations of the constellation of first-person narrator and Malina in Bachmann's novel, the female, nameless 'I' not only occupies the position of memory, of excitation, and of the other side of Reason, but also that of amazement: 'but my amazement is filled with curiosity (is Malina ever amazed? I increasingly think not) and it is restless' (Bachmann 1978: 3, 22). The relation between the positions of the first-person narrator and Malina involves, among other things, the dialectic between his knowledge 'without astonishment' (1978: 23) and her attitude of amazement. It is only by portraying this dialectic that Bachmann is able to construct a form of 'writing in amazement' – in a novel which, in its entirety, in many senses constitutes a boundary case.

Translated by Jeremy Gaines

Notes

INTRODUCTION

1 Thus his text 'On the Concept of History' is treated as moral philosophy or as philosophy of history, while his book on German tragic drama is assessed according to the criteria of literary historiography, and so on.

2 The German word *Aktualität* is ambiguous in meaning, and it is this very ambiguity which has permitted the frequent misrecognition of Benjamin's concept of 'actuality' which is addressed in Chapter 1. In order to retain this ambiguity, the term has for the most part been left in the German here. See also note 1, Chapter 1. (Translator's note.)

3 It is particularly useful as a way of surmounting the category of 'false consciousness' which has so often, in that it tends to ignore or misrecognize the imbroilment of thought (including one's own) in the structures of desire or of the unconscious, led up a blind alley, or at least, resulted in the formulation of moral value-judgements and in divisions between the subject and the object of the cognitive act.

4 See, for example, the siting of Benjamin's theory in the categories of a 'materialist aesthetic' which provides the central reference point for Habermas' 1972 commemorative lecture and is the basis for the misrecognition of Benjamin's concept of *Aktualität* in the reception of his work (discussed at length in Chapter 1).

5 The *Passagen-Werk*, Benjamin's last great project on an 'ur-history of modernity', has so far been only partially translated into English, and is usually given the title *Arcades* (or, with reference to the earliest part of the project, *The Paris Arcades*). 'Passagen' does indeed refer to these architectural features which for Benjamin became the topographical paradigm of modernity, but since the word also has connotations of paths and passageways, and thus of progression (among other things through the text, whether as writer or as reader), the German title *Passagen* has been retained throughout here. (Translator's note.)

6 See Weigel (1995b).

7 A concrete result of this marginalization is that among the institutional heirs of Critical Theory in today's Frankfurt Institute for Social Research (*Frankfurter Institut für Sozialforschung*) there is not a single expert in the field of Benjaminian theory.

8 In that aesthetics as a theory of sensuous perception was here reduced to a

mere theory of art or of the beautiful, it followed that it was then seen in opposition to the field of the political, the ethical, and the social.

9 It may well be that the delayed publication of Benjamin's writings (in the German original, let alone in translation) gave rise to the blind spot for a long time associated with his name in the French reception of German philosophy. In 1983 a major conference on the *Passagen* project took place in Paris: see Bolz and Faber (1985, 1986).

10 Derrida's reading of the 'Critique of Violence' was also, of course, motivated by a symposium at the Cardozo Law School in New York.

11 The term *Ähnlichkeit* in Benjamin is generally translated as 'similarity', and the related adjective *ähnlich* therefore as 'similar', as in 'The Doctrine of the Similar' (*Die Lehre vom Ähnlichen*). As is argued in this volume, Benjamin's use of the term is associated with his concept of the image, not as reproduction, but, in an older tradition, as likeness, resemblance, Latin *similitudinem*. 'Similitude', as a more narrowly circumscribed term (encompassing the meanings 'likeness, resemblance', and also, pertinently, 'counterpart'), would seem to offer a more precise rendition than 'similarity', as is also borne out by the use of this term in the English translation of Foucault (see Chapter 3). 'Similitude' (or occasionally 'resemblance') is thus the preferred translation here. (Translator's note.)

1 BENJAMIN'S 'WORLD OF UNIVERSAL AND INTEGRAL ACTUALITY'

1 In common usage, *Aktualität* generally means 'topicality' or 'contemporary relevance'; it may also mean something new (as in a news item) or up-to-date; to be *aktuell* may even be to be fashionable. In Benjamin's usage, *Aktualität* draws perhaps closer to the field of meanings suggested by the word 'actual' in English: real, literal, immediate, existing at the present moment. To retain this ambiguity of meaning, the word *Aktualität* has for the most part been left in the German here. (Translator's note.)

2 See, for example, the controversy between the journal *alternative* (vol. 56/57, 1967 and vol. 59/60, 1968) and the Frankfurt School concerning 'Benjamin's Marxism'.

3 The translators here quote from Benjamin, *Reflections*, ed. Peter Demetz (New York, 1978: 189). The translation in *OWS* is slightly different: see *OWS* 236. (Translator's note.)

4 See Chapter 2 for an account of the meaning and genesis of this concept.

5 *Gegenstrebige Fügung* is a rendering of the phrase from Heraclitus (Fragment 51) *palintropos harmonie* (sometimes given as *palintonos harmonie*) meaning, literally, a 'fitting together of opposing tensions'. The precise image is that of the archer's bow. (Translator's note.)

6 For an account of Benjamin's reading of Freud, see, above all, Chapters 8, 9, and 10 in the third section of this volume.

7 Similarly in the psychoanalytical re-reading of central Marxist terms – such as 'phantasmagoria' and 'fetish' – which are understood by Benjamin, in terms of the aspects of meaning and expression, as images and as it were given a certain independence.

8 Benjamin's concept of memory is discussed in Chapter 8.

9 For a discussion of the significance of descent (*Herkunft*) in the work of Benjamin and Foucault, see Chapter 3.

10 In his notes, Benjamin emphasizes the involuntary nature of mnemic images as he writes:

> The image of the past, flashing up in the Now of cognizability, is in terms of its wider definition a mnemic image. It resembles the images of his own past which come upon a person in a moment of danger. These images come, as one knows, involuntarily. History in its strict sense is thus an image springing from involuntary remembrance, an image that presents itself to the subject of history in a moment of danger.
>
> (*GS* I.3, 1243)

2 BODY- AND IMAGE-SPACE

1 Above all in his conceptions of the trace as the 'appearance of closeness, however distant the thing is which left it behind' and of aura as the 'appearance of distance, however close the thing is which produces it' (*GS* V.1, 560). But also in the famous quotation from Karl Kraus: 'The more closely one looks at a word, the more distantly it looks back' (*GS* I.2, 647; *Ill* 202, translation modified).

2 This is further emphasized by the use of military-style rhetoric, such as 'present commands' (*die heutige Order*) and 'to a man' (*Mann für Mann*).

3 See, for example, *GS* V, 577; *N* 49. The distinction between the archaic and the dialectical image is linked to a distinction between mythology and historical space. The constellation of awakening is constitutive of this distinction: Benjamin calls the moment of awakening the textbook example of dialectical thinking or the exemplary case of recollection.

4 See Laplanche and Pontalis (1985).

5 See Chapter 8 for a discussion of the theoretical differences between the concepts of memory in the first and second phases of the *Passagen* project.

6 'The Paris Arcades. A Dialectical Fairyland' (*Pariser Passagen. Eine dialektische Feerie*) was the title that Benjamin initially gave for the projected *Passagen* work in his correspondence with Scholem. His announcement that the profane motifs from 'One-Way Street' would in the *Passagen* work 'march past in a hellish intensification' could be applied with at least equal validity to the Surrealism essay which Benjamin himself described as a *Paravent* or screen in front of the *Passagen* project. See the letter of 30 January 1928 (Benjamin 1978: I, 455; see Benjamin 1995: 322).

7 Benjamin himself, in a letter to Scholem dated 30 January 1928, indicated his assumption that 'One-Way Street' would mark the beginning of a new production complex in his work; the proposed *Passagen* project was to mark the completion of this complex 'in the same way that the *Trauerspiel* book [*The Origin of German Tragic Drama*] marked the completion of the one concerned with German literature' (Benjamin 1978: I, 455; see Benjamin 1995: 322). Two years earlier, while he was at work on 'One-Way Street', Benjamin wrote to his friend that in that work his 'older and a more recent physiognomy' overlapped (letter of 5 April 1926: Benjamin 1978: I, 416; see Benjamin 1995: 293). The change from the production complex

concerned with German literature – notably the work on Romantic criticism, on Baroque tragic drama, on Hölderlin, and on Goethe's *Wahlverwandt-schaften* – to one concerned with modernity can be related to a biographical caesura, as the different dedications – that of the *Trauerspiel* book to his wife and that of 'One-Way Street' to Asja Lacis – suggest, a caesura which was, however, above all connected with his new situation as a freelance writer who, forced to relinquish his hopes for an academic career and faced at the same time with significant changes in his domestic situation, was now obliged to live exclusively by his pen. See also Fürnkäs (1988).

8   To my knowledge, the term first occurs in the 'Initial Notes' (*Erste Notizen*) for the 'Paris Arcades' (*Pariser Passagen*), the composition of which Tiedemann ascribes to the period 'mid-1927 to late 1929 or 1930' (*GS* V.2, 1073).

9   For example, 'On Painting or Sign and Mark' (*Über die Malerei oder Zeichen und Mal*) (*GS* II.2, 603ff.), probably composed, like the other notes on painting mentioned, around 1918.

10   For the history of this conception of the image, see Mitchell (1984: 521). For an account of Benjamin's concept of the image, see Chapter 4.

11   See Weigel (1990) for an account of the aspect of the connections between city topography, recollection, and gender difference.

12   This in effect reconciles the distinction between Adorno's interpretation of aura in terms of work and Benjamin's interpretation of it as the human dimension in things, a distinction drawn by Stoessel at the beginning of her study (1983: 27).

13   Benjamin's psychoanalytical reformulation of his language theory in the 'Doctrine of the Similar' is discussed in Chapters 8 and 9. For a discussion of the *structural* similarity between Benjamin's conception of the fall from paradise in language and Kristeva's structural model of psychoanalysis, see Chapter 5.

14   It seems that Benjamin's attempt at a theoretical and systematic opposition of the two terms for body, *Leib* and *Körper*, which still played a significant role in, for example, the 'Schemata on the Psychophysical Problem', took on far less importance in the course of this move. But a proper examination of Benjamin's usage with respect to these two terms has yet to be undertaken.

15   See Chapter 9 for an account of the significance of distortion as what might be termed a second caesura in the history of language, following the Fall of language-mind (*Sprachgeist*).

3 COMMUNICATING TUBES

1   See Introduction.

2   For a discussion of the relationship between Foucault and Benjamin with regard to the link between the city and the topography of the sexes, see Weigel (1990: 180–203).

3   'For opinion is the false subjectivity that can be separated from the person and incorporated into commodity circulation,' writes Benjamin in the Kraus essay (*GS* II.1, 343; *OWS* 266, translation modified).

4 In this respect Menninghaus speaks quite correctly of the 'structuralism in practice in the *Trauerspiel* book' (Menninghaus 1980: 127ff.).

5 The reference here is to the second of the revolutionary moments examined by Foucault: 'Now, this archaeological inquiry has revealed two great discontinuities in the *episteme* of Western culture: the first inaugurates the Classical age (roughly half-way through the seventeenth century) and the second, at the beginning of the nineteenth century, marks the beginning of the modern age' (Foucault 1970: xxii). In Benjamin's work these two historical caesurae mark the difference between allegory in *The Origin of German Tragic Drama* and his studies on the allegory of modernity. This is discussed in Chapter 7. See also Menninghaus (1980: 72ff.).

6 The fact that Foucault limits his investigations of the history of sexuality in antiquity to prescriptive texts has its problematical aspects. For as a result the movement of the *logos* is examined (see Foucault 1990: 106), but not the representation of the conflicts and reverse sides of this history which find expression in another form of language, in myth, for example, or in the tragedies. For a discussion of this aspect, see Weigel (1990: 187ff).

7 For example, Roland Barthes's structural portrait of the *Fragments of a Language of Love*, or Derrida's more recent texts with their marked tendency towards metaphor, or again the language games of Lacan, where the references to the symbolic or the corporeal remain far from unambiguous.

8 See in particular *Konvolut* N in the *Passagen* project.

9 On the translation of the Benjaminian term *Ähnlichkeit* adopted in this volume, see Introduction, note 11. (Translator's note.)

10 The comparison of the relationship between God, man, and nature which exists in paradisiac language in Benjamin's theory of language magic with this ternary, triadic sign system seems more appropriate than the comparison with the Oedipal triangle such as Stoessel undertakes (see Chapter 3). For a discussion of 'conjuncture' as a condition of possibility of Benjamin's theory of allegory, see Chapter 7.

11 For a discussion of the significance for Benjamin's concept of 'nonsensuous similitude' of distortion and of a second caesura in the history of language following the 'Fall of language-mind', see Chapter 9.

12 See, above all, Benjamin's critical discussion of Nietzsche's *The Birth of Tragedy* in his book on German tragic drama. At base, he accuses Nietzsche of failing to take account of the myth of tragedy from the point of view of the history of philosophy. Pfotenhauer has given a systematic account of the traces of Benjamin's readings of Nietzsche – see Pfotenhauer (1985).

13 See Chapter 2.

14 Benjamin's first sketches for the theses 'On the Concept of History' include the following note: 'Problem of tradition II/ For the proletariat the consciousness of the new mission had no historical correspondence. No recollection took place. (There was an attempt to produce it artificially, in works such as . . . ' (*GS* I.3, 1236; see also p. 1242).

15 For an account of the difference in the interpretation of masquerade between Marx and Benjamin, see Chapter 1. See also Foucault's passage on history as parody and farce:

The new historian, the genealogist, will know what to make of this masquerade. He will not be too serious to enjoy it; on the contrary, he will push the masquerade to its limit and prepare the great carnival of time where masks are constantly reappearing. . . . Genealogy is history in the form of a concerted carnival.

(Foucault 1977: 160–1)

16 For a discussion of the genealogy of Benjamin's topographical model of memory, see Chapter 8.

17 See Chapter 1.

18 Foucault admittedly proceeds from a conventional understanding of Freud, whereas his own dialectic, both with regard to the dream and to the primal fantasies, comes very close to Laplanche and Pontalis's re-reading of Freud's writings. See, for example, the figure of the dream as a drama and the embroilment of the dreamer in this dream-drama (Foucault 1992: 56ff.).

19 This is a connection which Benjamin carries over to the built, materialized wish-images of the collective consciousness; for example, in his exposé on the arcades (*Passagen*): 'They are residues of a dream world. The evaluation [*Verwertung*] of the elements of the dream upon waking is the textbook example of dialectical thinking' (*GS* V.1, 59; *CB* 176, translation modified).

4 THOUGHT-IMAGES

1 The relation between image and 'distorted similitude' (*entstellte Ähnlichkeit*) is discussed in Chapters 8 and 9.

2 The term *Ähnlichkeit* in Benjamin has hitherto generally been translated as 'similarity'. 'Similitude' has been preferred here as a more precise rendering. See Introduction, note 11. (Translator's note.)

3 Dürer's *Melancolia*, for example, caught Benjamin's interest as early as 1913, when he saw the picture during a museum visit in Basel; later, the allegorical reading of this image became an important building block in the *Trauerspiel* book (1928). And his twenty-year fascination with Klee's painting has, of course, made (theoretical) history. This is discussed below.

4 The method of writing characteristic of these thought-images can be particularly closely observed in the short prose texts collected under the title 'Short Shadows' (*Kurze Schatten*): for example, 'Platonic Love' (*Platonische Liebe*) or 'Once is Never' (*Einmal ist keinmal*), which trace the constitution of meaning in traditional love myths. See *GS* IV.1, 368–9.

5 The German is *Bekanntlich soll es einen Automaten gegeben haben . . .*, better rendered as 'It is well-known that there was once an automaton . . .'. (Translator's note.)

6 See Habermas (1973).

7 A phrase that Benjamin used in relation to Kafka (*GS* II.2, 678), but which could equally well be read as self-reflexive.

8 The figure derives from Heraclitus – see Chapter 1, note 5. *Gegenstrebige Fügung* is also the title of Jakob Taubes's book on the history of his fascination with Carl Schmitt.

9 For a more detailed discussion of this originary constellation in Benjamin's thinking-in-images, see Chapter 6.

10 Most recently in Lindner (1992: 254).

11 Compare Gershom Scholem's interpretation of the 'Angel of History'. The emphasis on Jewish tradition in Benjamin's thought, which was considerably influenced by his friendship with Scholem, is important for an understanding of Benjamin here. However, in his essay, Scholem chooses to disregard the differences between his own thought and Benjamin's when he ascribes to him a cyclical concept of history in which beginning and end meet (Scholem 1983: esp. 63 and 71).

12 Benjamin uses the word *Beaugenscheinigung* (beviewing or examination) to characterize the magical fixation of a certain kind of philology on the text (Benjamin 1978: 794). This is discussed in Chapter 5.

13 This allegory is discussed in more detail in Chapter 8.

14 See Hölderlin's letter to Wilmans of 28 September 1803 (Hölderlin 1992: II, 925).

5 TOWARDS A FEMALE DIALECTIC OF ENLIGHTENMENT

1 Where English distinguishes between 'the feminine' and 'the female', a distinction that has had repercussions for English-language gender discourse, where the former term is generally taken to indicate culturally constructed gender and the latter biological sex, German (like French) does not, having only one word, *Weiblichkeit* (and its related adjective *weiblich*), which encompasses both fields of meaning in the English. The translation of the terms *Weiblichkeit* and *weiblich* into English is thus always a matter of choice between the two terms, which should be borne in mind by the reader in what follows. (Translator's note.)

2 The commentaries on *Malina* fill shelves in the meantime; but although a completely new understanding of the novel has been worked out in recent years, the respective interpretations never manage to discuss more than individual levels of meaning at any one time. See Weigel (1994a: 232–63).

3 Gudrun Axeli-Knapp uses this term in her critique of recent social studies in feminist research in which particular feminine characteristics are valued positively and generalized. See Axeli-Knapp (1988).

4 Many German contributions on this topic give the impression that what is at issue is the taking of sides for or against enlightenment, or the declaration of oneself as an advocate or opponent of postmodernism, rather than the analysis of the historical changes in cultural development. For an alternative approach, see Fredric Jameson (1984).

5 This is not to say that Horkheimer and Adorno's text does not create any myths about woman; see especially the passage on the Megaera (Horkheimer and Adorno 1973).

6 The most impressive descriptions of the history of enlightenment taking into account the effects of this sacrificial structure for 'the feminine' are to be found in Heinrich (1985) and Kurnitzky's Oedipus study (Kurnitzky 1978).

7 This is particularly evident in her treatment of the figure and motif of the androgyne.

8 Benjamin's work on the image of the myth of creation is discussed in Chapter 6. See Weigel (1990) for an account of the perspectives this myth offers for cultural history.

9 In relation to this issue, see my case-study of the different preconditions governing male and female art production via the examples of Hans Bellmer and Unica Zürn (Weigel 1990: 67–114).

10 The Western orientation, or the 'Westernization of our cultural orientation and values', has been identified by Jürgen Habermas as one of the most prominent trends in the development of West German theory since 1945 (Habermas 1989). Even Seyla Benhabib forgets Benjamin in her history of Critical Theory; that is, she mentions him only briefly in the context of Habermas's critique of him (Benhabib 1986).

11 Notably in his essays 'On Language as Such and on the Language of Man' (1916), and 'On the Mimetic Faculty' and 'The Doctrine of the Similar' (1933).

12 The translation by Margaret Waller gives 'instinctual stases', 'instinctual functioning'; our translation is slightly different: 'stases of drives', 'functioning of drives'. (Translator's note.)

13 The position of the *infans*, described in both Freud and Lacan primarily in masculine terms, is examined by Kristeva also from the female perspective.

14 For example, in such phrases as 'virgins of the word', 'daughter of the father', 'daughter of the mother'; see 'From this Side', in Kristeva (1977).

15 Her *Tales of Love* refer to central myths in Christian-European culture, such as the Virgin Mary, Romeo and Juliet, and Don Juan. That German-language reception of Kristeva is a great deal more positive than the Anglo-American may have something to do with the fact that, in the former, *Revolution in Poetic Language* is taken as marking the beginning and providing the basis for her theoretical position. Her texts which look explicitly at 'the feminine' have never attained an importance on the scale of *Revolution*.

16 See the chapter on references to mythology and memory of history in my book on contemporary literature by women (Weigel 1987).

17 See Chapter 2.

18 His dialectical image makes reference (among other things) to the topographical description of the 'psychic apparatus' by Freud in his 'Note upon the "Mystic Writing-Pad"' (*Notiz über den 'Wunderblock'*). In this text, the non-synchronicity of 'perception-consciousness' (*Wahrnehmung-Bewußtsein*) and 'memory' is considered as both temporal and spatial. See Chapter 8 for a detailed discussion.

19 Benjamin's distinction between his position and Louis Aragon's *Paysan de Paris*, which he regarded both as model for *and* contrast to his own city-texts, should also be seen in this context. 'While an impressionistic element lingers on in Aragon ("mythology") – and this impressionism should be held responsible for the many nebulous philosophemes of the book – what matters here is the dissolution of "mythology" into the space of history' (*GS* V.1, 571; *N* 44–5).

20 This is discussed in Weigel (1987); see especially the chapter 'Literatur-geschichte in Bewegung'.

21 See Chapter 4.

22 I have tried to describe the specific place of women as being at one and the same time participants in and excluded from a culture as a 'double focus' (*schielender Blick*) and as an impossible constellation in the image of the 'voice of the Medusa' (*Stimme der Medusa*) – see Weigel (1983) and Weigel (1987). Amongst contemporary women writing in German, Anne

Duden especially treats women's position as both victims *and* perpetrators as a basic assumption. See her publications *Übergang* (Berlin, 1982) and *Das Judasschaf* (Berlin, 1985). See also the dialogue Duden and Weigel (1989).

23 If one were to superimpose the figuration of the angel of history on the historical situation of the so-called *Trümmerfrauen* in Germany after 1945, for example, then the feminist research concerned with recovering and remembering the history of these women would probably acquire a different perspective and emphasis. Whereas up to now the aspect emphasized has been that of unpaid female labour, particularly in the light of women subsequently being forced back into housework in the technically new and improved houses of the era of the 'economic miracle' (*Wirtschaftswunder*), the phenomenon can also be seen from another angle, that of these women's participation in building up the economy and clearing away the ruins and wreckage of the Nazi catastrophe. Women, too, are implicated, for example, in the question posed by Primo Levi in the text in which he remembers and describes his journey through the ruins of Germany as a survivor of the Auschwitz concentration camp:

> As I wandered around the streets of Munich, full of ruins, near the station where our train lay stranded once more, I felt I was moving amongst throngs of insolvent debtors, as if everybody owed me something, and refused to pay. I was among them, in the enemy camp, among the *Herrenvolk*; but the men were few, many were mutilated, many dressed in rags like us. I felt that everybody should interrogate us, read in our faces who we were and listen to our tale in humility. But no one looked us in the eyes, no one accepted the challenge; they were deaf, blind and dumb, imprisoned in their ruins, as in a fortress of wilful ignorance, still strong, still capable of hatred and contempt, still prisoners of their old tangle of pride and guilt.
>
> ('The Awakening', in Levi (1987: 376–7))

6 FROM IMAGES TO DIALECTICAL IMAGES

1 See Chapter 4.

2 One may call it language magic or language theology. Both aspects, the magical and the theological, are already contained in 'Conversation': 'The conversation of the genius is prayer, however. . . . The genius who speaks is more silent than the listener, just as the person at prayer is more silent than God' (*GS* II.1, 93).

3 On the translation of the Benjaminian term *Ähnlichkeit* adopted in this volume, see Introduction, note 11. (Translator's note.)

4 Benjamin points out that in the second version of the story of the creation in Genesis there is reference to the material from which man was made; he himself refers to the first version of the story, however, in order to discuss 'the relation of the creative act to language' (*GS* II.1, 148; *OWS* 115).

5 Stoessel's thesis of the 'forgotten human dimension' and of the Oedipal structure in the essay 'On Language as Such' is discussed in Chapter 3.

6 See, for example, the images of silence giving birth, of the deflowering gaze

(*GS* II.1, 92), of the conceiving landscape (*GS* II.1, 99), of the womb of time (*GS* II.1, 102), or of being pregnant with knowledge (*GS* II.1, 131).

7 The crassest example is the model of the 'bachelor machine' (*Jungge-sellenmaschine*); see Clair and Szeemann (1975).

8 In the 'Life of the Students' (*Das Leben der Studenten*) (*GS* II.1, 84), for example, or in 'Sokrates' (*GS* II.1, 130).

9 Prominent in the writings of the German *Sturm und Drang* movement, for example.

10 Suggestive for Benjamin's field of imagery here is Heinrich Heine's ironic word-play in the poem *Lotusblume*, written in 1855 on his sick-bed (forced against his will into the position of the genius, so to speak) on his mistress, 'die Mouche', and himself: *Doch statt des befruchtenden Lebens / empfängt sie nur ein Gedicht* ('But instead of fructifying life / she only receives a poem') (Heine 1993: 847). On the constellation Benjamin–Heine, see Briegleb (1988).

11 See Chapter 4.

12 See Weber (1991: 7–8).

13 The woman in question was the Dutch painter Toet Blaupot ten Cate. See Wil van Gerwen's lecture 'Walter Benjamin 1932/33 auf Ibiza', held at the Benjamin symposium in Osnabrück in June 1992.

14 Thus in the Hessel review; also, with slight deviations, in the early drafts of the *Passagen* written from 1927 on (*GS* V.2, 1052).

15 On Benjamin's reception of Bachofen, see Plumpe (1979).

16 The *Dirne* is predominant in his early writings which also allude to student experiences, and the *Hure* in the later works, whereby it is quite clear that the term *Hure* refers to the whore's status as image. However, Benjamin's usage is not uniform. He consistently uses *Dirne* in the texts up to and including 'One-Way Street' (1928), while at the same time the *Hure* makes her appearance in the early drafts of the *Passagen* (see, for example, *GS* V.2, 1023, 1057). But in his letter to Horkheimer of 1938 in which he sets out his concept for the Baudelaire book (Benjamin 1978: 752), as also in the first schematic plans for it (*GS* VII.2, 739), he refers once again to the *Dirne*.

17 See my article 'Traum – Stadt – Frau. Zur Weiblichkeit der Städte in der Schrift', in Weigel 1990: 204–29. For an English translation see Weigel (1996).

7 THE 'OTHER' IN ALLEGORY

1 The literary allegory, too, understood as extended or continued metaphor (*metaphora continua*, as for example in Quintilian, *Institutio oratoria* VIII, 8.40) or a sequence of metaphors, goes back to the transferred speech of metaphorical representations.

2 See Weigel (1990), in particular Section II.

3 This was the theme of a symposium, 'The Gender of Allegories' (*Das Geschlecht der Allegorien*), held at the Cultural Studies Institute in Essen in December 1991. See Schade *et al.* (1994).

4 The further pursuit of this question would involve looking more closely at the

various triangular relationships between (1) image or text, (2) meaning, and (3) subject, in order systematically to analyse or typologize their different possibilities and variants.

5 See, for example, the system of allegorical representations in the arts in Ripa's *Iconologia* of 1593.

6 Benjamin elaborates with some care the dialectic of elevation *and* devaluation of the profane world, as also the dialectic of transcendence and immanence. And yet, counter to the established way of regarding allegory, he stresses the aspect of devaluation. See also Steinhagen, in Haug (1979: 672).

7 Benjamin is here quoting Cysarz (1924: 31).

8 Julia Kristeva, by contrast, attempts in her reading of the Song of Songs to recuperate the simultaneity of literal/fleshly and allegorical/religious meaning. See Kristeva (1987).

9 In relation to this, see the excursus on the feminine form of allegory in Weigel (1990: 167ff.).

10 This connection is discussed in greater detail in Chapter 3.

11 See also Menke (1991: 180).

12 Heinz Schlaffer has drawn attention to the modernity which Benjamin projected into the Baroque book, but in so doing limits the historical validity of the work (Schlaffer 1989: 186–90). One could argue conversely – and, with Foucault, on an historical basis – that, with the aid of the illumination of 'now-time' (*Jetztzeit*), Benjamin discovered aspects in the Baroque *Trauerspiel* which anticipate the modern.

8 FROM TOPOGRAPHY TO WRITING

1 On the translation of the Benjaminian term *Ähnlichkeit* adopted in this volume, see Introduction, note 11. (Translator's note.)

2 Compare Freud's siting of his 'scientific renewal' as a third 'insult to human self-love', following the cosmological one brought about by the discoveries of Copernicus and the biological one brought about by the theory of natural selection – in 'On the History of the Psycho-Analytic Movement' (*Zur Geschichte der psychoanalytischen Bewegung*) (1914), in Freud 1963: 43–113 (see Freud 1953: XIV, 7–66). In relation to this, see also Weber 1991: 168ff.

3 The symbol (x) indicates a word omitted from the published text because it is illegible in the manuscript.

4 Thus the title given to the 'Notiz über den "Wunderblock"' in the *Standard Edition* of Freud's works. See Freud 1953: XIX, 225–32. (Translator's note.)

5 The translation given in the *Standard Edition* is simply 'instead of', thus erasing the ambiguity in the German. See Freud 1953: XVIII, 25. (Translator's note.)

6 The German translation of Ginzburg's essay bears the title *Spurensicherung*, meaning 'securing of clues' or, more literally, 'securing of traces'. (Translator's note.)

7 For Freud's reading of the Morelli method, see in particular 'The Moses of Michelangelo' (*Der Moses des Michelangelo*), in Freud (1969: X, 195–220) (see Freud 1953: XIII, 209–36). See also Weigel (1994b).

8   Benjamin's *Catalogue of Read Works* (*Verzeichnis der gelesenen Schriften*) lists only the following works by Sigmund Freud: 540) *Der Witz und seine Beziehung zum Unbewußten*; 549) 'Psychoanalytische Bemerkungen über einen autobiographisch beschriebenen Fall von Paranoia (Der Fall Schreber)', 'Einführung des Narzißmus'; 609) *Über Psychoanalyse: Fünf Vorlesungen*; 1076) *Jenseits des Lustprinzips* (*GS* VII.1, 438–76). That this catalogue has only limited value in terms of elucidating Benjamin's actual reading of Freud is already evident from the fact that further titles not listed here receive mention at various points, but above all from the fact that Benjamin integrated numerous Freudian terms into his theory.

9   See *GS* VI, 674 and Scholem (1973: 75). The university satires, 'Acta Muriensa', which Scholem and Benjamin exchanged following their period together in Bern, contain references indicating their study of Freud's 'joke' book, which had appeared in 1905 (see *GS* IV.2, 442). Benjamin evidently returned to a consideration of this work of Freud's again later, as is borne out by a note in one of the preparatory schemata for the essay on Karl Kraus of 1931 (see *GS* II.3, 1097).

10   This clearly refers to Freud's 'On Narcissism: An Introduction' (*Zur Einführung des Narzißmus*) of 1914.

11   That is, it can be dated between the resumption of the *Passagen* project from 1934 onwards and the inception of work on the Baudelaire essay, an offshoot of the *Passagen*, in 1937. This means that a conscious and systematic reading of psychoanalytical theory of memory in the mid-1930s is verifiable.

12   The concept of the unconscious is also of some significance for the 'Short History of Photography' (1931), where the 'instinctual unconscious' or, better, 'unconscious of drives' (*das Triebhaft-Unbewußte*) of psychoanalysis is brought into association with the 'optical unconscious' (*das Optisch-Unbewußte*) of photography (*GS* II.1, 371; *OWS* 243); also for the essay on 'The Work of Art in the Age of Mechanical Reproduction' (1938), which takes up this idea again in relation to film (*GS* I.2, 500; *Ill* 239).

13   It is not until Benjamin's work that awakening becomes a central constellation of memory, a constellation in which literary scenes, in particular ones deriving from his reading of Proust, and Freud's theory of dreams, intersect. It is to be noted, however, that Benjamin remarked upon the desideratum of a psychoanalysis of awakening, as his question directed at Adorno in June 1935 demonstrates: 'Incidentally, can you off-hand recall any point in his [Freud's] work or in his school at which a psychoanalysis of awakening is to be found? or studies on it?' (*GS* V.2, 1121) In Freud's *Interpretation of Dreams*, awakening appears once as an *in flagranti* constellation in which the 'transformation of thoughts into images' might be caught in the act (Freud 1969: II, 483; 1953: V, 503).

14   See Freud 1953: XIX, 231.

15   For this notion of an imagistic relationship between the Now and the has-been, a related passage in Freud's work might also be mentioned; namely, his concept of the 'time-mark' (*Zeitmarke*) of day-dream and fantasy: 'Thus what is past, what is present, and what lies in the future [*Vergangenes, Gegenwärtiges, Zukünftiges*] [are] lined up like beads on the string of the wish that runs through them' – In 'Creative Writers and Day-Dreaming' (*Der Dichter und das Phantasieren*) of 1908 (Freud 1969: X, 174).

16 See Chapter 2.
17 See, for example, the formulation 'motoric innervation' (*motorische Innervation*) in his 'Notes on a Theory of Play' (*Notizen zu einer Theorie des Spiels*) from 1929–30 (*GS* VI, 188) which stand in chronological proximity to the 'innervations of the collective' in the 'Surrealism' essay and prefigure ideas concerning the reflexive memory of the player in the Baudelaire studies.
18 In this text the topography of individual recollection is seen as distinct from the memory of the city which is as it were inscribed into the ground (see *GS* VI, 489; *OWS* 316). By contrast, in 'Berlin Childhood Around 1900' the emphasis is precisely on the correspondences between the memory of the subject and the topography of the city.
19 See Chapter 4.
20 See note 1 above.
21 See the chapter on the modes of representation of the dream in the *Interpretation of Dreams*.
22 See his request in a letter to Scholem to be sent the earlier essay on language 'to compare with these notes', since he had had to leave his copy amongst his 'Berlin papers' when he fled from Germany (Benjamin 1978: 575).
23 The translation in *DS* gives 'the sole basis on which the picture puzzle can form itself'; this represents a misunderstanding of the word *Fundus*, which means, not 'basis', but 'store' or 'repository'. A 'repository' is of course a place where things are preserved, like the archive, which is fully in keeping with the sense of the passage here. (Translator's note.)
24 This is discussed in Chapter 9.

9 THE READING THAT TAKES THE PLACE OF TRANSLATION

1 These works were characterized by Benjamin himself as his second production complex, following on and taking over from the earlier one on German literature, to which the essay on 'The Task of the Translator' may still be counted as belonging.
2 This marks the greatest contrast between the later works and the early writings. When, for example, the 'I' of 'The Diary' (*Das Tagebuch*) (1913) is surrounded by what is happening *as* by a landscape (*GS* II.1, 99), the events described are perceived within a mythical structure in which history appears as nature. Benjamin's efforts at dissolving mythology into the space of history (*GS* V.1, 571) provide the grounding for his concept of reading in which the images of the has-been become decipherable in the context of mnemic writing.
3 See Chapter 8.
4 On the translation of the Benjaminian term *Ähnlichkeit* adopted in this volume, see Introduction, note 11. (Translator's note.)
5 The German reads: *Die Übersetzung ... ruft ... das Original hinein, an demjenigen einzigen Orte hinein, wo jeweils das Echo in der eigenen den Widerhall eines Werkes der fremden Sprache zu geben vermag.* Zohn omits *das Original* from his translation of this passage altogether – thus making of it a translation without *das Original*. (Translator's note.)

6   On the translation of the word *'Fundus'* adopted here, see Chapter 8, note 23. (Translator's note.)
7   See in particular Chapter 2 of Foucault (1970), and Chapter 3 of this volume.
8   The formulation 'distorted similitude' is to be found in Benjamin's essay on Proust and in 'Berlin Childhood Around 1900'.
9   Zohn renders this phrase: 'There is, however, a stop.' That is, he reads the verbal noun 'Halten' as deriving from *halten* meaning 'to stop', rather than *halten* meaning 'to hold'. There is, of course, a certain ambiguity, perhaps better rendered by the translation 'hold' which in English also includes the suggestion of 'holding' as 'arresting'. In what follows, it is, however, important that the word is read in the sense of 'having something to hold onto', which prevents the plunge into the abyss. (Translator's note.)
10   See the discussion in Chapter 4.
11   The publication 'Walter Benjamin's "The Task of the Translator"' (de Man 1986: 73–105) is a transcription of a recording of a lecture held in 1983.
12   This image is discussed at greater length in Chapter 4.
13   De Man is quoting from *Illuminationen* (Frankfurt-on-Main, 1986), 262.

10 READABILITY

1   Quoted from the dual-language edition with translation by C. J. Rowe (Plato 1988: 123).
2   The passage from the *Phaedrus* appears as the epigraph in the book that initiated the series, Assmann and Hardmeier (1983); but is also quoted in Yates (1966: 38); Lachmann (1990: 14); Harth (1991a: 17).
3   Most notably in Derrida, who develops his theory of writing, 'grammatology', in distinction from the myth of a truth of the soul which is expressed in the *logos*, but in doing so rejects a sign system that preceded writing (Derrida 1976: 10ff.).
4   This is the title Derrida gives to his essay on Freud: see Derrida (1978: 196–231).
5   In fact, the old paradigm has, despite the new constellation of transition, evidently lost none of its appeal; see, for example, the opposition proposed between writing and trace versus the 'living heart of memory' in Nora (1990).
6   See, for example, de Certeau (1984); Assmann and Hölscher (1988); Assmann and Harth (1991a).
7   In particular in Yates (1966); Lachmann (1990); Assmann and Harth (1991b); and Haverkamp and Lachmann (1991).
8   This is the sub-title of the 1990 German translation of Yates's *The Art of Memory* (1966), which captures more accurately the content of her book than the misleading main title *Gedächtnis und Erinnern*.
9   See, for example, Klaus Reichert's analysis of Joyce's *Ulysses*, in Haverkamp and Lachmann (1991: 328–55).
10   Walter Hamilton's translation in the Penguin edition of the *Phaedrus* (Harmondsworth, 1977) has been preferred here for its greater fluency.
11   The *Kulturwissenschaftliche Bibliothek* was set up by Warburg in Hamburg in 1909. In the early 1920s, it was turned into a public institute which in 1933, when the Nazis came into power, was rescued into exile in London,

where it remains to this day as the Warburg Institute. See Warburg (1980) and Hofmann *et al*. (1980). For a more detailed discussion of Warburg, see Weigel (1995a).

12 See in particular Saxl (1980: 419–32).

13 On the significance of taxonomies for the ordering of knowledge in the age of representation, see Foucault (1970).

14 It was only in the subsequent reception Warburg's work – that is, with the establishment of a Warburg *school* – that the tendency towards the codification and encyclopaedic systematization of the pathos formulae took hold, whereby the latter came to be read as symbols rather than memory traces.

15 Of course, Freud was not the first to cast doubt on this: see Lavater's earlier critics, such as Lichtenberg and Lessing; or Bergson's notion of senso-motorically stored images of past experience which can be understood as haptic recollection; or also Nietzsche.

16 See Freud's monograph on aphasia (1891), cited in Freud (1969: III, 165–7).

17 This process is treated by Starobinski in his *Kleine Geschichte des Körpergefühls* (*Short History of Body Sensation*) (Starobinski 1991).

18 For an account of Benjamin's increasing use of psychoanalytical terminology around 1930, see Chapters 8 and 9.

19 On this point, see Chapter 9.

20 See Chapter 11.

21 See Chapter 4.

11 NON-PHILOSOPHICAL AMAZEMENT

1 Benjamin's own title uses the term 'concept' (*Über den Begriff der Geschichte*) and not 'philosophy'. The title of the English translation, 'Theses on the Philosophy of History', follows the title *Geschichts-philosophische Thesen* given by Adorno and Horkheimer.

2 Be it capitalism, patriarchy, destruction of nature, colonialism, or scientific revolution.

3 Benjamin's term '*Erkenntnis*' emphasizes the moment of cognition or realization, whilst the English translation 'knowledge' too much connotes already existing or established ideas. (Translator's note.)

4 'As unity and totality, the time that begins and completes, i.e. the sphere of historical discourse, is full of sense: in a double sense of having direction and intelligibility' (Chatelet 1975: 205).

5 For example, Karl Löwith's description in his historico-philosophical *opus magnum*, in its analysis of the problems of eschatological thinking in modernity, is based on the paradigm of *crisis* instead of reflecting the limits of the philosophy of history.

6 A reading of Thesis IX on the angel of history as a dialectical image is presented in Chapter 4.

7 In his analysis of history and salvation, Karl Löwith, in referring to Hermann Cohen's *Religion der Vernunft aus den Quellen des Judentums* (*Religion of Reason from the Sources of Judaism*), obscures precisely the differences between Christian eschatology and Jewish prophetism (see Löwith 1983: 28). Therefore his critique of the philosophy of history

remains immanent, referring to the concept of crisis (see note 5). A counter-argument could be constructed on the basis of Gershom Scholem's work; he had already shown the tendency to exclude the apocalypse in the case of Maimonides' attempt to describe Jewish revelation as a consistent system of a religion of Reason (see Scholem 1963). However, the incompatibility and the 'radical difference between the unredeemed world of historiography and Messianic redemption' (1963: 36) structures Benjamin's thinking and is the basis of his text 'On the Concept of History'.

8 On the concept of primal scene (*Urszene*), see Laplanche and Pontalis (1985).

9 See Claussen (1988). Claussen reflects Adorno's writing as a reference to Auschwitz, but without analysing the historical distance between *Minima Moralia* (1951) and *Negative Dialectics* (1966), that is, the genealogy of Adorno's shaping of his thoughts and language on Auschwitz.

10 The phrase 'even the past is no longer safe from the present' is a variation on Benjamin's Thesis VI that '*even the dead* will not be safe from the enemy if he wins' (*GS* I.2, 695; *Ill* 257).

11 This is also still the case for Leo Löwenthal's text *Individuum und Terror* (*The Individual and Terror*) (1944). On the problem of the self-limitation of 'Critical Theory', see Briegleb (1993, esp. 24ff.).

12 For a thorough philosophical analysis of Adorno after Auschwitz, in relation to Heidegger's *Germanien*, see Garcia Düttmann (1991).

13 See 'Juvenal's error' in Adorno (1974).

14 See Burgard (1992).

15 See Bohleber's overview on this paradigm (Bohleber 1990).

16 See the Broszat–Friedländer debate. Concerning the *topos* of 'writing after Auschwitz', see the differentiation of the various forms of silence in Heller (1993).

17 Diner postulates a 'negative historics' cognition of history:

> Since historians must first become aware of the cancellation of assumptions of rationality in historical reconstruction before they can venture to engage in the enterprise of historicization. Or, to phrase it differently: due to the loss of its imaginability, it is necessary first to *think* Auschwitz before it can be written about historically.
>
> (1992: 142)

18 This is discussed in greater detail in my article on desire and traumatization in Bachmann's writing (Weigel 1994a: 232–63).

19 See Weigel (1994a: 232–63).

20 On intertextuality between Benjamin and Bachmann, see also my article in Weigel (1994a: 81–101).

Bibliography

ABBREVIATIONS

Short references in the text refer to the following editions of Walter Benjamin's writings:

CB   *Charles Baudelaire: A Lyric Poet in the Era of High Capitalism*, trans. Harry Zohn, London: Verso, 1976.

DS   'Doctrine of the Similar', trans. Knut Tarnowski, *New German Critique* 17 (Spring 1979): 60–69.

GS   *Gesammelte Schriften*, ed. Rolf Tiedemann and Hermann Schweppenhäuser, 7 vols, Frankfurt am Main: Suhrkamp, 1980–9.

Ill   *Illuminations*, ed. Hannah Arendt, trans. Harry Zohn, Glasgow: Fontana/Collins, 1973.

N   'N [Re The Theory of Knowledge, Theory of Progress]', trans. Leigh Hafrey and Richard Sieburth, in Gary Smith (ed.) *Benjamin. Philosophy, History, Aesthetics*, Chicago and London: Chicago University Press, 1989, 38–83.

OGT   *The Origin of German Tragic Drama*, trans. John Osborne, introduction by George Steiner, London: New Left Books, 1977.

OWS   *One-Way Street and Other Writings*, trans. Edmund Jephcott and Kingsley Shorter, London: Verso, 1985.

Adorno, Theodor (1973) *Negative Dialectics*, trans. E. B. Ashton, New York: Seabury Press.

—— (1974) *Minima Moralia*, trans. E. Jephcott, London: New Left Books.

—— (1981) *Prisms*, trans. S. and S. Weber, Cambridge, MA: MIT Press.

Agamben, Giorgio (1990) 'Das unvordenkliche Bild', in Volker Bohn (ed.) *Bildlichkeit: Internationale Beiträge zur Poetik 3*, Frankfurt am Main: Suhrkamp, pp. 534–53.

—— (1992) 'Noten zur Geste', in Jutta Georg-Lauer (ed.) *Postmoderne und Politik*, Tübingen: edition diskord, pp. 97–107.

Arendt, Hannah (1986) *Zur Zeit: Politische Essays*, ed. M. L. Knott, Berlin: Rotbuch.

Aristotle (1984) 'De Anima', in *The Complete Works of Aristotle*, ed. Jonathan Barnes, Princeton, NJ: Princeton University Press, pp. 641–92.

Assmann, Aleida and Hardmeier, Jan-Christof (eds) (1983) *Schrift und Gedächtnis: Archäologie der literarischen Kommunikation I*, Munich: Fink.

Assmann, Aleida and Harth, Dietrich (eds) (1991a) *Kultur als Lebenswelt und Monument*, Frankfurt am Main: Fischer Taschenbuch.

—— (1991b) *Mnemosyne: Formen und Funktionen der kulturellen Erinnerung*, Frankfurt am Main: Fischer Taschenbuch.

Assmann, Jan and Hölscher, Tonio (eds) (1988) *Kultur und Gedächtnis*, Frankfurt am Main: Suhrkamp.

Axeli-Knapp, Gudrun (1988) 'Die vergessene Differenz', *Feministische Studien* 6, 1: 12–31.

Babylon: Beiträge zur jüdischen Gegenwart, Frankfurt am Main, pp. 1986ff.

Bachmann, Ingeborg (1978) *Werke*, ed. Christine Koschel, Inge von Weidenbaum, and Clemens Münster, 4 vols, Munich, Zurich: Piper.

—— (1983) *Wir müssen wahre Sätze finden: Gespräche und Interviews*, ed. Christine Koschel and Inge von Weidenbaum, Munich, Zurich: Piper.

Bachofen, Johann Jakob (1948) *Das Mutterrecht*, ed. Meuli, Basle: Schwabe.

Benhabib, Seyla (1986) *Critique, Norm and Utopia*, Guildford, New York: Columbia University Press.

Benjamin, Walter (1955) *Schriften*, ed. Theodor W. and Gretel Adorno, 2 vols, Frankfurt am Main: Suhrkamp.

—— (1978) *Briefe*, ed. Gershom Scholem and Theodor W. Adorno, 2 vols, Frankfurt am Main: Suhrkamp; translated as Benjamin (1995).

—— (1979) *Text + Kritik* 31/32, ed. Heinz Ludwig Arnold, Munich: Edition Text + Kritik.

—— (1987) *Berliner Kindheit um Neunzehnhundert*, Frankfurt am Main: Suhrkamp.

—— (1995) *The Correspondence of Walter Benjamin, 1990–1940*, trans. Manfred R. Jacobson and Evelyn M. Jacobson, Chicago: University of Chicago Press.

Blumenberg, Hans (1981) *Die Lesbarkeit der Welt*, Frankfurt am Main: Suhrkamp.

Bohleber, Werner (1990) 'Das Fortwirken des Nationalsozialismus in der zweiten und dritten Generation nach Auschwitz', *Babylon: Beiträge zur jüdischen Gegenwart* 7: 70–84.

Bohn, Volker (ed.) (1990) *Bildlichkeit: Internationale Beiträge zur Poetik 3*, Frankfurt am Main: Suhrkamp.

Bolz, Norbert W. and Faber, Richard (eds) (1985) *Walter Benjamin: Profane Erleuchtung und rettende Kritik*, Würzburg: Königshausen & Neumann.

—— (eds) (1986) *Antike und Moderne: Zu Walter Benjamins 'Passagen'*, Würzburg: Königshausen & Neumann.

Bolz, Norbert and Witte, Bernd (eds) (1984) *Passagen: Walter Benjamins Urgeschichte des XIX. Jahrhunderts*, Munich: Fink.

Briegleb, Klaus (1988) '"Paris, den . . .": Heinrich Heines Tagesberichte. Eine Skizze', *Der Deutschunterricht* 40, 1: 39–50.

—— (1993) 'Leo Löwenthal – Literatursoziologie unmittelbar zur Epoche', *Mitteilungen des Instituts für Sozialforschung* 3: 12–29.

Buci-Glucksmann, Christine (1994) *Baroque Reason: The Aesthetics of Modernity*, trans. Patrick Camiller, London: Sage Publications.

Buck-Morss, Susan (1989) *The Dialectics of Seeing: Walter Benjamin and the Arcades Project*, Cambridge, MA: MIT Press.

Bulthaup, Peter (ed.) (1975) *Materialien zu Benjamins Thesen 'Über den Begriff der Geschichte': Beiträge und Interpretationen*, Frankfurt am Main: Suhrkamp.

Burgard, Peter J. (1992) 'Adorno, Goethe, and the politics of the essay', *Deutsche Vierteljahrsschrift für Literaturwissenschaft und Geistesgeschichte* 66, 1: 160–91.

Certeau, Michel de (1984) *The Practice of Everyday Life*, Berkeley: University of California Press.

Chatelet, François (1975) 'Die Geschichte', *Geschichte der Philosophie*, vol. VII, Frankfurt am Main, Vienna, Berlin: Ullstein.

Clair, Jean and Szeemann, Harald (eds) (1975) *Junggesellenmaschinen/Les Machines Célibataires* (Ausstellungskatalog), Berne.

Claussen, Detlev (1988) 'Nach Auschwitz: Ein Essay über die Aktualität Adornos', in Dan Diner (ed.) *Zivilisationsbruch: Denken nach Auschwitz*, Frankfurt am Main: Fischer Taschenbuch, pp. 54–88.

Cysarz, Herbert (1924) *Deutsche Barockdichtung: Renaissance, Barock, Rokoko*, Leipzig: Haessel.

Deleuze, Gilles and Guattari, Félix (1984) *Anti-Oedipus: Capitalism and Schizophrenia*, trans. Robert Hurley, Mark Seem, and Helen R. Lane, preface by Michel Foucault, London: The Athlone Press.

Derrida, Jacques (1976) *Of Grammatology*, trans. Gayatri Chakravorty Spivak, Baltimore, London: Johns Hopkins University Press.

—— (1978) *Writing and Difference*, trans. Alan Bass, London, Henley: Routledge & Kegan Paul.

—— (1990) 'Force de loi: Le "fondement mystique de l'autorité"/Force of law: The "mystical foundation of authority"', trans. Mary Quaintance, *Cardozo Law Review* 11 (1989–90): 919–1045.

Diner, Dan (ed.) (1988) *Zivilisationsbruch: Denken nach Auschwitz*, Frankfurt am Main: Fischer Taschenbuch.

—— (1992) 'Historical understanding and counterrationality: the *Judenrat* as epistemological vantage', in Saul Friedlander (ed.) *Probing the Limits of Representation: Nazism and the 'Final Solution'*, Cambridge, MA: Harvard University Press.

Douglas, Mary (1986) *Ritual, Tabu und Körpersymbolik: Sozialanthropologische Studien in Industriegesellschaft und Stammeskultur* (1973), Frankfurt am Main: Suhrkamp.

Duden, Anne and Weigel, Sigrid (1989) 'Schrei und Körper – Zum Verhältnis von Bildern und Schrift: Ein Gespräch über *Das Judasschaf*', in Thomas Koebner (ed.) *Laokoon und kein Ende: Der Wettstreit der Künste*, Munich: Edition Text + Kritik, pp. 113–41.

Duden, Barbara (1989) 'A repertory of body history', in Michel Feher et al. (eds) *Zone 5. Fragments for a History of the Human Body 3*, New York: Urzone, pp. 470–578.

Flusser, Vilém (1987) *Die Schrift: Hat Schreiben Zukunft?*, Göttingen: Edition Immatrix.

—— (1991) *Gesten: Versuch einer Phänomenologie*, Düsseldorf, Bensheim: Bollmann.

Foucault, Michel (1970) *The Order of Things: An Archaeology of the Human Sciences*, trans. from the French, London: Tavistock.

—— (1972) *The Archaeology of Knowledge*, trans. A. M. Sheridan Smith, London: Tavistock.

—— (1977) *Language, Counter-Memory, Practice: Selected Essays and Interviews*, ed. Donald F. Bouchard, trans. Donald F. Bouchard and Sherry Simon, Ithaca, NY: Cornell University Press (Cornell Paperback edn, 1980).

—— (1981a) *The History of Sexuality*, vol. 1: *An Introduction*, trans. Robert Hurley, London and Harmondsworth: Penguin.

—— (1981b) 'The order of discourse', trans. Ian McLeod, in Robert Young (ed.) *Untying the Text: A Post-Structuralist Reader*, Boston, London, Henley: Routledge & Kegan Paul, pp. 48–78.

—— (1984) 'Nietzsche, genealogy, history', trans. Donald F. Bouchard and Sherry Simon, in Paul Rabinow (ed.) *The Foucault Reader*, London: Penguin.

—— (1987) *The History of Sexuality*, vol. 2: *The Uses of Pleasure*, trans. Robert Hurley, London and Harmondsworth: Penguin Books.

—— (1990) *The History of Sexuality*, vol. 3: *The Care of the Self*, trans. Robert Hurley, London and Harmondsworth: Penguin Books.

—— (1992) 'Einleitung', in Ludwig Binswanger *Traum und Existenz* (1954), Berne, Berlin: Gachnang & Springer, pp. 7–93.

Fox Keller, Evelyn (1986) *Liebe, Macht und Erkenntnis: Männliche oder weibliche Wissenschaft?*, Munich: Hauser.

Freud, Sigmund (1953) *The Standard Edition of the Complete Psychological Works of Sigmund Freud*, ed. and trans. James Strachey *et al.*, 24 vol., London: Hogarth Press and the Institute of Psycho-Analysis, 1953–74.

—— (1963) *Gesammelte Werke*, vol. X: *Werke aus den Jahren 1913–1917*, ed. Anna Freud *et al.*, Frankfurt am Main: Fischer (3rd edn).

—— (1964) *Gesammelte Werke*, vol. I: *Werke aus den Jahren 1892–1899* (2nd edn).

—— (1969) *Studienausgabe*, ed. Alexander Mitscherlich *et al.*, 10 vols., Frankfurt am Main: Fischer, 1969–75.

—— (1986) *Briefe an Wilhelm Fliess, 1887–1904*, Frankfurt am Main: Fischer.

—— (1987) *Gesammelte Werke*, supplementary vol.: *Texte aus den Jahren 1885–1938*, ed. Anna Freud *et al.*, Frankfurt am Main: Fischer.

Freud, Sigmund and Breuer, Josef (1970) *Studien zur Hysterie*, Frankfurt am Main: Fischer.

Fürnkäs, Josef (1988) *Surrealismus als Erkenntnis: Walter Benjamin – Weimarer Einbahnstraße und Pariser Passagen*, Stuttgart: Metzler.

Garcia Düttmann, Alexander (1991) *Das Gedächtnis des Denkens: Versuch über Heidegger und Adorno*, Frankfurt am Main: Suhrkamp.

Geertz, Clifford (1973) *The Interpretation of Cultures: Selected Essays*, New York: Basic Books.

Ginzburg, Carlo (1990) *Myths, Emblems, Clues*, trans. John and Anne C. Tedeschi, London: Hutchinson Radius.

Goux, Jean-Joseph (1990) *Symbolic Economies: After Freud and Marx*, trans. Jennifer Curtiss Gage, Ithaca, NY: Cornell University Press.

Habermas, Jürgen (1972) 'Bewußtmachende oder rettende Kritik – Die Aktualität Walter Benjamins', in Siegried Unseld (ed.) *Zur Aktualität Walter Benjamins. Aus Anlaß des 80. Geburtstags von Walter Benjamin*, Frankfurt am Main: Suhrkamp, pp. 173–223; quoted here from 'Conscious-ness-raising or redemptive criticism – the contemporaneity of Walter

Benjamin', trans. Philip Brewster and Carl Howard Buchner, *New German Critique* 17 (Spring 1979): 30–59.

—— (1973) *Kultur und Kritik*, Frankfurt am Main: Suhrkamp.

—— (1989) 'Verwundete Nation – oder lernende Gesellschaft?', *Frankfurter Rundschau*, 11 April 1989, p. 9.

Harth, Dietrich (ed.) (1991a) *Die Erfindung des Gedächtnisses*, Frankfurt am Main: Keip.

—— (1991b) 'Der aufrechte Gang – Monument der Kultur? Über die Lesbarkeit des Leibes und einige andere Voraussetzungen der Kulturanalyse', in Aleida Assmann and Dietrich Hardt (eds) *Kultur als Lebenswelt und Monument*, Frankfurt am Main, Fischer Taschenbach, pp. 75–111.

Haß, Ulrike (1993) *Militante Pastorale: Zur Literatur der antimodernen Bewegungen im frühen 20. Jahrhundert*, Munich: Fink.

Haug, Walter (ed.) (1979) *Formen und Funktionen der Allegorie*, Stuttgart: Metzler.

Haverkamp, Anselm and Lachmann, Renate (eds) (1991) *Gedächtniskunst: Raum–Bild–Schrift. Studien zur Mnemotechnik*, Frankfurt am Main: Suhrkamp.

—— (1993) *Memoria: Vergessen und Erinnern. Poetik und Hermeneutik XV*, Munich: Fink.

Heine, Heinrich (1993) *Sämtliche Gedichte in zeitlicher Folge*, ed. Klaus Briegleb, Frankfurt am Main, Leipzig: Insel.

Heinrich, Klaus (1985) 'Das Floss der Medusa', in Renate Schlesier (ed.) *Faszination des Mythos: Studien zu antiken und modernen Interpretationen*, Basle, Frankfurt am Main: Roter Stern, pp. 335–98.

Heller, Agnes (1993) 'Die Weltzeituhr stand still: Schreiben nach Auschwitz? Schweigen nach Auschwitz? Philosophische Betrachtungen eines Tabus', *Die Zeit*, 7 May 1993, p. 61.

Hofman, Werner, Syamken, Georg, and Warnke, Martin (1980) *Die Menschenrechte des Auges: Über Aby Warburg*, Frankfurt am Main: Europäische Verlagsanstalt.

Hölderlin, Friedrich (1992) *Sämtliche Werke und Briefe*, ed. Michael Knaupp, 3 vols, Munich: Hanser.

Horkheimer, Max, and Adorno, Theodor W. (1973) *Dialectic of Enlightenment*, trans. John Cumming, London: Allen Lane.

Irigaray, Luce (1985) *This Sex which is Not One*, trans. Catherine Porter with Carolyn Burke, Ithaca, NY: Cornell University Press.

Jameson, Fredric (1984) 'Postmodernism, or the cultural logic of late capitalism', *New Left Review* 146: 53–93.

Kafka, Franz (1971) *Sämtliche Erzählungen*, Frankfurt am Main: Fischer.

Kemp, Wolfgang (1985) 'Fernbilder, Benjamin und die Kunstwissenschaft', in Burkhardt Lindner (ed.) *Walter Benjamin im Kontext*, Königstein/Ts: Athenäum (2nd, extended, edn), pp. 224–57.

—— (ed.) (1989) *Der Text des Bildes: Möglichkeiten und Mittel eigenständiger Bilderzählung*, Munich: Edition Text + Kritik.

Kippenberg, Hans G. and Luchesi, Brigitte (eds) (1978) *Magie: Die sozialwissenschaftliche Kontroverse über das Verstehen fremden Denkens*, Frankfurt am Main: Suhrkamp.

Klee, Paul (1990) *50 Werke aus 50 Jahren (1890–1940)*, ed. Werner Hofmann (Ausstellungskatalog), Hamburg.

Kott, Jan (1990) *Das Gedächtnis des Körpers: Essays zu Theater und Literatur*, Berlin: Alexander.

Kristeva, Julia (1976) 'Die Produktivität der Frau: Interview mit Elaine Boucquey', in *Das Lächeln der Medusa* (*alternative* 108/109), pp. 166–72.

—— (1977) *About Chinese Women*, trans. Anita Barrows, London: Marion Boyers.

—— (1984) *Revolution in Poetic Language*, trans. Margaret Waller, New York: Columbia University Press.

—— (1987) *Tales of Love*, trans. Leon S. Roudiez, New York: Columbia University Press.

Kuhn, Hugo (1979) 'Allegorie und Erzählstruktur', in Walter Haug (ed.) *Formen und Funktionen der Allegorie*, Stuttgart: Metzler, pp. 206–18.

Kurnitzky, Horst (1978) *Ödipus. Ein Held der westlichen Welt: Über die zerstörerischen Grundlagen der Zivilisation*, Berlin: Wagenbach.

Lachmann, Renate (1990) *Gedächtnis und Literatur: Intertextualität in der russischen Moderne*, Frankfurt am Main: Suhrkamp.

Laplanche, J. and Pontalis, J.-B. (1985) *Fantasme originaire: Fantasmes des origines, originale du fantasme*, Evreus: Hachette.

—— (1988) *The Language of Psychoanalysis*, trans. Donald Nicholson-Smith, London: Karnac Books.

Lavater, Johann Caspar (1984) *Physiognomische Fragmente zur Beförderung der Menschenkenntnis und Menschenliebe* (1775), Stuttgart: Reclam.

Levi, Primo (1987) *'If This Is a Man' and 'The Truce'*, trans. Stuart Woolf, London: Sphere Books.

Lindner, Burkhardt (ed.) (1985) *Walter Benjamin im Kontext*, Königstein/Ts.: Athenäum (2nd, extended edn).

—— (1992) 'Engel und Zwerg: Benjamins geschichtsphilosophische Rätselfigur und die Herausforderung des Mythos', in Lorenz Jäger and Thomas Regehly (eds) *'Was nie geschrieben wurde, lesen': Frankfurter Benjamin-Vorträge*, Bielefeld: Aisthesis, pp. 236–65.

Löwith, Karl (1983) *Sämtliche Schriften*, vol. 2: *Weltgeschichte und Heilsgeschehen: Zur Kritik der Geschichtsphilosophie* (1949), Stuttgart: Kohlhammer.

Man, Paul de (1986) 'Conclusions: Walter Benjamin's "The task of the translator"', in *The Resistance to Theory*, Minneapolis, MN: University of Minnesota Press, pp. 73–105.

Marx, Karl (1979) 'The Eighteenth Brumaire of Louis Bonaparte', in Karl Marx and Friedrich Engels, *Collected Works*, vol. 11: *Marx and Engels 1851–53*, London: Lawrence & Wishart.

Menke, Bettina (1991) *Sprachfiguren: Name-Allegorie-Bild nach Walter Benjamin*, Munich: Fink.

Menninghaus, Winfried (1980) *Walter Benjamins Theorie der Sprachmagie*, Frankfurt am Main: Suhrkamp.

Mitchell, W. J. T. (1984) 'What is an image?', *New Literary History* XV (Spring 1984), 3: 503–37.

—— (1990) 'Was ist ein Bild?', in Volker Bohn (ed.) *Bildlichkeit: Internationale Beiträge zur Poetik 3*, Frankfurt am Main: Suhrkamp, pp. 17–68 (rev., expanded version of Mitchell 1984).

Nägele, Rainer (1991) *Theater, Theory, Speculation: Walter Benjamin and the Scenes of Modernity*, Baltimore, London: Johns Hopkins University Press.

Nietzsche, Friedrich (1980) *Werke in sechs Bänden*, ed. Karl Schlechta, Munich, Vienna: Hanser.

Nora, Pierre (1990) *Zwischen Geschichte und Gedächtnis*, Berlin: Wagenbach.

Pfotenhauer, Helmut (1985) 'Benjamin und Nietzsche', in Burkhardt Lindner (ed.) *Walter Benjamin im Kontext*, Königstein/Ts.: Athenäum (2nd, expanded, edn), pp. 100–26.

Plato (1988) *Phaedrus*, trans. C. J. Rowe, Warminster: Aris & Phillips (2nd, corrected, edn).

Plumpe, Gerhard (1979) 'Die Entdeckung der Vorwelt: Erläuterungen zu Benjamins Bachofenlektüre', in Walter Benjamin *Text + Kritik* 31/32, ed. Heinz Ludwig Arnold, Munich: Edition Text + Kritik, pp. 19–27.

Pontalis, J.-B. (1992) *Die Macht der Anziehung: Psychoanalyse des Traums, der Übertragung und der Wörter*, Frankfurt am Main: Fischer Taschenbuch.

Raulff, Ulrich (ed.) (1986) *Vom Umschreiben der Geschichte: Neue historische Perspektiven*, Berlin: Wagenbach.

Saxl, Fritz (1980) 'Die Ausdrucksgebärden der bildenden Kunst' (1932), in Aby M. Warburg *Ausgewählte Schriften und Würdigungen*, ed. Dieter Wuttke, Baden-Baden: Koerner, pp. 419–32.

Schade, Sigrid, Wagner, Monika, and Weigel, Sigrid (eds) (1994) *Allegorie und Geschlechterdifferenz*, Cologne: Böhlau.

Schlaffer, Heinz (1989) *Faust Zweiter Teil: Die Allegorie des 19. Jahrhunderts*, Stuttgart: Metzler.

Schmitt, Carl (1988) *Political Theology: Four Chapters on the Concept of Sovereignty*, trans. George Schwab, Cambridge, MA: MIT Press.

Scholem, Gershom (1963) 'Zum Verständnis der messianischen Idee im Judentum' (1953), in Gershom Scholem, *Judaica I*, Frankfurt am Main: Suhrkamp, pp. 7–74.

—— (1973) *Zur Kabbala und ihrer Symbolik*, Frankfurt am Main: Suhrkamp.

—— (1980) *Die jüdische Mystik* (1941), Frankfurt am Main: Suhrkamp.

—— (1983) *Walter Benjamin und sein Engel*, Frankfurt am Main: Suhrkamp.

Starobinski, Jean (1991) *Kleine Geschichte des Körpergefühls*, Frankfurt am Main: Fischer Taschenbuch.

Steiner, George (1987) 'The Long Life of Metaphor: An Approach to the Shoah', *Encounter* 68(2): 55–61.

Stoessel, Marlen (1983) *Aura. Das vergessene Menschliche: Zu Sprache und Erfahrung bei Walter Benjamin*, Munich, Vienna: Hanser.

Unseld, Siegfried (ed.) (1972) *Zur Aktualität Walter Benjamins: Aus Anlaß des 80. Geburtstags von Walter Benjamin*, Frankfurt am Main: Suhrkamp.

Warburg, Aby M. (1980) *Ausgewählte Schriften und Würdigungen*, ed. Dieter Wuttke, Baden-Baden: Koerner.

Weber, Samuel M. (1991) *Return to Freud: Jacques Lacan's Dislocation of Psychoanalysis*, trans. Michael Levine, Cambridge: Cambridge University Press.

Weigel, Sigrid (1983) 'Der schielende Blick: Zur Geschichte weiblicher Schreibpraxis', in Inge Stephan and Sigrid Weigel *Die verborgene Frau*, Berlin: Argument (abridged version in English in Gisela Ecker (ed.) *Feminist Aesthetics*, trans. Harriet Anderson, London: Women's Press, 1986, pp. 59–80).

—— (1987) *Die Stimme der Medusa: Schreibweisen in der Gegenwarts-*

literatur von Frauen, Dülmen-Hiddingsel: Tende (Reinbek bei Hamburg: Rowohlt, 1989).

—— (1990) *Topographien der Geschlechter: Kulturgeschichtliche Studien zur Literatur*, Reinbek bei Hamburg: Rowohlt.

—— (ed.) (1992) *Leib- und Bildraum: Lektüren nach Walter Benjamin*, Cologne: Böhlau.

—— (1994a) *Bilder des kulturellen Gedächtnisses: Beiträge zur Gegenwartsliteratur*, Dülmen-Hiddingsel: Tende.

—— (1994b) 'The wreathed beard of Moses: body language between interpretation and reading', in Sigrid Schade (ed.) *Andere Körper/Different Bodies: Katalog der Ausstellung im Offenen Kulturhaus Linz*, Vienna, pp. 36–45

—— (1995a) 'Aby Warburg's *Schlangenritual*: reading culture and reading written texts', *New German Critique* 65 (Spring/Summer 1995): 135–53.

—— (ed.) (1995b) *Flaschenpost und Postkarte: Korrespondenzen zwischen Kritischer Theorie und Poststrukturalismus*, Cologne: Böhlau.

—— (1996) 'Reading/writing the feminine city: Calvino, Hessel, Benjamin', pp. 85–98.' in Gerhard Fischer (ed.) *With the Sharpened Axe of Reason: Approaches to Walter Benjamin*, Oxford: Berg, pp. 85–98.

White, Hayden (1990) *Die Bedeutung der Form: Erzählstrukturen in der Geschichtsschreibung*, Frankfurt am Main: Fischer Taschenbuch.

Wiegmann, Jutta (1989) *Psychoanalytische Geschichtstheorie: Eine Studie zur Freud-Rezeption Walter Benjamins*, Bonn: Bouvier.

Wind, Edgar (1983) 'Warburg's concept of *Kulturwissenschaft* and its meaning for aesthetics' (1931), in Edgar Wind *The Eloquence of Symbols: Studies in Humanist Art*, ed. J. Anderson, Oxford: Clarendon Press.

Wohlfarth, Irving (1993) 'The measure of the possible, the weight of the real and the heat of the moment: Benjamin's actuality today', *New Formations* 20 (Summer): 1–20.

Yates, Frances A. (1966) *The Art of Memory*, London: Routledge & Kegan Paul.

Yerushalmi, Yosef Hayim (1988) *Zachor. Erinnere Dich! Jüdische Geschichte und jüdisches Gedächtnis* (1982), Berlin: Wagenbach.

Index

excitation (*Erreguung*) xi, 12, 26,
115, 122, 125, 151–2, 173

facilitation (*Bahnung*) xvi, 48, 71,
118, 122–3, 137
false consciousness 12, 59, 121
fascism 22
feminine, the xvii, 25, 63–70, 80,
90–1, 96
feminist theory 66, 70, 73
'final solution' 164, 170
flâneur 17, 96
forgetting xv, 27–8, 121, 124, 154
Foucault, M. xiii–xiv, 30–48, 71, 81,
100–1, 136; *The Archaeology of
Knowledge* 36; *The History of
Sexuality* 30–2, 36; introduction
to Binswanger, *Traum und
Existenz* 47–8; *The Order of
Things* xvii, 33, 36–41;
'Nietzsche, Geneaology and
History' 42–5
fragment 38, 150
Frankfurt School xiii, 70
French Revolution 12–13, 46
Freud, S. xii–xiv, 10–11, 23, 25, 28,
46, 48, 59, 73, 93, 103–4, 111,
113–27, 129, 152–5, 167;
Benjamin's study of 25, 116–17;
'Beyond the Pleasure Principle'
114, 117; 'Dream-Work' 121; *The
Interpretation of Dreams* 11,
47–8, 115, 133, 153; 'Note Upon
the "Mystic Writing-Pad" ' 59,
114; 'Totem and Taboo' 121

Geertz, C. 150
gegenstrebige Fügung 9, 54–5, 82,
143, 162
gender: difference xii, 32, 63, 80,
83, 87, 90, 96; discourse 63;
language and 64; relations 63–6,
87, 96
genealogy 5, 31, 43–4
Genesis: Book of 39–40, 84, 129,
136
genius 84, 88–9, 142
gesture 4, 25, 27–8, 73, 127–8, 151,
154
Ginzburg, C. 115–16

Goethe, J. W. von 33
grammatology 52
Greenblatt, S. 30
Guattari, F. 153

Habermas, J. xiii, 5–9, 145
has-been, the (*das Gewesene*) xvii,
17, 48, 50, 69, 76–7, 90–1, 93,
109, 112–13, 120, 128–9, 137–8,
155–6
Hegel, G. W. F. 52, 161
Heidegger, M. xiv, 169
hieroglyphics 103
historical index xii, 101, 119, 156
historical materialism xv, 6, 8,
10–12, 53, 55
Historikerstreit 167
historiography 29, 42, 46, 77,
109–10, 121, 156, 162
history 22, 29–30, 36, 38, 41–7, 53,
58–9, 73, 76–7, 79, 112–13,
142–4, 155, 157–9; Benjamin's
concept of 12, 14, 35–6, 42, 141,
159–62; as continuum 12–13, 33,
42, 58, 77; dialectical
representation of 12; images of x,
11–12, 23, 34, 46, 110, 162; as
scene 46–7
Hölderlin, F. xiv, xvi, 33, 52, 59–60,
138, 140–1
homosexuality 32
Horkheimer, M. 67, 75, 104, 161,
163, 169, 173; *Dialectic of
Enlightenment* 67, 162–4, 166,
169–70, 173
hunchback 29, 141
Husserl, E. xiv
Hyppolite, J. 42

ideology critique xi, 5–6, 31
image: Benjamin's concept of ix, 23,
49–51, 109, 124; as 'third' ix–x,
49–50
image-desire (*Bildbegehren*) xi, xiv,
50, 58–9
image-space (*Bildraum*) x, 7–10,
12–14, 18, 22–3, 25, 44, 76, 94,
155
imagination (*Imagination*) 47–8
immediacy 8–9, 13, 25, 39–40, 72,